ANTICLAUDIANUS

This work was completed with the aid of a Canada Council Senior Fellowship and published with a subsidy from the De Rancé Foundation.

ISBN-O-88844-263-7

Printed by UNIVERSA — WETTEREN — BELGIUM

ALAN OF LILLE

ANTICLAUDIANUS
OR
THE GOOD AND PERFECT MAN

TRANSLATION AND COMMENTARY

by

James J. SHERIDAN
St. Michael's College

PONTIFICAL INSTITUTE OF MEDIAEVAL STUDIES
TORONTO
1973

FOREWORD

A translation of the Anticlaudianus of Alan of Lille is a difficult task. His sentence-structure is involved. The wealth of synonyms available to him in Latin and the fact that it is an inflected language save his repetitions from evoking a too unfavourable reaction from a reader of the original. An attempt at accurate translation often results in inelegance. He abounds in word-plays. It is often impossible to transfer these to English and, in his attempts to pun, he sometimes becomes obscure. Moreover, he wrote for his contemporaries. They were fully conversant with the twelfth century, its outlook, theories and disputes. What was clear to them often proves puzzling to us. In my notes I have made a modest attempt to help the reader reconstruct the background against which Alan wrote but I could not hope to give more than a glimpse of a section of that challenging century.

I owe a deep debt of gratitude to many friends who generously placed their time and talents at my disposal. Professor N. M. Häring of the Pontifical Institute of Mediaeval Studies read the entire work in manuscript and his expertise in matters pertaining to the twelfth century has contributed much to whatever value the work may have. Rev. L. K. Shook of the Pontifical Institute and Sister M. Blandina of the Classics staff of St. Michael's College also read the manuscript and supplied many valuable suggestions and corrections. I gladly acknowledge my indebtedness to Professor E. A. Synan of the Pontifical Institute, Professor A. Hughes of the Faculty of Music in the University of Toronto, Professor P. G. Walsh of the University of Edinburgh, my niece, Nuala Gallogley and her co-workers, Hornsey Library, Harringay, London and the staff of the National Library of Ireland, Kildare St., Dublin.

James J. Sheridan

St. Michael's College,
Toronto.

All references to the *Anticlaudianus* are, unless otherwise indicated, to *Alain de Lille, Anticlaudianus, Texte critique avec une Introduction et des Tables,* par R. Bossuat (Paris 1955).

ABBREVIATIONS

Archives	*Archives d'Histoire Doctrinale et Littéraire du Moyen Age.*
Beiträge	*Beiträge zur Geschichte der Philosophie und Theologie des Mittelalters.*
CSEL	*Corpus Scriptorum Ecclesiasticorum Latinorum.*
MGH	*Monumenta Germaniae Historica.*
PG	Migne, *Patrologiae Cursus Completus, Series Graeca.*
PL	Migne, *Patrologiae Cursus Completus, Series Latina.*
RE	Pauly-Wissowa, *Realencyclopädie der Classischen Altertumswissenschaft.*
W	Thomas Wright, *The Anglo-Latin Satirical Poets and Epigrammatists of the Twelfth Century,* Rolls Series 59.2 (London 1872).

INTRODUCTION

LIFE

EXTERNAL EVIDENCE:

1. Ralph of Longchamp dedicated his commentary on the *Anticlaudianus* to Arnaud Amalric, Archbishop of Narbonne from 1212 to 1225. He states: "I began this work for various reasons — to give a deeper understanding of the *Anticlaudianus* of Alan, the memory of whose love and friendship often forces me to tears ... to help those who have made comparatively little progress and to show my joy in your knowledge and patronage."[1]

2. Otho of Sankt Blasien (before 1223): "At this time Masters Peter Cantor and Alan and Prepositinus flourished ... One in his writings dealt with many subjects: among other things he wrote the work, entitled *Anticlaudianus*, and *The Rules of Heavenly Law, Against Heretics, On Virtues and Vices, On the Art of Preaching, Book of Sermons* and many other sound and catholic works."[2]

3. Alberic of Trois-Fontaines (before 1241): "This year Master Alan of Lille died at the house of the Cistercians. He was a teacher of renown and the author of the *Anticlaudianus*" (Chronicle for 1202).[3]

4. John of Garland (1252): "The inspired bard, Alan, a son of Flanders, herded the heretics together and was the first to tame them. Greater than Virgil, more reliable than Homer, he enhanced the wealth of learning at Paris."[4]

[1] MS Paris, BN lat. 8083. Cf. B. Hauréau, *Notices et Extraits de quelque Manuscrits Latins de la Bibliothèque Nationale* (Paris 1890) 1, 325 ff.

[2] MGH, SS 20, 326.

[3] MGH, SS 23, 881. Peter Cantor died in 1197 and Prepositinus in 1206.

[4] *Joannis de Garlandia, De Triumphis Ecclesiae Libri Octo*, ed. T. Wright (London 1856) 74.

5. A monk of Affligem (1270-4): " Alan, a native of Lille, an expert in the Liberal Arts, was head of an ecclesiastical school in Paris. He left monuments to his genius. He wrote a compendium of great value in fulfilling the obligation of preaching. As he was a man of outstanding ability in versification, he wrote a composition in verse, based on a thorough examination of the subject of the completely good man, perfect in all things. He entitled this work Anticlaudianus."[5]

6. The epitaph of Alan at Citeaux reads: "Short life brought Alan to a little tomb. He knew the two, he knew the seven, he knew all that could be known."[6] Later, probably in the sixteenth century, four lines were added: "Despising the goods of a world that was going to ruin, he became poor. Turning his heart to other things, he devoted himself to feeding the flock. Faithful to Christ, he laid aside his mortal frame in 1294. The acceptance of these lines as genuine by some scholars led to serious confusion in accounts of his life. Some even postulated two Alans as the only way out of the difficulty.[7]

Internal evidence:

1. The *Contra Haereticos* is dedicated to William VIII of Montpellier (1152-1202).[8] The same work contains two references to the

[5] *Catalogus Virorum Illustrium* 21, ed. N. M. Häring, "Der Literaturkatalog von Affligem," *Revue Bénédictine* 80 (1970) 82. The author is probably Henry of Brussels. The work was for long attributed to Henry of Ghent. See Hauréau, *Notices et extraits* 6, 162-173; F. Pelster, "Der Heinrich von Gent zugeschriebene Catalogus virorum illustrium und sein wirklicher Verfasser," *Historisches Jahrbuch* 39 (1918/1919) 253-265.

[6] The *Two* refers to Philosophy and Theology; the *Seven* to the Liberal Arts. In "Découverte du Tombeau du bienheureux Alain de Lille," *Collectanea Ordinis Cisterciensium Reformatorum* 23 (1961) 259-260, M. Lebeau states that the original epitaph contained only the first sentence and that the second was added by Jean de Cirey when he had the tomb constructed in 1482. He does not make it clear whether or not he is besing his statement on something found in the tomb. R. Bossuat has found the second sentence in a Manuscript of the *De Planctu Naturae* which dates back to the thirteenth century and also in a thirteenth century manuscript of the *Anticlaudianus*: ed. *Anticlaudianus* (Paris 1955) 15, 18. "He knew all that could be known" is frequently found in epitaphs. It is found twice in one of the epitaphs of Abelard: *PL* 178. 103D. Alan's reputation for learning was such that it was inevitable that someone should apply these words to him soon after his death, even if they were not part of his actual epitaph.

[7] Carolus de Visch discusses this addition and other epitaphs in *PL* 210.10 ff.

[8] *PL* 210.305-308.

Aphorismi de Essentia Summae Bonitatis.[9] This is the *Liber de Causis,* a translation from the Arabic made by Gerard of Cremona at Toledo between 1167 and 1187.

2. The *Liber in Distinctionibus Dictionum Theologicalium* is dedicated to Hermengald, Abbot of St. Giles (1179-1195).[10] The *Liber Poenitentialis* is dedicated to Henry of Sully, Archbishop of Bourges (1183-1200).[11]

3. One of his sermons is entitled: "For the Annunciation of the Blessed Virgin when it falls on Palm Sunday."[12] This concurrence of feasts took place in 1179 and 1184[13] when Alan was still a layman. The fact that such a sermon was acceptable from him shows that he was by then revered both for learning and piety.

4. Arguments of varying cogency have been used to establish the date of some of Alan's works. The *Regulae* is assigned to 1160, the *Summa Quoniam Homines* to 1160-1165, *De Planctu Naturae* to 1165-1182, *Anticlaudianus* to 1182-1184, *Contra Hereticos* to 1184-1195, *Distinctiones* to 1195, *Liber Poenitentialis* to 1199-1202.[14]

What is set down here is, by and large, the material available for a life of Alan until 1960. Scholars did what they could with it. The main dates in Alan's life were reconstructed as follows: Alberic of Trois-Fontaines gives 1202 as the date of his death. Alberic was using the Paschal method of reckoning years.[15] We know, then, that Alan died between April 14, 1202 and April 5, 1203.[16] He studied in Paris but

[9] *PL* 210.332C and 334B.

[10] *PL* 210.685A-688A.

[11] Ed. J. Longère.

[12] *PL* 210.199B-203B.

[13] See J-P. Escoffier, *Calendrier Perpétuel* (Paris 1880) 137, 140. Cf. A. Cappelli, *Cronologia, Cronografia e Calendario Perpetuo* (Milan 1930) 259.

[14] R. Delage, *Alain de Lille, Poète du XIIe Siècle* (Montreal and Paris 1951) 29, 32; C. Vasoli, "Studi recenti su Alano di Lilla," *Bullettino dell'Instituto Storico Italiano per il Medio Evo e Archivio Muratoriano* 72 (1960) 53; *Alain de Lille Liber Poenitentialis*, ed. J. Longère, *Analecta Mediaevalia Namurcensia,* 17, 18 (Louvain 1961) 1.213-216.

[15] In this method Easter Sunday = previous Jan. 1 of our reckoning.

[16] Cappelli, *Cronologia*, 260. There is some reason for thinking that Alan was buried on July 16, 1202. In 1666 C. Charlemont brought out at Paris a work entitled *Series Sanctorum et Beatorum Virorum Sacri Ordinis Cisterciensium.* He has an entry on Alain (240-241). He gives the date for his *depositio* in the old Roman and Gregorian style but

must have come there in 1148 or later as John of Salisbury who left Paris that year does not mention him.[17] It was assumed that he came to Paris in 1148 or very soon after and that he was about twenty, the usual age, when he arrived there. This placed his birth around 1128.

On June 22, 1960, Marcel Lebeau, a monk of Citeaux, completed the uncovering of Alan's grave.[18] His body was exhumed. There can be no doubt about the identity of the grave or the body. The opinion of an expert in forensic medicine was that Alan had died at the age of eighty-six.[19] This would put the date of his birth in 1116 or 1117, much earlier than many had thought.

We must try to reconstruct his life in view of this new evidence. He was born at Lille in Flanders c. 1116.[20] He, no doubt, went to the well-known school of St. Peter in his native city.[21] He came to Paris c. 1136. John of Salisbury's failure to mention him may be due to Alan's

the dates do not correspond. He states that Alan was buried "on the seventeenth day before the Calends of August, July 15th". The seventeenth day before the Calends of August is July 16. The fifteenth of July is the Ides of July. He very likely had the old Roman date and miscalculated. His account of Alan in general is inaccurate and replete with legends. Perhaps the date too should be suspect. B. Hauréau, *Notices et extraits* (Paris 1890) I, 327 states that Alan died in July, 1202, but does not say on what he bases this opinion.

17 This argument from silence was never a very strong one. John of Salisbury does not claim that he is giving an exhaustive list.

18 M. Lebeau, "Découverte du Tombeau du bienheureux Alain de Lille", *Collectanea Ordinis Cisterciensium Reformatorum* 23 (1961) 254-260. The exhumation verified the tradition that he was of small stature. His height was slightly over 5 ft. 4 1/2 ins. He had suffered a fracture of the right humerus at some time in his life. The broken parts had not been set too expertly; there was a slight overlap but they had knitted well. He must have been rather young at the time of the fracture.

19 Ph. Delhaye, "Pour la Fiche Alain de Lille," *Mélanges de Science Religieuse* 20 (1963) 39-51. In the *New Catholic Encyclopedia* (1967), s.v. Alan, 1, 239, P. Glorieux states that the skeleton indicated a man of eighty-eight to ninety-two years. He gives no reason for diverging from the age mentioned by Delhaye.

20 Other countries have claimed Alan as one of their sons — Germany, Spain, Sicily, Scotland, England, — but none of these claims can now be taken seriously. An account of the claims and their grounds can be found in A. Dupuis, *Alain de Lille, Etude de Philosophie Scolastique* (Lille 1859); B. Hauréau, *Histoire de la Philosophie* (Paris 1872) 1.521-532 and "Mémoire sur la vie et quelques œuvres d'Alain de Lille," *Mémoires de l'Académie des Inscriptions et Belles Lettres* 32 (1886) 1-27.

21 E. Lesne, *Les Ecoles de la fin du VIIIe siècle a la fin du XIIe* (Lille 1940), *Histoire de la Propriété Ecclésiastique en France* 5 (Lille 1940) 338-340.

anti-English attitude or even to jealousy.[22] After studies at Paris, and possibly at Chartres,[23] he taught in Paris and almost certainly at Montpellier.[24] He spent some years in Bas-Languedoc but it is impossible to determine the years with any accuracy.[25] It is quite possible that a close contact was established with the Cistercians during these years as they had gone into that area to combat heresy. He entered Citeaux some time before his death. It is impossible to determine how long he was in this Monastery. There was in the twelfth century a marked disposition on the part of bishops, abbots, priests, rulers and noted laymen to spend their last years with the Cistercians. In many cases where dates are available, it seems that the stay in the monastery was quite short.[26] However, even if Alan went to Citeaux only to prepare for death, any estimate of the years he spent there leaves a wide margin for error in either direction.

There is the question of Alan's teachers. The greatest single influence on him seems to have been Gilbert of Poitiers. In the *Anticlaudianus* alone the influence can be seen in such expressions as: *concrecio* (1. 458), *unio nativa* (1. 459), *scema reducit* (3. 133), *repetit ... distribuit ... colligit* (3. 317), *radius ... splendor ... calor* (6.

[22] For Alan's anti-English attitude, see Book I. 171 and notes. John, who would have liked to be a philosopher and theologian but did not quite succeed in his ambition, may have been jealous of Alan's well-deserved reputation.

[23] He was certainly influenced by the school of Chartres. He could have heard the lectures of Thierry of Chartres in Paris or he may have gone for a time to the famous school.

[24] Ralph of Longchamp states that he was personally acquainted with Alan (MS Paris, BN lat. 8083). He does not say that their contact was at Montpellier, although it is very likely that they met there.

[25] Alan's dedication of the *Contra Haereticos* to William VIII of Montpellier and the familiar terms used in the dedication (*PL* 210.305A ff.) show that Alan spent time at Montpellier in some capacity. Stephen of Bourbon (died c. 1261) gives two versions of a legend referring to Alan as a teacher at Montpellier, *Tractatus de diversis materiis predicabilibus*, 293, 426, ed. A. Lecoy de La Marche, *Anecdotes Historiques, Légendes et Apologues tirés du Recueil Inédit d'Etienne de Bourbon, Dominicain du XIIIe Siècle*, (Paris 1877) 246, 370-371. In both versions Alan takes soldiers to task for robbery in terms akin to those used in his sermon, *Ad Milites, PL* 210.186B-C.

[26] M. A. Dimier, "Mourir à Clairvaux," *Collectanea Ordinis Cisterciensium Reformatorum* 17 (1955) 272-285.

254-264), *tacendo strangulet* (7. 128-129),[27] Gilbert taught in Paris until 1142: Alan mentions him and was almost certainly one of his pupils.[28] If he was not, then he certainly scrutinized his works carefully.

Thierry of Chartres and his school had a marked influence on Alan. In the *Anticlaudianus* this influence is manifested in such expressions as: *labilis unda* (1. 206), *materie fluxus* (2. 483), *numerus numerans, numerus numeratus* (3. 316), *notam requirit materiem* (5. 38-9), *efficiens causa ... formalis ... finalis* (5.294-5), *credulitas* for *fides* (6. 29), *leges Parcarum ... Tonantis* (6. 217), *purus aer ... purior ignis* (7. 14-5), *ultra ... citrave* (8. 140-1). The Platonism which is so dominant in the *Anticlaudianus* derives from Thierry or his school.[29] Alan may have attended Thierry's lectures in Paris or may have gone for a time to Chartres. Gilbert of Poitiers was almost thirty years dead when Alan began to write the *Anticlaudianus*. Thierry of Chartres had retired to a monastery probably between 1151 and 1156 : nothing is known of him after this. These revered teachers must have become hallowed memories for the now aging Alan. Of Alan's relations with another contemporary, Bernardus Silvestris, we know nothing. Indeed, all we know about Bernardus is that he flourished c. 1150. Although practically everything in his *De Universitate Mundi*[30] is quoted by Alan, there is nothing to indicate that Bernardus had had any great personal influence on Alan. Bernardus seems only to have supplied Alan with material and information much as Martianus Capella[31] did.

[27] The references to the passages in Gilbert and Thierry will be given in the notes on these words and phrases.

[28] "Quoniam Homines", ed. P. Glorieux, *Archives* (1953) 162. He says "Magister Gilibertus dicebat ..." The use of *dicebat* "used to say" makes it practically certain that he is repeating what he heard *viva voce*. When referring to written works, he uses the present tense or, in rare instances, the perfect.

[29] V. Cilento, *Alano di Lilla, Poeta e Teologo del Sec. XII* (Naples 1958) 7 ff., 42; E. Jeauneau, "Macrobe, source du Platonisme chartrain," *Studi Medievali* 3a Serie I, 1 (1960) 3-24; D. Knowles, *The Evolution of Medieval Thought* (London 1960) 131 ff.

[30] *De Mundi Universitate sive Megacosmus et Microcosmus*, edd. C. Barach and J. Wrobel (Innsbruck 1876: Minerva Reprint (Frankfurt a. M. 1964).

[31] *Martianus Capella*, ed. A. Dick, Republication with addenda by Jean Préaux (Stuttgart 1969).

Works

Non-literary works

Summa quoniam homines (Since Men)

This work is named from its opening words.[32] Its purpose seems to be to give a more rigid structure to the science of Theology.[33] It is an incomplete and poorly organized work on God, the Trinity, Angelology and Man. The Prologue envisages a treatment of the subject under three heads: Creator, Creature (angels and men), Recreation (Redemption). Part III is missing and may never have been written. Part II is incomplete.

De Virtutibus et Vitiis (On Virtues and Vices): *De Virtutibus et de Vitiis et de Donis Spiritus Sancti* (On Virtues and on Vices and on the Gifts of the Holy Ghost).

MS Paris, BN, lat. 323F preserves a short work, *On Virtues and Vices*, attributed in the manuscript to Alan of Lille. This has been edited by J. Huizinga.[34] MS London, Royal 9E.XII has a much longer work, *On Virtues and Vices and on the Gifts of the Holy Ghost.* This work is not specifically attributed to Alan but is followed immediately in the manuscript by the *Quoniam Homines*, which P. Glorieux has established as a work of Alan.[35] The work has been edited by O. Lottin.[36] The sections on Virtues and Vices are practically identical and there is no reason to question Alan's authorship here. There are dif-

[32] Ed. P. Glorieux, "La Somme Quoniam Homines d'Alain de Lille," *Archives d'histoire Doctrinale et Littéraire du Moyen Age* 20 (1953) 113-359. The text of this edition is defective. Among other things, *ullus* appears for *nullus* in more than fifty instances. See N. Häring, "The Liberal Arts in the Sermons of Garnerius," *Mediaeval Studies* 30 (1968) 71, n. 3.

[33] C. Vasoli, *La Filosofia Medioevale* (Milan 1961) 159 ff.; J. M. Parent, "Un nouveau témoin de la théologie dionysienne au XIIe siècle," *Beiträge*, Suppl. 3.1. (1935) 289-309.

[34] *Über die Verknüpfung des Poetischen mit dem Theologischen bei Alanus de Insulis* (Amsterdam 1932) 95-110.

[35] "L'Auteur de la Somme Quoniam Homines," *Recherches de Théologie ancienne et medievale* 17 (1950) 29-45.

[36] "Le Traité d'Alain de Lille sur les Vertus, les Vices et les Dons du Saint-Esprit," *Mediaeval Studies* 12 (1950) 20-56.

ficulties. Which came first? Is the shorter work an extract from the longer? Is the longer work an amplification of the shorter? If so, is the amplification due, in whole or in part, to Alan? It is difficult to find an entirely satisfactory answer to these questions. It would seem that the longer work antedates the shorter. The abrupt beginning and end of the shorter work are not in keeping with Alan's usual method. Some things in the shorter work would be unintelligible if we did not have the longer version.[37] The shorter work may well be an extract made for, or by, students, interested in a maximum of factual information with a minimum of speculation. There is another difficulty. The style of some parts of the longer work is widely different from the style of the rest of it and is so laboriously like the style of parts of the *Quoniam Homines* that it gives the impression of having been written by someone trying to imitate Alan, even trying to out-Alan Alan. One might mention: the build-up of short arguments introduced by *item,* the continual use of *ad hoc dicimus* or some variant of it, the strange use of *instantia*, the casting of the arguments in a dry logical form, the dialectical gymnastics of some parts of the work, the marked tendency to omit *est, probatur, ait,* the jerkiness of the style in general. Could it be a parody on some lecturer or on a Disputation in the Schools? It can hardly be a serious imitation of Alan. An efficient imitator would have produced a more convincing piece of work.

Theologicae Regulae (Maxims of Theology).

This is a remarkable work,[38] characterised by a novel approach to Theology as a science. When Alan dealt with the Seven Liberal Arts in the *Anticlaudianus*, Geometry was given the most superficial treatment of all. Nevertheless, in the *Regulae* the approach to Theology is based on the method used in Geometry. A theorem is established and from this deductions are made. From these further deductions are drawn. For example, Regula 3 begins: "This *Regula* arises from the previous

[37] We are told that there are eight species of lies. The author then continues: "the first species is mortal and is to be given a very wide berth." No further information is given about it. It is only from the longer version that we learn that the reference is to spreading false religious doctrines: Huizinga 108; Lottin 43.

[38] *PL* 210.618-684. C. Vasoli thinks that Alan's purpose here too is to give a more rigid structure to Theology, *La Filosofia Medioevale*, 159. Cf. V. Cilento, *Alano di Lilla,* 10 ff.; M. D. Chenu, "Un Essai de Méthode Théologique au XIIe Siècle," *Revue des Sciences Philosophiques et Théologiques* 24 (1935) 258-267.

one." Regula 4: "This *Regula* is derived from the third one." Regula 5: "This *Regula* arises from the first one." He could well apply to this work what he said of Euclid: "(He) joins the parts, so to speak, with a rope of reason and one would think that the subsequent parts followed from just one original." The edited text is very defective. Moreover, the part dealing with Theology ends at *Regula* 115[39] and the text, with no indication of a change, goes on to deal with natural philosophy. It is regrettable that so little has been done on this work.

Liber in distinctionibus Dictionum theologicalium (A Work on the Various Meanings of Theological Terms).

This is a dictionary of the Bible,[40] giving the literal, allegorical and moral connotation of various words. The work shows a thorough knowledge of the Bible and a fertile imagination but some of the explanations are bizarre. Statements are often made that Alan in this work confused *ibis* (a bird, sacred to the Egyptians, akin to the stork and heron) and *ibex* (a mountain-goat). Alan was too good a Latinist to think that *ibices* could be the plural of *ibis*. Copyists, confused no doubt by the irregularities in the declension of *ibis*, compressed two entries into one. There is an addendum to *ibex*, which in Migne reads: "called stempock in the vernacular." Alan wrote "capestang", the Provençal equivalent for *ibex*. A German editor changed it to "Steinbock", the German equivalent. Successive corruptions have brought it to "stempock".

Elucidatio in Cantica Canticorum (Elucidation of the Canticle of Canticles).

A note at the end of the oldest manuscript states that this work[41] was written at the request of the Prior of Cluny. Throughout this interpretation the Spouse of the Canticle is the Blessed Virgin Mary. De Lage points out that several of the verses here applied to the Blessed

[39] *PL* 210, 686.
[40] *PL* 210.686-1012.
[41] *PL* 210.51-110.

Virgin are referred to the Church in the *Distinctiones.*[42] For this reason he questions its authenticity. However, there is no reason that a term may not be referred allegorically to more than one object, especially if there is a kinship between the objects. A number of terms in the *Distinctiones* have several references. In the Prologue to the *Elucidatio*, we find: "Thus although the Canticle of love ... is referred to the Church in a special and spiritual way, yet it applies to the glorious Virgin in a very spiritual and very special way." In view of the close relationship in mediaeval thought between the Blessed Virgin and the Church, there is nothing anomalous in Alan's referring certain terms now to one, now to the other. It is a question of emphasis. No doubt the Prior of Cluny had asked for an *elucidatio* associating the Canticle with the Blessed Virgin.[43]

Expositio super symbolum apostolicum et Nicenum (Explanation of the Apostles' Creed and the Nicene Creed).

The Prologue to this work defines its scope.[44] It is to be an investigation of five points: the different meanings of *symbolum*; its meaning in the terms "Apostles' Creed" and "Nicene Creed"; the authors of these Creeds the difference between them: their conformity. He gives an etymological explanation of *symbolum* that is more detailed, but no more correct, than the one given in *Distinctiones* 964 C-D. He accepts the tradition, recorded in Rufinus of Aquileia[45] and Isidore of Seville[46] that the Apostles' Creed owed its origin to the Apostles, each contributing a section. He states that the Blessed Virgin and Mary Magdalen were present at its composition.

[42] G. R. De Lage, *Alain de Lille, poète du XIIe siècle* (Montreal 1951) 15.

[43] There does not seem to be any compelling reason for postulating a special relationship between Alan and the Cluniacs. Alan was the outstanding theologian and writer of the day. He had a deep devotion to the Blessed Virgin. It was only natural that the Prior of Cluny should ask him to write a work on this subject.

[44] Ed. M; T. d'Alverny, *Textes Inédits*, 194-217. Recently N. M. Häring has studied an *Expositio super Symbolum Quicumque* and convincingly argues that it is a work of Alan of Lille. Text and discussion will appear in an article entitled "A Poem by Alan of Lille on the Pseudo-Athanasian Creed", in: *Revue d'Histoire des Textes* (1974).

[45] *PL* 21, 337.

[46] *PL* 83, 815-816.

Expositio Prosae de Angelis (Explanation of the *Prosa* on the Angels).

The *Prosa* is a composition in rhythmic prose, written as a Sequence for the feast of St. Michael.[47] It is attributed to Notker in *PL* 131. 1018-1019.[48] Alan attributes it to Gerbertus.[49]

The text used by Alan differs in minor details from any of the traditional texts. Alan uses the *Prosa* as a basis for a disquisition on a favourite subject, the various hierarchies, their work and their knowledge of God. This matter is treated also in the *Quoniam Homines* and in the *Hierarchia*; these works help us to understand better the reference to *Theophania* in the Prose Prologue and the account of the Choirs of Angels in Book 5. 406 ff.

Hierarchia (Hierarchy).

In this work[50] Alan speaks of a three-fold Hierarchy : supercelestial (the Trinity), celestial (the Angels), subcelestial (ecclesiastical). The celestial Hierarchy is treated in detail. The distinction he makes between the knowledge of the three hierarchies is worth noting. Theosophy is the wisdom of God. Theophany is the Angels' knowledge of God. Theology is man's knowledge of God. The definition of Theophany is of special interest in view of the *theophaniae coelestis emblema* mentioned in the *Prose Prologue* of the *Anticlaudianus*.

De Arte Praedicatoria (On the Art of Preaching).

This work contains forty-eight sermons on various subjects.[51] The text in Migne is confused and defective. The sermons are Alan's but the compilation of them is later. Not enough research has been done on this work to warrant further statements on it.

Sermones (Sermons).

This work contains eleven complete sermons and a fragment of a

[47] Ed. M. T. d'Alverny, *Textes Inédits*, 194-217.

[48] See W. von den Steinen, *Notker der Dichter und seine geistige Welt* (Bern 1948) 334 ff.

[49] For Gerbertus, see Book 3.378 and notes.

[50] Ed. M. T. d'Alverny, *Textes Inédits*, 219-235.

[51] *PL* 210.110-198.

sermon. "On the Birthday of St. Augustine."[52] A critical edition of the full text of this sermon and of eight others has been published by M. T. d'Alverny.[53] There are also critical editions of four other sermons: "For the Day of the Assumption of the Blessed Virgin,"[54] "On St. Peter."[55] "On the Contempt of the World;" "On a Theme from Virgil."[56]

Epistola magistri Alani quod non est celebrandum bis in die (Letter of Alan that Mass is not to be celebrated twice on the same day).

This letter[57] was written to his "venerable friend, P." The P. may well be Peter Cantor who was interested in this point of discipline.[58] Two practices are condemned: outright bination and the fusion of two Masses into one, e.g. beginning with a Mass of the Day and changing to a Mass of the Dead.

Liber Poenitentialis (Work on the Sacrament of Penance).

This work is a manual for Confessors, who sorely needed it if we are to believe the introductory remarks.[59] In one place Alan says that

[52] *PL* 210.197-228. Non-critical texts of two sermons appear in B. Hauréau: a Lenten sermon in *Mémoires de l'Académie des Inscriptions et Belles Lettres* 32 (Paris 1886) 18-19 and a Christmas sermon in *Notices et Extraits* 6 (Paris 1893) 194-195. Alan himself was a noted preacher. A story has come down that on one occasion he omitted his usual prayer to God for help and his salutation of the Blessed Virgin at the beginning of a sermon and for a time lost his power of speech, E. Martène, *Veterum Scriptorum et Monumentorum Amplissima Collectio* (Paris 1729) 6.52. Cf. *Histoire Littéraire de la France* 16.412.

[53] *Textes Inédits*, 241-306.

[54] P. Glorieux, "Alain de Lille, docteur de l'Assomption," *Mélanges de Science Religieuse* 8 (1951) 16-18.

[55] L. Hödl, "Eine unbekannte Predigtsammlung des Alanus von Lille," *Zeitschrift für katholische Theologie* 80 (1958) 516-527.

[56] M. T. d'Alverny, "Un Sermon de Alain de Lille sur la misère de l'homme," *The classical Tradition, Literary and Historical Studies in Honor of Harry Caplan*, ed. L. Wallach (Ithaca 1966) 515-535. "Variations sur un thème de Virgile dans un sermon d'Alain de Lille," in: *Mélanges offerts à André Piganiol* (Paris 1966) 1517-1528.

[57] Ed. M. T. d'Alverny, *Textes Inédits*, 290-294.

[58] *PL* 205.110A ; *Pierre le Chantre, Summa de Sacramentis et Animae Consiliis*, ed. J. A. Dugauquier, *Analecta Mediaevalia Namurcensia* 7 (Louvain 1957) 2.411.

[59] There are two redactions of this work. The shorter one is in *PL* 210.304 and in an edition by J. Longère, *Alain de Lille, Liber Poenitentialis, Les Traditions Moyenne et Courte, Archives* 32 (1965) 169-242. The longer one is edited by J. Longère, *Alain de*

priests are spiritual physicians and should pattern their approach to the penitent after the practice of wordly physicians.[60] There follows a short and delightful account of the "bedside manner" of the competent medical practitioner. Among other things he identifies with the patient (*se conformat infirmo*): this must be one of the earliest references to the "how-are-we-to-day?" approach. There follows a well-detailed account of the physician's method of obtaining a case-history, his diagnosis and his remedies which appear to be restricted to prescribing a diet.

De Sex Alis Cherubim (On the Six Wings of the Cherubim).

This work[61] is based on Isaias 6.1-10. Isaias had a vision of the Lord sitting on a throne. Above him were Seraphim (not Cherubim), each with six wings. They kept calling, one to another, "holy, holy, holy is the Lord of hosts; the whole earth is full of his glory." The prophet realized his own sinfulness and the sinfulness of the men with whom he associated and he acknowledged this sinfulness. One of the Seraphim came to him with a burning coal and touching his mouth with it, told him that his sins were forgiven and that, though God did not wish it, He must forgive the sins of the people if they turned to Him. Alan explains the vision and then logically goes on to refer each of the five feathers of each of the six wings to the Sacrament of Penance, man's means of obtaining forgiveness. Part of the work has been at times attributed to St. Bonaventure[62] and part of it to Clement of Llanthony. There seems to be no reason to doubt its authenticity and no necessity to divide it into two separate works as some suggest.[63]

De Fide Catholica contra Haereticos (On the Catholic Faith, Against Heretics).

This is a work against heretics.[64] It is in four books and a book is

Lille, Liber Poenitentialis, 2 volumes, *Analecta Mediaevalia Namurcensia* 17, 18 (Louvain 1965). For the incompetence of confessors, see *Sermo ad Scholares,* ed. M. T. d'Alverny, *Textes Inédits,* 274.

60 *PL* 210.285C; ed. J. Longère, 2.25.

61 *PL* 210.265-280.

62 The work was probably confused with the *De Sex Alis Seraphim* of St. Bonaventure. *S. Bonaventure Opera Omnia,* ed. A. Laver (Quaracchi 1898) 8.131-151.

63 L. Hödl, *Die Geschichte der scholastischen Literatur und der Theologie der Schlüsselgewalt* (Münster 1960: *Beiträge* 38.4) 232.

64 *PL* 210.307-430.

devoted to each of four heretical bodies, the Albigensians, the Waldensians, the Jews, the Mohammedans.[65] The text is in very poor condition.

Sermo de Sphera intelligibili (Discourse on the Intelligible Circle).

This work[66] begins from the much discussed statement, already found in Regula 7 : "God is a circle whose centre is everywhere and whose circumference is nowhere."[67] Four types of Being are discussed : Actual Being, Primordial Matter, Forms, the Divine. There is a type of knowledge corresponding to each type of Being.

Literary works

De Planctu Naturae (On the Plaint of Nature).

This is a work in Menippean form.[68] It presents a vision seen by Alan in sleep. The opening verses express the poet's sympathy for Nature faced with the prevalence of the unnatural vice of sodomy. Nature then comes on the scene. Everything about her is described in the most minute detail. In a long address she tells Alan all about herself, her relation to God, her powers, her limitations, finally discussing the relation between Faith and Reason and admitting Faith's superiority. The next section is devoted to a series of questions and answers between Alan and Nature. Here the main theme, sodomy, is reintroduced. Nature has come to regularize sex relations. In a Plato-like myth she explains the emergence of sodomy. God, the Creator, had decreed that life on earth should continue by a birth-and-death

[65] V. Cilento, *Alano di Lilla,* 68-71; J. Russell, "Interpretations of the Origins of Medieval Heresy," *Mediaeval Studies* 25 (1963) 26-53. Christine Thouzellier, *Hérésie et Hérétiques* (Rome 1969); W. L. Wakefield and A. P. Evans, *Heresies of the High Middle Ages* (New York and London 1969). Much valuable, detailed and interesting information on contemporary heresies can be found in Stephen of Bourbon, *Tractatus de diversis materiis predicabilibus*, 327-352, ed. A. Lecoy de La Marche, 274-314.

[66] Ed. M. T. d'Alverny, *Textes Inédits,* 297-306.

[67] *PL* 210.627A. The statement goes back to the *Book of the XXIV Philosophers, Beiträge* 25 (1927) 208.

[68] *PL* 210.429-486. T. Wright, *The Anglo-Latin Satirical Poets and Epigrammatists of the Twelfth Century*, Rolls Series, 59.2 (London 1872) 429-522. English Translation: D. M. Moffat, *The Complaint of Nature, Yale Studies in English* (New York 1908).

process. Nature, His delegate, was to see to it that this process continued. Overburdened with work already and choosing to live in heaven, she subdelegated this part of the work to Venus with detailed instructions as to how she should fulfill her role. The rest of the explanation is somewhat Ovidean. Venus had a legitimate son, Desire, by Hymenaeus ; by Antigamus she had an illegitimate son, named (*per antiphrasim*) Joke. From him arose forbidden love and other vices. Nature answers a number of questions for Alan and at Alan's request discusses a number of vices. A number of Virtues are introduced and described. In keeping with both the Platonic and Christian tradition, it is maintained that a man cannot have just one virtue or one vice. He has all or none. Finally Genius comes on the scene. On his robe he paints images of characters from ancient history and ancient literature, each representing a virtue or a vice. Finally he pronounces a long excommunication on all sinners. The vision fades and the poet wakes up.

Much of the work is couched in the terminology of Grammar. This requires great skill but it soon becomes tiresome. The *Plaint of Nature* has more in common with the *Anticlaudianus* than any other work of Alan. It is a much earlier work. Alan's vigour, his delight in words, a near-unintelligibility which seems at times deliberate, even the subject matter, sex, seem to betoken a much younger man than the writer of the later Epic.

Liber Parabolarum (Book of Parables).

This is a short work in elegiacs consisting of a series of proverb-like statements with very definite scriptural and classical echoes.[69] The maxims are practically all of a moral nature or, more correctly, the second line of each couplet gives a moral application to the general maxim of the first line. Maxims dealing with the same subject are collected together and the work could be a ready-reference source for one in search of pithy statements to suit any occasion. Works specializing in the dicta of worldly wisdom had a great vogue from Hesiod to comparatively recent times. They were committed to memory, made their way through every strata of society and furnished quotations for many who had no idea of their source. It is not surprising that this was for long the most popular work of Alan. There were two French and two German translations of it and it was quoted by many famous men, including Rabelais.[70] Even to-day Glorieux considers the *Parables* "a near-classic".[71] In general, however, works of this kind are no longer popular; these sententious pearls of wisdom are treated as clichés. We can agree with De Lage that we now find the *Parables* tiresome but that should not dispose us to think that this work cannot have come from an author we like. De Lage points out that the work is stylistically flat.[72] The flatness, however, is confined to the second line of the couplets, which tends to be anticlimactic and marred by "fillers" (*eo, ibi, idem*, etc.) introduced to accommodate the metre. The rigidity of the structure demanded for this line is largely responsible for the "fillers" and partially explains the anticlimactic element. It would seem that the author collected and elaborated a number of proverbs. These he put in dactylic hexameters. To each hexameter he added a pentameter line giving the hexameter a moral application. One cannot read the work without being continually reminded of Alan. There are verbal similarities with his other works. The rare twelfth century Arabic derivative *cifr* is found in the *Parables*.[73] This word literally means "zero" and figuratively "useless", "of no consequence", "a nothing". It is found in *The Plaint of Nature* referring to the bat[74] and in the *Anticlaudianus* referring to the letter *H*.[75] In the *Parables* Alan is talking of the vagaries of an incompetent writer who finds himself in difficulties both as regards matter and arrangement. He says that "he is delighted to find himself involved in figures that signify nothing and is often anxious to get ahead of himself." There is too a strong resemblance between the thoughts and terminology of *Parables* 594 A-C, *De Arte Preadicatoria*, 117 A-B

[70] *Gargantua*, Ch. 14, *Oeuvres de François Rabelais*, ed. A. Lefranc (Paris 1913) 1.141. Alan's work is referred to as *Alanus in Parabolis*. There is a tradition that Charles I of England, shortly before his death, said: "He who lies on the ground can fall no farther." These words, once incorrectly attributed to Ovid, come from *Parables* 584A: *Histoire Littéraire de la France* 16.411.

[71] Article in *New Catholic Encyclopedia*, s.v.

[72] *Alain de Lille*, 16.

[73] *PL* 210.586C. Alan seems to have been the first to use the word.

[74] *PL* 210.436D; W: 439.

[75] 2.438.

and the Sermon, *Memorare Novissima Tua.*[76] Apart from these verbal similarities we recognize Alan's interest in schools and teaching, his preoccupation with fire, water, waves, storms, his fear of heights, his love of youth, his idea of the role chance plays in life, and his desire for peace. There seems to be no reason for doubting the authenticity of the *Parables.*

Rhythmus de Incarnatione Christi (Poem on the Incarnation of Christ).

This work views the Incarnation from the standpoint of the Seven Liberal Arts and shows that it defies all the laws of Nature.[77]

Rhythmus de Natura Hominis fluxa et caduca (Poem on the transitory and mortal Nature of Man).

Man passes away like the grass of the field. He should remember this and direct his life accordingly.[78]

The Anticlaudianus

Name and genre

The full title of the work is *Anticlaudianus de Antirufino*, "The Antithesis of Claudian's *Against Rufinus*."[79] It is not a refutation of Claudian's work but rather the opposite of it. Claudian depicted the completely evil man. Alan will depict the completely good man. The work consists of a Prose Prologue, a Verse Prologue and nine books containing 4385 lines in dactylic hexameter, the metre of epic.

76 M. T. Alverny, *Textes Inédits*, 267-273.

77 *PL* 210.577. M. T. d'Alverny, "Alain de Lille et la 'Theologia'", *L'Homme devant Dieu, Mélanges offerts au Père Henri de Lubac*, vol. 2 (Aubier 1964) 126-128.

78 *PL* 210.579. G. M. Dreves and C. Blume, *Ein Jahrtausend lateinischer Hymnendichtung* (Leipzig 1909) 1.238.

79 Manuscripts carry a second title: *De Officio Viri Boni et Perfecti Libri Novem.*

Date

We have to rely exclusively on internal evidence for the date of the *Anticlaudianus.*

Alan refers to the work of one M(a)evius who wrote an Epic on the feats of Alexander of Macedon (*gesta ducis Macedum*). Maevius, a poetaster of the Augustan Age, is a thinly veiled reference to Walter of Châtillon whose Alexandreid begins with the words *Gesta ducis Macedum.*[80] A retort from Walter, equating Alan with Bavius, a contemporary and coequal of Maevius is preserved by De La Monnoye.[81] The *Anticlaudianus,* then, is later than the Alexandreid. According to experts on Walter of Châtillon, the Alexandreid was begun in 1176. Walter himself states that he spent five years on its composition.[82] It was completed, then in 1181. Since the reference to Walter is in Book I, the *Anticlaudianus* was begun no earlier than 1181.[83]

The *Architrenius*[84] of John of Altavilla is based on the *Anticlaudianus.* There are resemblances to the *Anticlaudianus* in the opening forty lines of the *Architrenius.* Possibly we would need to be consciously in search of them to advert to them. However, when we come to *at ne desidia Musae mihi sapiat ignes* and go on to read that the existence of great works does not preclude more modest efforts, just as Apollo's laurel does not render the lowly tamarisk superfluous, we are back with Alan and are for the rest of the work continually reminded of him. John's attempts to vary Alan's examples are too obvious to escape attention. Even in their disagreements, the influence of

[80] *PL* 209.463.

[81] *Jugemens de savans sur les principaux ouvrages des auteurs* (Amsterdam 1725) 4.261. Cf. *Hist. Litt. de France* 16, 408.

[82] *PL* 209.463A. The concluding lines of Book 5, *PL* 209.518C, refer to Philip II of France and must have been written shortly after his coronation in Reims on November 1, 1179 and certainly before the death of his father, Louis VII, on September 19, 1180.

[83] In "L'Anticlaudianus d'Alain de Lille, Etude de Chronologie", *Romania* 50 (1924) 1-13, C. M. Hutchings expresses the opinion that only part of the *Alexandreid* had been written before the *Anticlaudianus.* He bases his opinion on the words : "... *in primo limine fessus/Haeret ...*" The metaphor is from racing and refers to a horse so slow that he has no chance of winning. It does not suggest that the horse stops and does not finish the course.

[84] *Johannis de Altavilla Architrenius,* ed. T. Wright in *Satirical Poets and Epigrammatists of the Twelfth Century,* Rolls Series 59.1 (London 1872) 240-392. John of Altavilla is commonly styled *Jean de Hanville* or *John of Hanville.*

the *Anticlaudianus* can be recognized. Henry II in Alan blasts the world like a thunderbolt, gives himself up to crime and exudes an iniquitous miasma that infects the whole world.[85] Henry II in the *Architrenius* is so worried by the iniquity of the world that his hair is grey and his face furrowed. He is the boast of England, the joy and glory of Normandy. From the fount of his natural goodness a stream spreads gently over the world.[86]

Book One of the *Architrenius* was written when Walter of Coutance was being transferred from the See of Lincoln to that of Rouen.[87] The official date of the transference was 19 December, 1184.[88]

The *Anticlaudianus* was written, then, between 1181 and 1184.

Argument

Nature, realizing that every product of hers is somehow defective, longs to cooperate in the production of a perfect man. She realizes that the work is too difficult for her and first calls in the Virtues to aid her. They come down to earth, to a garden-paradise, where Nature has her home. Murals show specimens of Nature's handiwork, both of her better efforts and her failures. Nature addresses the Virtues and tells them of her dream of the "divine man" and suggests that they should unite their efforts to bring him into existence. Prudence approves of Nature's project but points out that, while they can fashion his body, his soul must be directly created by God. What can be done about this? Prudence appeals to Reason for clarification and directions (1). Reason speaks. She advises that an ambassador be chosen to go to Heaven and to ask God for a soul. She suggests that Prudence undertake this office. Prudence demurs, claiming that the task is too great for her. The others urge her to accept the office. She wavers. Concord addresses the assembly. She emphasizes the dangers of disunity, pleads for a combined effort on the part of the Virtues and begs Prudence to accept the office. Prudence agrees. Reason orders the Seven Liberal Arts to build

[85] 1.171 ff. Here Nero represents Henry II.

[86] Book 5, ed. Wright, 311. The *Architrenius* shows the influence of other works of Alan. Cf. *Architrenius,* ed. Wright, 249 (change of sex, anvil, etc.) and *De Planctu Naturae, PL* 210.431A, B; W: 429, 430.

[87] Ed. Wright, 245 ff.

[88] P. Gams, *Series Episcoporum* (Leipzig 1931) 192.

a chariot to take Prudence to heaven. They willingly cooperate (2). The chariot is constructed, part by part. Concord fits the parts together. Reason, acting for Nature, brings forward five horses (the five senses) and hitches them to the chariot. Prudence mounts the chariot, her sisters bid her farewell and the trip begins. Prudence, accompanied by Reason, passes through Air, investigates the background of many natural phenomena and sees the demons that haunt this realm. She proceeds to Ether, enjoys its peace, learns much about the planets (3-4). She reaches the Firmanent, sees the Constellations and the Signs of the Zodiac. She is now at the limits of our Universe. The horses refuse to go farther and the road ahead is confusing and dangerous. She realizes that she can go no further on her own. Theology comes into view. Her home-territory is the top of the world and she can ascend far up from there. Prudence begs her to be her guide and she agrees. (The poet here, in Vergilian tradition, speaks in his own person and begs help from heaven in the difficult task of describing the strange things that he is to see). Prudence, guided and enlightened by Theology, goes further into the heavens and is able to investigate problems about fire water, dew, and hail. Through more beautiful and happier regions she is led to realms of joy[89] (5). When she tries to continue her course, the light proves too bright for her eyes and the impact of this new realm benumbs her mind. A trance comes over her. When Theology fails to rouse her completely from her lethargy, she seeks the aid of Faith. A short account is given of the relationship between Faith and Reason. Faith restores Prudence to consciousness but, realizing that what is to come would be too much for human eyes, she supplies her with a mirror in which she will see things tempered by reflection. When she cannot understand what she sees, Faith comes to her aid with explanations. Prudence sees the angels and saints. She tries to understand how Mary can be both Virgin and Mother. Faith finally warns her that human laws and causality as understood by human reason cannot be applied to everything in Heaven. There the final and ultimate determinant is the will of God, Who is free from every restriction encountered on earth. This Prudence keeps in mind for the remainder of

[89] Here, Alan, speaking in his own person, gives an account of heaven, its beauty, the choirs of angels, the saints, the Blessed Virgin, Jesus Christ.

her stay in Heaven. She continues on her course and finally enters the palace of God. Here she receives further enlightenment. She realizes why there is so great a difference between the lots of men on earth, the reason for the vocations of various well-known characters. She reaches a glimmer of understanding of the Trinity. Finally, face to face with God, she explains her mission and begs God for the soul she seeks. He agrees to grant her request. Noys seeks an exemplar for the soul and presents it to God Who creates the soul and hands it over to Prudence with instructions to guard it well. She sets out on the return journey and rejoins Reason. They bid farewell to Theology and Faith, make their way back to the chariot and return to earth. The Virtues welcome Prudence and are astonished at the beauty of the soul (6).

Nature fashions a body from choice parts of earth, water, air, and fire and gives every endowment within her power. Concord, aided by Arithmetic and Music, joins soul and body. The New Man is in existence. The Virtues and the Liberal Arts make their contribution to his perfection. Nobility wishes to make a contribution but has nothing of her own to offer. She decides to consult her mother, Fortune. An account is given of the rock where Fortune's house is built (7). The house itself and its mistress are described. Nobility begs her mother for a gift. Fortune accompanies her daughter to Nature's home. Under Reason's surveillance Nobility passes on the gifts of Fortune to the New Man. He is now complete.

Rumour spreads abroad the news of Nature's great work. Allecto hears of it. She calls the Vices and their retinues together and urges them to make war on the New Man. They agree. Nature and the Virtues rally to his aid (8). The battle takes place. The New Man is victorious and becomes the ruler of earth. The Virtues decide to live on earth where there are now peace, harmony and plenty.

The author wishes his book well, speaks of his hopes and fears for it and is ultimately consoled by the thought that malicious attacks on it will cease after his death, if not sooner (9).

Interpretation

In his Prose Prologue Alan states that his work can be approached on three levels. Boys will find in it a delightful adventure story; the ascetically minded will be benefited by instruction and exhortation; the fully matured intellect will appreciate the allegorical meaning. The third approach is the only one that calls for examination. The *Anticlaudianus* is an allegory. What lies behind the literal meaning? To answer this we must consider the *Anticlaudianus* as an epic. Traditionally an epic is an account of the exploits of a hero, a man idealized in different ways according to the outlook of the poet and his times. Who is the hero of the *Anticlaudianus* ? De Lage would make the New Man the hero and speaks of the work as "an Odyssey without an Iliad". This is putting it mildly. It would be almost "an Odyssey without an Odysseus". The idea of a New Man is first put forth in definite terms at Book 1.236. From this point to Book 2.324, he would be in the reader's mind, although he is not mentioned by name. With the introduction of the Seven Liberal Arts he tends to fade out completely. The emphasis is on knowledge: the mission of Phronesis is to "investigate the secrets of Noys" (2.371). The Liberal Arts and the five senses are treated. Phronesis investigates the phenomena of Air, Ether and the Firmament. The equivalent of approximately three books passes before the New Man is mentioned again at 5.202 when Phronesis explains her mission to Theology. Aided by Faith and her mirror, Phronesis finally reaches the reality that lies behind the mutable things of earth; she sees the permanent and unchanging, the celestial ideas, the causes of causes. Admitted to the presence of God, she again explains her mission and asks for the soul for the New Man. She obtains it and returns to earth. A body is formed, the soul is joined to it. Finally the New Man emerges at 7.74. From 7.77 to the end of Book 8, he remains passive (a most unepic state) while the Virtues, the Seven Liberal Arts and finally Fortune (in response to the request of her daughter, Nobility) are bestowing their gifts on him, the Vices are rallying to Allecto's aid, the Virtues are arming him and the preliminaries of the battle are taking place. Only in Book 9 does he emerge as a possible epic figure.[90]

The epic figure that predominates is Phronesis. Her quest is for real knowledge. Allegorically Phronesis' trip to heaven and back is a Christian version, lengthened and more detailed of Plato's account of the cave-dweller's emergence into the light of day and into the world that lies behind the shadows and his return to his underground

[90] Even here he seldom takes the initiative. His role is largely passive.

home.[91] It is the ascent and descent of Plato's Philosopher-King told in a Christian context.[92] The cave-dweller and the Philosopher-King, when they return to their natural habitat, see the same things as they have seen before their journey but the significance of these things is forever changed. Plato identified knowledge and virtue.[93] If one accepts Plato's outlook here, the one who is seeking the man with all virtue is seeking the man with all knowledge. The five senses, the Liberal Arts, Philosophy, Theology and Faith unite to lead man to a knowledge of God. This knowledge makes the universe intelligible and places perfection within man's reach.

Background

The perfect man

Psychologically everyone has a desire for perfection and an idea of

[91] Plato, *Republic* 7.514-517. Some men are chained in a cave in such a way that they can see only a wall in front of them. There is a fire behind them and a low wall between them and the fire. Men, some talking, some silent, pass along the wall carrying all sorts of vessels, statues, figures of animals. All the chained men see are the reflections of these objects on the wall opposite them. They attribute the sounds they hear to these shadows. For them the shadows are the sole reality. One is released and brought up from the cave. At first he cannot stand the light; he looks at objects reflected in water. Gradually he is able to took at real objects and finally at the sun and he understands its power. When he returns to the cave and sees the shadows, they have an entirely different meaning for him. Plato states that the emergence of the cave-dweller represents the ascent of the soul to the intellectual region (*εἰς τὸν νοητὸν τόπον*, "to the realm of Noys"). There, finally and with difficulty, it perceives the essential Form of Good and realizes that it is the source of all that is right and beautiful, of the sun and light in the visible world, of reason and truth in the intellectual world.

[92] Plato, *Republic* 7, 521C-541B. The future ruler is to study Arithmetic, Geometry, Astronomy and Dialectic as a preparation for the Philosophy that will bring him to a knowledge of the essential Form of Good, the source of all knowledge and of all virtue. Alan did not know Greek. He could have known about Plato's *Republic* without knowing Greek. However, the consensus seems to be that he was entirely unacquainted with the *Republic*. The similarity between him and Plato here is amazing and becomes more so when we consider the similarity between the description of the System of Stars in *De Planctu Naturae* and the vision of Er in the *Republic*. See Duhem, *Le Système du Monde*, 3, 228. In dealing with Euclidean geometry, Alan does not go beyond what could be mastered by an average student in a month. Plato, *Rep.*, 526D-E, says that very little of this geometry will suffice in the education of the Philosopher-King.

[93] See M. J. O'Brien, *The Socratic Paradoxes and the Greek Mind* (Chapel Hill 1967) 198 ff.

what would constitute this perfection. The heroes of Homer, set before Greek boys for their imitation,[94] had each his own special accomplishment. With the possible exception of Odysseus, none of them could lay claim to an all-round perfection. Simonides, in a fragment preserved in Plato's *Protagoras*, brings up the idea of a "truly good man, fashioned without a flaw, four-square in hands, feet and mind".[95] The heroes and heroines of Greek tragedy may be near perfect but Aristotle points out that it is essential to tragedy that each hero or heroine have a fatal flaw.[96] Certain virtues were connected with youth, others with old age. Gradually there emerged the idea of a perfection combining the vigour of youth with the maturity of age. The conflict between young and old is prominent in Aristophanes where there are references to young men with old ideas and old men with young ideas.[97] While such references were to recur in most writers of classical antiquity, it is not until Virgil that we find definite reference to a boy with a wisdom beyond his years. Young Iulus has "a man's mind and a sense of responsibility beyond his years".[98] Ovid says that young Gaius Caesar could handle wars that no boy should handle. His ability comes from heaven and its growth cannot be reckoned by years.[99] Statius, speaking of the deceased foster-son of Melior, says that he had a discretion, propriety and probity beyond his years.[100] Apuleius speaks of a youth with the wisdom of an old man.[101] Claudian makes mention of a fiery youth who tempered his impetuosity with a wisdom matured by responsibilities.[102] Gregory the Great's Life of St. Benedict was very popular in the Middle Ages. It begins by stating that St. Benedict, even as a boy, had the understanding of an old man.[103]

[94] Plato, *Protagoras* 325E-326C.

[95] 339B.

[96] *Poetics* 13. 1453a7-16.

[97] *Clouds* 821, *Birds* 255.

[98] *Aeneid* 9.311. For much of what follows I am indebted to E. R. Curtius, *Europäische Literatur und lateinisches Mittelalter* (Bern 1948): English Translation by W. R. Trask, *European Literature and the Latin Middle Ages* (London 1953).

[99] *Ars Amatoria* 1.185.

[100] *Silvae* 2.1.40.

[101] *Florida* 9.38.

[102] *Panegyric on Probinus and Olybrius* 1.154-155.

[103] *PL* 66.126A. English Translation: O. J. Zimmerman, O.S.B. and V. R. Avery, O.S.B., *Life and Miracles of St. Benedict* (Collegeville, Minnesota 1949) 1. The reference to the premature wisdom of St. Benedict is not in the Greek text in *PL* 66.

This idea of the young-old man is prominent in Alan's description of the New Man. When Youth is bestowing her gifts on him, she "adopts grave ways and patterns herself on the characteristics of an aged man".[104] Reason bestows on the youth "the character of a man full of years".[105] It has been suggested that Alan based his concept of the New Man on Adam before the Fall[106] or on Christ.[107] He may have derived the idea of a *perfect* body and *perfect* mind from these sources, but basically he is using the young-old man topos.[108]

It might be added for completeness' sake that there is also a tradition of the young-old woman. Pliny bemoans the death of a young girl who had the wisdom of an old woman and the gravity of a matron.[109] Six of the Liberal Arts in Martianus Capella show traits of youth and age.[110] *Mundus* in Peter of Compostella is a young-old woman.[111] Philosophy in Boethius is an old woman with the vitality of youth.[112] This tradition influenced Alan's description of Faith.[113]

[104] 7.94-95.

[105] 7.170-171.

[106] Duhem, *Système du Monde*, 3.223. Some idea of Alan's concept of Adam before the Fall can be got from "On Virtues and on Vices and on the Gifts of the Holy Ghost," ed. O. Lottin, 37-38.

[107] The accound of the attack of Venus in 9.228 ff., and especially the New Man's fear and flight could not have been referred to Christ by one who believed that He was God. The same applies to several details of the Psychomachia.

[108] Alan bitterly attacks the opposite of the boy with the wisdom of years, i.e., the childish old man, *Liber Poenitentialis, PL* 210.183B; ed. J. Longère, 2.21. He complains that many priests *senes sunt et pueri*. He uses the phrase *maledictus elementarius senex* as if it were in the Scriptures and meant "cursed be (or is) the childish old man." The word *elementarius* is not in the Bible. Seneca uses it in *Letter* 36.4 for an old man who has not yet learned the alphabet. In *Distinctiones, PL* 210.941B, he has *maledictus eleemosynarius senex*. This, he says, is a phrase used to designate a fool. *Eleemosynarius* seems to mean here "a man who lives on alms". The word is not found in the Bible but is found in commentaries. I have failed to find it with this meaning.

[109] *Epistles* 5.16.

[110] Ed. Dick 82.11; 151.15; 211.10; 291.7; 365.5; 422.5.

[111] *Petri Compostellani de Consolatione Rationis Libri Duo*, ed. P. B. Soto, Beiträge 8 (1912) 54.

[112] *De Cons. Phil.* Bk. 1, Prose 1.

[113] 6.64-72.

Literary antecedents

The celestial journey

Martianus Capella, in a work containing nine books, gives an account of the marriage of Mercury and Philology. In the first two books Virtue, Mercury and Apollo, attended by the Muses, ascend to the palace of Jupiter to arrange for the marriage. A council of the gods approves the marriage. The Seven Liberal Arts are given to Philology as a wedding present and the remaining seven books deal with the Arts, one book being assigned to each Art. Alan drew heavily on this work.

Bernardus Silvestris gives an account of the perfecting of primordial matter and the creation of man. The creation of man necessitates a journey to heaven. Nature makes the trip and man is created. It is easy to see that the *Anticlaudianus*, dealing with the perfecting of man, is a development of this work. Practically every line of Bernard's work is quoted or echoed in Alan. However, there is a significant transformation in outlook. Bernardus Silvestris is, to all intents and purposes, a pagan humanist;[114] Alan is a Christian humanist.

The celestial car

There are a few minor references to cars, by way of metaphor, in Alan's contemporaries. Hildebert, in a letter of moral exhortation to a widow, speaks of the cardinal virtues as the wheels of the chariot that carries us to heaven.[115] His metaphor is so spread out that he forgets to mention specifically that Fortitude is the second wheel although he deals with that virtue in detail. Walter of Châtillon complains that many want a free ride on the car of science.[116] Alan got nothing from Hildebert or Walter of Châtillon, but their statements show that the car motif was common in the twelfth century.

[114] J. R. O'Donnell in the entry on Bernardus Silvestris in the *New Catholic Encyclopedia* (1967) aptly points out that Alan is a Christian who is no longer afraid of a detrimental influence on Christianity from pagan culture.

[115] *PL* 171.163B-166B. His terminology, e.g. *Haec ea est quadriga,* shows that the car motif was common.

[116] Ed. Karl Strecker, *Moralisch-Satirische Gedichte Walters von Chàtillon* (Heidelberg 1929) 68.

The evil man

Claudian tells the tale of Rufinus, the completely evil man.[117] Allecto, disturbed by the growth of Virtue on earth, calls a council of the Vices and urges that they devise a crime worthy of their august assembly. After some disagreement Megaera directs their attention to Rufinus, pointing out that "all the wickedness that is ours in common is his alone"[118] and she offers to conduct him to the kingly palace of the Emperor of the world. They agree. Megaera goes to Elusa in Gaul, Rufinus' birthplace and promises him that if he will obey her, she will make him lord of the world. On her instruction he makes a journey to the East and finally worms his way into the imperial palace. Here he embarks on a career of treachery, disruption and self-aggrandisement. Stilicho led two campaigns against him and his barbarian supporters. Finally Rufinus was killed. Minos in the underworld could not bear the sight of him, sentenced him to every possible punishment and sent him to the lowest hell.

Martianus, Bernardus and, to a lesser extent, Claudian influenced the format of Alan's *Anticlaudianus* and supplied him with numerous quotations. In addition to this he borrows whatever material he thinks suitable from every source known to him. There are easily recognizable borrowings from Cicero, Virgil, Horace, Propertius, Tibullus, Ovid, Quintilian, Persius, Juvenal, Apuleius, Hyginus, Hilary of Poitiers, Prudentius, Donatus, Claudian, Sidonius, Boethius, Avitus, Priscian, Gilbert of Poitiers, Thierry of Chartres and Michael Psellos.[119] It must be kept in mind that Alan makes it clear in his Prose Prologue that he considers his adaptation of elements from previous writers one of the great merits of his work. He adapts his borrowings to his own special purpose. The borrowed phrase or word may have a wider application than it had in the original or it may have a narrower; it may retain all of its original meaning, some of it or none of it.

Dionysius of Halicarnassus compares the writer to a builder: "When a builder has provided himself with the material from which he intends

117 *In Rufinum*, Loeb edition of Claudian's works by M. Platnauer (Cambridge, Mass., 1922: Reprint of 1956) 1.24-97.

118 1.111, ed. Platnauer, 34.

119 Alan made no distinction between Classical, Silver Age, and later writers.

to construct a house — stones, timbers, tiling, and all the rest, he then puts together the structure from these, studying the following three things: what stone, timber and brick can be united with what other stone, timber and brick; next how each piece of the material that is being so united should be set, and on which of its faces; thirdly, if anything fits badly, how that particular thing can be chipped and trimmed and made to fit exactly. A like course should, I affirm, be followed by those who are to succeed in literary composition".[120] In Alan's structure, the plan, the roof and the mortar are all his own.[121] Many bricks have been newly fashioned for this particular building. Others have been used before, some of them several times. These he reshapes skilfully when the need arises. He arranges and places his bricks, old and new, to the best advantage. The resultant edifice may not be an architectural gem. However, there is nothing bizarre about it. It is sound and serviceable and fulfills admirably the noble purpose for which it was intended.

The Anticlaudianus as an Epic

The plot of the *Anticlaudianus* is simple and unified. It contains an account of the events leading up to Phronesis' mission, the journey to heaven, the events there, the return journey and the results of the successful mission. On the whole, the work is free from the long digressions, loosely connected with the main theme, which abound in many epic poems. His transitions are smooth, a somewhat rare virtue in Latin writers. We pass from the Liberal Arts to Theology and on to Faith without being conscious of anything abrupt, strained or over-contained. The description of the Liberal Arts may bore us but we must keep in mind that they appear here in a new role and have a special significance. Without them man cannot begin his ascent to the world of supramundane Forms and to God. Thus they merit a somewhat detailed treatment. The description of heaven is long and

[120] *On Literary Composition*, Ch. 6, ed. W. Rhys-Roberts (London 1910) 107.

[121] For the first time we have a systematic account of man's use of his five senses to proceed from the Liberal Arts to Philosophy, Theology and Faith. Man's knowledge becomes whole and integrated. See V. Cilento, *Alano di Lilla*, 21 ff. Cf. *Quoniam Homines*, ed. Glorieux, 120.

somewhat repetitious but since the days of Homer, writers have had to consider the interests of their audience.

Phronesis is the heroine of Alan's Epic. His portrayal of her is subtle and skilful. He emphasizes her close kinship with Reason. Yet almost imperceptibly the gap between them so widens, in accidentals, not essentials, that our reactions to them become widely different. Reason shows no feeling; she appeals to our intellect but not to our emotions. Phronesis shows feeling; she is loving and lovable, and we find that we can identify with her. She is represented as opening wide her arms to embrace all who will come to her.[122] In her speech she has nothing but praise for Nature and Reason.[123] This very praise, however, portrays Reason as lacking feelings, especially the feeling of wonder that is so necessary for one seeking knowledge. Reason's speech emphasizes Nature's limitations,[124] rather unnecessarily, since Nature herself has already admitted these limitations.[125] Phronesis is praised for qualities that appeal to us and that are associated with an epic hero — indomitable courage and unflagging perseverance in the face of apparently insuperable difficulties. These qualities make for leadership. Concord emphasizes that the Virtues rightly expect that Phronesis will rally them when they are discouraged and disheartened by the seeming impossibility of the proposed project.[126] The result is that by the time Phronesis sets out on her journey, we are ready to espouse her cause and share her difficulties and triumph. We rejoice at the success of her mission. We are thrilled by her gifts to the New Man — "a treasury of intellect and all riches of soul".[127] She gives him knowledge. It is immune to the decay and the destructive factors that beset all other things of earth. The more it is shared, the greater it grows. By comparison Reason gives good advice. Finally, when the New Man is being armed for the battle, Phronesis gives him a helmet to protect his head, the part of him that is of vital importance if he is to use his gift for his own benefit and for the benefit of others.[128]

[122] 1.292-293.
[123] 1.326-424.
[124] 2.7-157.
[125] 1.214-265.
[126] 2.296-309.
[127] 7.228 ff.
[128] 8.326.

The other "characters" in the Epic manifest love and respect for Phronesis. Nature and Concord had to call for silence before their speeches.[129] As soon as Phronesis rose, she had the immediate attention of the assembly.[130] The Liberal Arts are enthusiastic about working for her.[131] When all is ready for the journey, the Virtues can hardly bear to see Phronesis go.[132] The long farewell scene is finally cut short by Reason. Mention has already been made of the praises bestowed on her by Reason and Concord. Phronesis, with her love, her eagerness, her sense of wonder, her enthusiasm, her perseverance, her willingness to lead or to follow is a heroic image of man's eternal struggle to get to the source of all knowledge and all virtue.

John of Altavilla imitated Alan very closely. He was not without ability as a writer. Compared with Alan, however, he lacks depth. The imitation of Alan is superficial and little more than an imitation of method. Walter of Châtillon and, to a lesser extent, Joseph of Exeter, may impress us by their skill and dexterity in using the Latin language, by an occasional flash of near-genius and by their enthusiastic attempts to resurrect the old mythologico-historical Epic. Side by side with the *Anticlaudianus,* their works seem like mere learned trifling.

"Understand your subject: the words will come to you" was a piece of advice given early in Roman times to writers.[133] Alan merited his title of *Doctor Universalis.* He knew his subject and his power of expression is magnificent. His style and diction change to suit the sense. Minor examples of this abound in the *Anticlaudianus.* However, the most impressive and sustained change comes where Alan begins his account of Heaven. He abandons all attempts to be clever, to make an impression by stylized manipulation of words and to resort to the types of ornament that are the stock-in-trade of so many writers of his

[129] 1.212; 2.210.

[130] 1.318-25.

[131] 2.329-30.

[132] 4.231-9.

[133] Cato the elder wrote a treatise on Rhetoric. All that has come down to us is the precept, *rem tene, verba sequentur* and the definition of an orator, "a virtuous man skilled in speaking" (*Vir Bonus dicendi peritus*). J. W. H. Atkins, *Literary Criticism in Antiquity* (London 1934) 2.16.

day.[134] He is dealing with the highest Reality and the ultimate End for both Christian and Platonist and he accommodates his style to his subject. Here one can see what Alan might have done had he freed himself in all his writing from the literary mannerisms that had accumulated over the centuries and had come to be regarded as indispensable adjuncts of effective writing.

Greek literary theory was poetry-centred; Latin literary theory was prose-centred. The prose was Rhetoric. Rhetoric is firmly established in Epic by Lucan's time. Christian writers, dealing with Christian themes, felt that they had an obligation to teach and to lead feelings in the right direction. This outlook ennobled the already firmly established Rhetoric. Alan is permeated with this Rhetoric. At times however, he shows an admirable restraint. Curtius cites Alan's account of the surroundings of Nature's house as an example of the rhetorical topos of the pleasance (*locus amoenus*).[135] In reality it has little or no connection with this topos. One has only to compare Alan here with the selection from Tiberianus given by Curtius. Tiberianus' imagery is confused and cloying: one could not possibly envisage, except in the haziest way, the place he describes. Alan's account is clear and vivid: We can see the place. His description of the birds is a gem of keen observation and attention to detail. Moreover, his approach is realistic. If asked to give our ideas of what would constitute for us a delightful place, we would inevitably mention some things we would wish not to see there. Alan emphasizes the absence of decay, old age, extremes of heat and cold, a forest floor defaced by fallen branches. The garden produces plants that help us fight disease; the river irrigates the soil and promotes growth and fruitfulness. Tiberianus' imaginings read like the description of an hallucination, "where neither head nor foot can be assigned to a single shape".[136] Alan's account evokes the picture of a lover of nature with excellent powers of observations and a keen eye for beauty. Alan's description of the grove of Fortune[137] is cited as an example of the topos of the *impossible* (adynaton). However, the realm

[134] 5.265-6.488. There seems to be a break in this at 5.342-347 where Alan seems to become over-excited about theories of falling moisture and perhaps at 6.83-88 where Faith takes on the role of doctor.

[135] 1.55 ff. Curtius, *European Literature*, 196-198.

[136] Horace, *A.P.* 8-9.

[137] 7.419 ff.

of Fortune is the realm of the impossible, the unexpected, the inexplicable, and this grove is in keeping with its mistress.

The Figures of Rhetoric increased in number from late classical antiquity until the disappearance of Latin as a literary medium. By Alan's time Figures of Speech and Figures of Thought together numbered more than sixty.[138] Examples of every one of these can be found in Alan. Citation of these would be tiresome and would contribute nothing to the understanding or appreciation of the *Anticlaudianus*. Indeed, readers accustomed to a modern language would not regard many of them as Figures at all. Perhaps mention should be made of a type of *commoratio* (repetition) that is common in Alan but does not seem to appear in his contemporaries. He makes a statement literally, repeats it twice or oftener figuratively and before leaving it repeats it literally in different words. This is probably due to Alan's experience as a lecturer to younger students.

Alan's management of the dactylic hexameter is mechanically adequate. Caesura in the third foot is the regular practice. Monosyllabic words are normally avoided at the end of lines. Lines that violate the metrical rules of hexameter are in some instances due to corruption of the text. Divergence in quantity from the norms of classical Latin is in accord with the usage of his time. His hexameter is, however, monotonous and lacks flexibility, pitfalls in Latin hexameter which Virgil alone entirely escaped. Elision is extremely rare. *Hic, ille, ipse, iste* are constantly used as fillers to accommodate a line to the metrical scheme. Singulars and plurals are interchanged and proper nouns are given odd quantities for the same purpose.[139]

Speaking of the best authors Quintilian says: "At times they lapse and bend beneath their burden, indulge their own tendencies or relax their efforts".[140] We should not concentrate on an author's defects, for, as Longinus points out, "we should not blame the man for his omissions but rather praise him for his intention and his earnestness".[141] These in Alan's case cannot be questioned.

138 See C. S. Baldwin, *Medieval Rhetoric and Poetic* (New York 1928) 304-5.

139 For some adverse criticism of Alan's prosody, see Ch. Thurot, *Extraits de divers Manuscrits Latins pour servir à l'histoire des doctrines grammaticales au moyen âge* (Paris 1869; Minerva Reprint, Frankfurt am Main, 1964) 429, 432, 434, 436.

140 *Institutio Oratoria* 10.1.24.

141 *On the Sublime* 1.2.

PROSE PROLOGUE

The lightning's bolt does not deign to spend its force on the twig but dislodges the proud outgrowths of full-grown trees.[1] The mighty rage of the wind does not waste its anger on the reed but stirs up the furious attacks of its mad blast against the highest of high things. The glare of envy does not flash through our flawed and lowly book; the wind of detraction does not bring down our poor and stunted work in which misery shipwrecked invokes the harbour of pity to a greater extent than success evokes the sting of envy. Let the reader, eschewing the madness of a yelping attack and improving the work with the file of correction, cut out what is superfluous[2] and bring to completion what is under-developed as long as it returns for correction with a blemish on it, is brought back to the workshop unrefined, is returned to its artificer as inartistic, comes back to the right anvil as badly turned.[3] But however much the irregularity of the artifact points an accusing finger at the ineptitude of the artist, however much the hand of the artisan leaves traces of ignorance in an ignoble product, let the work nevertheless beg forgiveness for its faults since the tiny fire of human reason[4] is darkened by many mistakes arising from ignorance and the spark of natural ability

[1] This Prologue contains an apologia for the work, a plea for consideration of a very human effort, a brief summary, a request for constructive criticism and a far from conciliatory statement as to who are not competent to judge the work. The Prologue apparently was meant to accompany copies of the Ms. sent to selected schools, perhaps to selected individuals, before the final release of the work to ask for advice and suggestions. Alan's vocabulary shows that he had in mind the advice given to writers by Horace in the *Ars Poetica* concerning the advisability of submitting a work before publication to frank and competent critics and accepting their advice. Bk. 9.410-426 was written when the work was being finally released. Alan had received some biased criticism and expected more.

[2] Horace, *A.P.* 447.

[3] *Ib.* 441.

[4] Cf. Boethius, *De Trin.*, 1 (Stewart-Rand 2).

fades away into the numerous clouds of error.[5] Therefore let the reader in his approach to this work be not influenced by disdain from a finicky mind or agitated by the ferment of fault-finding but enticed by a love of something new, so that, although the book does not bloom with the purple of flowering eloquence and is not lit up with the stars of flashing dicta, the sweetness of honey may nevertheless be found in a small and fragile reed and parching thirst may be slaked from a small and falling rivulet. Let the work not be considered in any way cheap and common or suffer the bite of blame by a claim that it smacks of the ignorance of the moderns, who prefer the flower of native genius and inter the merits of diligent study:[6] the lowly dwarf, placed on the shoulder of the enormous giant, outdoes the giant in height[7] and a stream, gushing forth from a spring, increases and grows into a torrent. Let those not dare to show disdain for this work who are still wailing in the cradles of the nurses and are being suckled at the breasts of the lower arts.[8] Let those not try to detract from this work who are just giving promise of a service in the higher arts.[9] Let those not presume to undo this work who are beating the doors of heaven with their philosophic heads.[10] For in this work the sweetnees of the literal sense will

[5] Hor., *A.P.* 347-53. Cf. 359: "even good Homer nods".

[6] *Ib.* 408-411. See Verse Prologue, note 1. Cf. *Quoniam Homines*, ed. P. Glorieux, 120.

[7] The question of Ancients versus Moderns was debated for many centuries. See Gilbert Highet, *The Classical Tradition* (Oxford 1949) 261-288. John of Salisbury states: "Bernard of Chartres used to say that we are like dwarfs resting on the schoulders of giants so that we can see more and further than they, not indeed by the keenness of our own vision or by our stature of body but because we are raised on high and kept aloft by the giant's height". *Metalogicon,* 3.4, ed. C.I.C. Webb, *Joannis Saresberiensis Episcopi Carnotensis, Metalogicon* (Oxford 1929) 136. See E. Jeauneau, "Nani gigantum humeris insidentes. Essai d'interpretation de Bernard de Chartres." *Vivarium,* 5.2 (1967) 79-99.

[8] Grammar, Logic, Rhetoric.

[9] Arithmetic, Music, Geometry, Astronomy.

[10] See the account of the relation between Faith and Reason in Bk. 6.14-28. Cf. 7.150. In Bk. 1.96-107 Reason states that Prudence can make her way to heaven and learn the secrets of God. The description of Prudence in 1.300-302 points out that she operates at the lowest level of human intelligence but at times disappears into the heavens

soothe the ears of boys, the moral instruction will inspire the mind on the road to perfection, the sharper subtlety of the allegory will whet the advanced intellect.[11] Let those be denied access to this work who pursue only sense-images and do not reach out for the truth that comes from reason, lest what is holy, being set before dogs be soiled, lest the pearl, trampled under the feet of swine be lost,[12] lest the esoteric be impaired if its grandeur is revealed to the unworthy.[13]

Since there emerge in this work the rules of grammatical syntax, the maxims of dialectical discourse, the accepted ideas of oratorical rhetoric, the wonders of mathematical lore, the melody of music, the principles of geometry, theories about writing,[14] the excellence of the dignity of astronomy,[15] a view of

where ordinary human vision cannot follow her. This is an allegory, borrowed from *Wisdom* 18.15-16: "Lord. down leaped thy word omnipotent ... thy word that trod earth, yet reached up to heaven". Cf. Boethius' description of Philosophy, *De Cons.* 1. Pr. 1 (Stewart-Rand 130). In Alan it represents the struggle of natural philosophy to reach out beyond the human and make contact with the science of the divine, Theology. This contact is finally made in Bk. 5.81 ff. When this contact is made, human knowledge is perfected and its terms take on a new and higher meaning. Cf. *Reg.*, 621B; *Quoniam Homines*, ed. P. Glorieux, 119-120. Alan will not accept the judgement of anyone who has not this perfected knowledge. If we may judge from his *Sermo ad Scholares*, few, even among clerics, made a serious study of Theology: M. T. d'Alverny, *Textes Inédits*, 274. For the preliminary studies necessary for Theology see *Quoniam Homines*, ed. P. Glorieux, 119-120.

[11] Sacred Scripture was interpreted in four senses — literal, moral, allegorical, mystical. We have three of the four senses here.

[12] Matthew, 7.6.

[13] Cf. Bk. 3.117-128.

[14] Bk. 7.245-284.

[15] In his account of the contents of the work, Alan tries to juxtapose Latin and Greek terms, *grammatice syntaseos ... musice melos*, etc. He speaks of *astronomice ebdomadis excellentia* and we might expect that *ebdomadis* had for Alan some connotation of excellence. Strange as it seems, this is so. In *Reg.* 622A he tells us that *hebdomades* mean *dignitates* and that there is a Greek word *hebdam* meaning the same as the Latin *Dignitas*. He is mistaken. *Hebdomas* has no meaning of excellence and *hebdam* not only does not exist in Greek but would be impossible. I wonder, however, if he may not be the victim of a copyist's error. He uses *ebdomadis* as the genitive singular, *hebdomades* as the accusative plural and *hebdomadibus* as the ablative plural. He must have known that *hebdomas* was the nominative singular and this may have been the reading where we now have *hebdam*.

the celestial theophany,[16] let not men without taste thrust their own interpretations on this work, men who cannot extend their course beyond the bounds of sense-knowledge, who, in the wake of dreams of the imagination, either remember what they have seen or, as contrivers of figments, discuss what they have never learned. Let those, however, who do not allow their reflexions to dwell on disgraceful imaginings but have the courage to raise them to a view of forms above the heavens,[17] enter the strait paths of my work, weighing with the reliable scales of discernment what deserves to be spread far and wide for public hearing, what deserves to be buried deep in silence.[18] Just as I do not fear deliberate attacks of destructive criticism from some, so too I do not expect a favouring breeze of praise from others. It was no congestion of inward pride trying to belch its way out to the public that drove me to compose this work, nor was it the desire for the favour of popular applause that summoned me to unwonted toil, but a desire to prevent my discourses from growing rusty from the long intervals between my treatment of them and to save myself from overexerting myself in labour and study for the benefit of others.[19]

[16] The account of heaven in Bk. 6.133 ff. *Theophania* would refer particularly to God's showing Himself; such a manifestation would bring the viewer the entire essence of Theology. See *Hierarchia Alani* for distinction between *Theosophia, Theophania* and *Theologia:* M. T. d'Alverny, *Textes Inédits*, 227; Cf. *Quoniam Homines*, ed. P. Glorieux, 121.

[17] Cf. *mentibus ab imaginibus defecatis* in *Prosa de Angelis*, ed. M. T. d'Alverny, *Textes Inédits*, 205.

[18] Cf. *Quoniam Homines*, ed. P. Glorieux, 120.

[19] It seems that Alan's lectures were being appropriated by others. See M. T. d'Alverny, *Textes Inédits*, 110.

VERSE PROLOGUE

The pen of the author and the ornaments of the poet I beg,[1] lest Clio,[2] my Muse, depressed by indolence,[3] wane in power and the pen lie idle rough with mould. The aged parchment rejoices to renew its youth with fresh writing, smiles in its desire to leave its ancient hiding place and the Muse plays on a slender reed.[4] Drench your poet, Apollo,[5] with the waters of your fountain that the parched mind, watered by your stream, may favour us with new growths and bring the tended growths to their final fruit.

[1] As early as Pindar the question was raised as to whether a good poem was the work of art or inspiration. By the time of Horace the accepted theory, under Peripatetic influence, was that both art and inspiration are necessary. Alan here prays to Apollo for inspiration. In Hellenistic times inspiration was spoken of as a draught from a sacred fountain. Alan varies the metaphor and speaks of inspiration as a watering of parched land. which will then produce a crop. He has great love for growing things and takes many metaphors from them. See Pind., *Olym.* 2.86-88; Hor., *A.P.* 295-296, 333, 408; Callim., *Scholia* ad Fr. 2, R. Pfeiffer, *Callimachus* (Oxford 1949) I.11; Apoll., *Argon.*, 1.1-4. The motif of the *Book of Wisdom* is that wisdom comes from God alone and comes in answer to the prayer of the innocent. In *Ecclesiasticus* there are frequent references to wisdom as a fount and stream, culminating in Wisdom's beautiful and poetic description of herself in terms of flowing waters in 24.35-44. Cf. *Sancti Thomae Aquinatis Commentum* in *Primum Librum Sententiarum Magistri Petri Lombardi,* ed. P. F. Mandonnet (Paris 1929) 2-5; Ninck, M. H., *Die Bedeutung des Wassers in Kult und Leben der Alten*, 2nd. ed. (Darmstadt 1960).

[2] One of the Muses, generally connected with history.

[3] Reading *dejecta.*

[4] Vir., *Buc.* 6.8.

[5] A Greek god associated with many things, including music, prophecy, medicine, development of civilization, codes of law, high moral and religious principles and philosophy. See Herod., 1.65.6; Aelian, *VH* 3.44. His shrine at Delphi was the most famous of Greek shrines.

BOOK I

That her gifts combined in one may more clearly re-echo her voice and the combination favour us with her own special gift, energetic and enthusiastic Nature[1] gathers together for one person the gifts which she has here and there bestowed on others individually. She seeks to fashion a work by which every other work is thrown into the shade. In this one work she would make amends for her mistakes of old, so that in this she may repair her failures elsewhere. As she nurses this work along, she begs for it the aid of every grace and in her desire to be adorned with the gift of a favour so great,[2] she calls for the anvil's[3] aid. But the anvil is overtasked and feeble when it expends its energies on projects so great. Nature is eager for a power that is beyond her and she plans herself a work that is above her ability. Thus she strains to be superior to other artisans and admits that she has

[1] In *Dist.* 871 A-D., Alan gives eleven definitions of Nature. For its meaning in the *Anticlaudianus*, see G. Raynaud De Lage, *Alain de Lille, Poète du XIIe Siècle*, (Montréal and Paris 1951) 59-67. His summary is worth quoting: "C'est Dieu même qui a institué un réseau de causes secondes, qui a défini leur domaine en même temps qu'il a orienté leur action; mais, une fois le système constitué, le Créateur respecte son autonomie et normalement n'intervient pas dans son fonctionnement. Nature représente ce système, personifie la regularité et continuité de son action, résume l'orientation correcte de ses tendances dans l'ordre moral comme dans l'ordre physique, reflète enfin l'autorité divine qui lui été déléguée et qui justifie la rayonnement dont le poète l'a parée". See also Tullio Gregory, *Anima Mundi, La Filosofia di Guglielmo di Conches e la Scuola di Chartres* (Florence 1955) 175-246; *La Filosofia della Nature nel Medioevo, Atti del Terzo Congresso Internazionale di Filosofia Medioevale* (Milan 1965) 255-259, 279-296, 320-326. Cf. M. Baumgartner, *Die Philosophie des Alanus de Insulis, Beiträge* 11 (Münster 1896) 76-84. For Alan all virtues have their foundation in Nature. In *De Virtutibus et Viciis*, he says that vengeance and severity are not virtues, "since every virtue has its foundation, *inicium*, in Nature", and they spring from infirmity. See edition by J. Huizinga, as appendix to *Über die Verknüpfung des Poetischen mit dem theologischen bei Alanus de Insulis* (Amsterdam 1932) 99-100. Cf. *De Pl. Nat.* 432A-442A: W. 431-437. Not all of Alan's contemporaries would agree that Nature was fundamentally and essentially good. See E. Gilson, *La Philosophie au Moyen Age*, 2nd. Ed. (Paris 1947) 317 ff.

[2] Cf. August., *Ps.* 95.12, *PL* 37.1596 ff., *Sermo* 4.31, *PL*38.50.

[3] The anvil signifies the pains the poet must take with his work.

over-reached herself. Feeling these sudden stirrings in her mind, she does not straightway rush into this work but considers whether she is equal to it and weighs every detail in the scales of reason.[4]

Forthwith, then, she calls her sisters to hear her prayers,[5] begging that the rule of worthy counsel come directly down from them and restrain the ardour of her mind so that thus she may, with the support of the pruning knife of reason, bring her mind's ideas to fulfilment in actual works or revise,[6] improve and reshape plans long conceived. Thus not disdaining the hard road of seeking advice, she calls the heavenly Council. The elite of the heavenly army leave their home on high, calm earth with their light and deign to honour the land with their blessed steps. The court of heaven, enduring its disdain of our world, descends from its splendour above. As they grant earth their own particular light for a time, the land is surprised to experience new footsteps: it rejoices at the burden, but the weight of a burden is judged in relation to the honour it brings.

Concord, Peace's foster-child, is first to get under way: then comes Plenty pouring all sorts of things from a full horn,[7] Favour, Youth bedecked with many a grace, Laughter that banishes the gloomy clouds from our minds, Temperance,[8] Moderation content within set limits, Reason, the measure of good (to her happy Honesty ever clings and accompanies her

[4] Cf. Hor., *A.P.* 441.

[5] Vir., *Aen.,* 5.234.

[6] The file, *lima,* was used to make erasures on wax tablets. Thus the "labour of the file" (*labor limae,* Hor., *A.P.* 291) means revision. Cf. *De Pl. Nat.* 451C: W. 465; Ovid, *Tr.* 1.5.19; 1.7.30.

[7] *Copia Cornu.* Amalthea was a she-goat, nurse of Zeus. Her horns flowed with nectar and ambrosia. One broke off, was filled with fruit and given to Zeus. This is "the horn of plenty". For another version of the legend, see Ovid, *Met.* 9.88 ff.

[8] *Pudor.* This is glossed as *Temperantia* in one Manuscript. *Temperantia* could not be fitted into a dactylic line. In view of the attention devoted to Temperance and to excesses in food and drink in *De Pl. Nat.* 461C-463D, 473C-474A: W. 484-488, 506-507, Alan would not omit it from his list.

with joyous tread), Decorum, Prudence weighing all things in her scales, Piety, Sincerity[9] that cannot, under the cloak of deception, simulate a hypocritical love for us and the Virtue[10] which scatters riches and pours out gifts: with her, wealth knows not a lazy peace nor can the pile of buried treasure sleep, but going abroad again and again, it changes from master to master. Finally Nobility,[11] below the best in renown for beauty, follows their steps from afar. Although there is something distinguished in her mien, her face could not in every detail match the beauty of the others. She is more favoured in gifts from Fortune but the Graces[12] shed Nature's endowments on her with a somewhat sparing hand. These children of the gods haste their steps to Nature's citadel and the chorus breathes its special honour on the house.

There is a place apart,[13] far distant from our region, a place that smiles at the turmoils of our lands. That place by itself has

[9] *vera Fides.* This is not the theological virtue of faith that appears in Bk. 6.23 ff. *Fides* in general means trustworthiness. Truth (*Veritas*), Sincerity (*Sinceritas*), Loyalty (*Fidelitas*) are aspects of it. Neither *Veritas, Sinceritas* nor *Fidelitas* could be fitted into the metre. In Bk. 9.349 *Fides* is the Virtue opposed to Fraud or Deception (*Fraus*) and here it refers to genuineness of feeling. Sincerity seems the best rendering. Alan was not the first to be faced with the necessity of using a periphrasis to identify something that would not fit the metre. See Hor., *Serm.* 1.5.87.

[10] A gloss correctly identifies this as *Largitas*, Generosity. *Largitas* would not fit into the metrical scheme. As Alan here uses *virtus* in references to one of Nature's sisters, it might be well to consider in what sense he regards them as *virtutes*. Prudence (2.355 ff.) emphasizes that the work of Nature and her sisters is restricted to the formation of man's body. In Bk. 1.33-54, then, we have personifications of factors or qualities that contribute to the perfection of man's body. This explains the presence of Plenty, Youth and Laughter. Huizinga (66) is mistaken in thinking that *vera fides* is the theological virtue of Faith. Alan's terminology makes it clear that he had in mind the council of Allecto and her sisters in Claud., *In Ruf.* 1.25 ff. To that council came Discord, Hunger, Old Age, Disease, Envy, Sorrow, Fear, Luxury, Want, Cares, Avarice.

[11] *Nobilitas*, the daughter of Fortune, refers in Alan to external things; it has nothing to do with nobility of soul. It means High Estate or Noble Lineage. She has an abundance of the gifts of Fortune but fewer of the interior gifts that come from the Graces. Cf. the *Latia nobilitate* of Nero in Bern. Silv., 1.3.48.

[12] *Gracia.* For the use of the singular for the plural, see Ovid, *Met.* 6.429.

[13] For description of Nature's garden, see accounts of the Golden Age in Cat., 64; Vir., *Buc.* 2.6; Ovid, *Met.* 1. 89 ff.; Avitus, *De Mundi Initio, De Originali Peccato* (1-34)

the power of all other places combined; what is in short supply in the others will be found in greater abundance in this one place. In this place Nature shows what her bounteous hand can do and where she is most pleased to pour out her gifts. There the earth, clothed in flowers of tender down, glittering with its own stars, afire with the purple of roses, tries to fashion[14] a second heaven. There the charm of the budding flower does not perish by a birth-death, for the rose is not a maid at morn, a tired crone by eve, but rejoicing in a never-changing appearance, stays young with the gift of eternal Spring. Winter does not nip this flower nor Summer parch it. The fury of mad Boreas does not rage there; Notus does not bring his lightning nor do hail-darts beat upon it. That place of places has and holds everything that feasts the eye, intoxicates the ear,[15] beguiles the taste, catches the nose with its aroma and soothes the touch. Untroubled by ploughshare, this land produces everything that wars against disease and, banishing the bane of harassing illness, restores our health. Without the extraneous aid of husbandman, content with Nature's hand and the favouring Zephyrus, the land bears and gives birth not indeed to common produce but to things wondrous and it prides itself on a progeny so large.

A wood, made to resemble a wall in arrangement, encompasses the place, a wood rejoicing in fresh flowers, topped with green foliage, uneroded by decay, not subject to the axe's ire, not levelled to the ground, not made inaccessible by strewn branches. Winter, that feeds on fresh young blooms, does not plunder its wealth of flowers nor shear its foliage-tresses.

in *MGH* Poetae 6.2., 203-213. Cf. F. J. E. Raby, *A History of Christian-Latin Poetry from the Beginnings to the Close of the Middle Ages* (Oxford 1927) 78. Claud., *In Ruf.* 1.380-387 gives an account of a Golden Age but it is no longer a rustic one. Rivers of wine, lakes of oil and sea-weed filled with jewels are features of it. The significance of the garden motif is discussed in P. Piehler, *The Visionary Landscape* (London 1971).

[14] *Pingere.* For the use of this word in Alan, see Huizinga, 60-66.

[15] The odd expression, *intoxicare aurem,* is found in Juv., 9.113, but is more apt there as a drunkard is being described.

Whatever tree cannot pay Nature's tribute of seed and fruit pays the penalty of exile, but every tree, anxious to purchase by better fruit the favour of Nature and to outdo the others in its gift, ever keeps produce in mind.

The Sirens of the grove, Spring's harpists, the birds, have congregated in this place and all around sing their honey-sweet songs as they pipe from pulsing throats; they reproduce in song the lyre's notes and as the hearer drinks in these songs, the sound brings sweet feast to his ears.

The land at its centre weeps and shedding tears in blessed woe, produces a fount of never-failing water and sobs forth sweet draughts. The silvery stream rids itself of connatal dregs as it comes again under the laws of a pure element; separating itself from foreign dross, it sparkles in its native brightness. Draughts from it inebriate the bosom of the fertile land and speed fulfilment of Earth-Mother's prayer for progeny. Like draughts the land generously bestows on trees and prompts in them the desire for offspring.

At the grove's centre a mountain, topped with high plateau, rises to the sky and kisses the clouds. Here the home of Nature rises on high, if indeed one may call it by that name since by its god-like majesty it can surpass the starry dwellings and the abode of the gods and does not deign to compare itself with kings' palaces. Set apart from our dwellings, a happier hall, sustained by long columns, cleaves the air. It flashes bright with clusters of gems and glows with gold, nor is it less graced with silver's distinctive adornment. Material, which is inferior to these and is subject to degeneration in its beauty, has no rights here. Here a charming mural depicts men's character.[16] The

[16] The paintings show specimens of Nature's handiwork. Of those figuring in the descriptions of the paintings, Paris, Hippolytus, Priam, Turnus, Odysseus, Hercules, Cicero, Virgil, Nero, Plato appear in that order in Bern. Silv., 1.3.42-52. Turnus, Odysseus, Plato, Cicero, Aristotle, Paris, Ennius appear in *De Pl. Nat.* 479D-480A: W. 517.

painting faithfully fastens its attention on its special project so that its representation of the subject may the less depart from reality. Oh painting with your new wonders! [17] What can have no real existence comes into being and painting, aping reality and diverting itself with a strange art, turns the shadows of things into things and changes every lie to truth.

Thus this art's power subtly checks logic's arguments and triumphs over logic's sophisms. Logic gives proofs, painting creates; logic argues, painting brings to pass everything that can exist. Thus, both wish the false to appear true but painting pursues this end more faithfully. In that mural Aristotle [18] prepares arms for the logician and presents his school of logic, but Plato's [19] profound mind has a more inspired vision of the secrets of heaven and earth and he tries to search the mind of God. In his own way Seneca,[20] the best cultivator of morals and husbandman of reason, forges character by reason. Ptolemy,[21]

[17] *O nova picture miracula.* The idea of art's power to astonishing and seemingly impossible things dates back to Homer, where there is a reference to a *miraculum* (*θαῦμα*) in that the land on Achilles' shield seemed black though the shield was of gold (*Il.* 18.549). At a very simple level this example could clarify what Alan has to say about painting. What can have no real existence comes into being, e.g. black gold. The painter turns the shadow of things into things; one looking at the shield would say "there is ploughed land". Every lie is turned into truth: "yellow gold is black" is false but true as regards the artistic representation. However, Alan is echoing the thoroughly Platonic idea that the world of Art is a second (for Plato, a third) and misleading world, connected with the real word by way of imitation or mimesis.

[18] Aristotle's *Prior Analytics* was the first great work on formal Logic. Alan has no great admiration for him. Cf. 3.115 ff., *De Pl. Nat.*, 479D: W. 517. Before the School of Chartres integrated philosophical speculation and the liberal arts, Logic tended to be a mere dialectical exercise. John of Salisbury insists that logic is of great value if used with other subjects but futile if used by itself. *Metalogicon* 2.9; 2.10. Webb 76, 83.

[19] Alan shows a high regard for Plato. Cf. 2.345; *De Pl. Nat.*, 468C: W. 497: 479D: W 517. His only criticism of him is in *Quoniam Homines*, ed. P. Glorieux, 126, where he finds fault with some of his ideas on God. For Alan's attitude to Plato and Aristotle, see Baumgartner, 9-12.

[20] Tutor and for a time political adviser to Nero. The bulk of his prose work is philosophical and abounds in moral exhortation.

[21] His *Almagest* was the recognised authority on Astronomy until the late Middle Ages.

with his overflowing stream of genius, is carried in the chariot of reason to the citadels on high: he considers the harmony of the stars, their places, times and courses. Tullius,[22] makes up for the limitations of a language by the splendour of his style and flashes forth, distinguished by witticisms. Virgil's[23] Muse shades many a lie and from the appearance of truth weaves a cloak for falsehood. Here strength and discretion weight out their gifts with equal balance. Strength is the arms of the descendant of Alceus,[24] discretion of Ulysses.[25] Lest his feast of riches agitate his mind, Titus[26] pours out his wealth with lavish hand and forces his gifts on their way. The bold and impetuous Turnus[27] ever

[22] Boethius, *Contra Eutychen* 3 (Stewart-Rand 88), says that Cicero maintains that the Latin language is not equal to the task of expressing Greek philosophical ideas. Cicero attributed this opinion to others. *De Nat. Deorum*, 1.4., but he refuses to subscribe to it, *ib.*, 3.2. Lucretius, on the other hand, bewails the poverty of Latin in regard to conveying the philosophical ideas of the Greeks: *De Rerum Natura,* 1.136-9, 832-5. Cf. *Quoniam Homines,* ed. P. Glorieux, 171.

[23] In the sixth century B.C., Xenophanes, the poet of the Ionian intellectual enlightenment, unfortunately set out to evaluate Homer as a teacher of theology and found that his whole concept of the gods was unacceptable. Anaximander and Anaximenes showed that Homer's cosmology was inaccurate. Soon the "lies of Homer" became proverbial. The basic mistake lay in looking at Homer merely as a teacher. With few exceptions (notably Aristotle and Eratosthenes), literary critics devoted far too much attention to accuracy in poetry. This was to continue down to and into vernacular literature. Alan has a long section in *De Pl. Nat.* devoted to an explanation of the lies of the poets. Xenophanes, *Fr.* 11 (Diehls); Arist., *Poet.* 25.1460b; *De Pl. Nat.*, 451A-452A: W. 465-466. Perhaps the most forthright statement about the lies of poetry comes from Gundisalvus: "It is the special function of poetry to use words to make one imagine that something is attractive or repulsive when it is not so ... Often a man's learning or knowledge wars with his imagination and in such cases he directs his actions by his imagination, not by what he knows or thinks": *De Scientiis* 2, ed. M. A. Alonso (Madrid-Granada 1954) 75. Cf. Chaucer, *House of Fame* 3.1477-80. See W. Wetherbee, "The Function of Poetry in the De Planctu Naturae of Alain de Lille". *Traditio* 25 (1969) 87-125.

[24] Hercules.

[25] King of Ithaca, a Greek hero at the siege of Troy. He was known as a master of intrigue and stratagem and a very persuasive speaker. See Hom., *Il.* 3.200 ff.

[26] Roman Emperor. He had a reputation for liberality, though most of it consisted in a rather free use of public funds (Suet, *Titus* 7). See Wilhelm Rath, *Bernardus Silvestris, über die allumfassende Einheit der Welt* (Stuttgart s.d.) 56, n. 21.

[27] King of the Rutulians. His fight against Aeneas is found in Vir., *Aen.* 7-12.

presses on to battle with clashing sword: he knows not fear and is careless of his life. The chaste Hippolytus[28] rejoices at his escape from the reins of Venus[29] and the Cytherean[30] goddess bemoans a chastity beyond her control.

The palace with its mural has these appearances of things, these figures and phantoms of truth and it is gay with so much beauty. However, a saddish painting, displaying a less noble aspect of beauty, covers the most recently allotted space there. You would think that the painting had not carried its game[31] far enough or at least had been affected by dreams and had felt the subtle winds of madness, or rather you would imagine that Nature had failed in this instance by forgetting the work she had in hand. The painting's face seems distracted and to be begging a better form, but neither the glitter of gems, day-bright in splendour, nor the gleam of silver nor gold with its more attractive sheen can serve as a defence for the full-blown crime represented in the painting or keep it from growing dull and pale amidst its gold. There our own Ennius[32] in a patch-work poem writes for the mob and thunders forth the fortunes of Priam.[33] There Maevius,[34] daring to raise a dumb mouth to heaven, tries

[28] Alan has the version of the legend found in Euripides, *Hippolytus*. Hippolytus had no interest in sex. His stepmother, Phaedra, became enamoured of him. He rejected her. She committed suicide, leaving a letter accusing him. When his father, Theseus, returned, he banished Hippolytus and used one of three wishes given him by Poseidon to ensure his doom. A sea-monster terrified Hippolytus' horses. He fell from the chariot and was dragged by the horses to such an extent that he died in a very short time.

[29] Goddess of love.

[30] Venus. The title comes from Cythera, an island in the Aegean, a prominent centre of her cult.

[31] In line 124 he spoke of painting as playing with the shadows of things.

[32] Alan had little regard from Ennius. See *De Pl. Nat.*, 480A: W. 518. Cf. Hor., *A.P.* 260. A gloss of William of Auxerre states that Alan was here referring to Joseph of Exeter, who wrote a *De Bello Troiano.*

[33] King of Troy.

[34] Maevius or Mevius, a poetaster, contemporary of Virgil and Horace. He is attacked in Virg., *Buc.* 3.90 and in Hor., *Ep.* 10. Alan is undoubtedly referring to Walter of Châtillon whose *Alexandreis* begins: *Gesta ducis Macedum.* For Alan's opposition to Joseph of Exeter and Walter of Châtillon, see De Lage, 22 ff.

to portray the exploits of the Macedonian leader in a dark and shadowy ode; tired he is slowed down at the very beginning of the course and complains that his muse grows slow and listless. There Nero[35] with swift thunderbolt shakes the world, gives himself up to crime and drives his madness to wish for more than madness by itself would desire; whatever evil he exudes spreads itself over the whole world. There the rich man is in need: Midas[36] in the very midst of gold, thirsts for gold and sets no limit to his desire for more possessions. Ajax,[37] outsoldiering soldiery, goes beyond the requirements for soldiers and the soldier's stability degenerates into madness. Paris,[38] overcome by love, melted on Venus's fire, fights to retain his Venus; when

[35] Nero's excesses became a byword. M. Hutchings maintains that Nero, Midas, Ajax, Paris, Davus refer respectively to Henry II of England and his sons, Henry, Richard-Cœur-de-Lion, Geoffrey, John: "L'Anticlaudianus d'Alain de Lille, Etude de Chronologie," *Romania* 50 (1924), 1-13. The references to Paris seem based on definite episodes in the *Iliad*. It is not easy to see that a comparison with Ajax could be regarded as an attack. Achilles might have been a more apt choice. However, Alan definitely had some contemporary characters in mind and undoubtedly Hutchings is correct in his identification.

[36] A legendary Phrygian king. There are several legends connected with him. Alan is following the one that says that Dionysus offered him anything he wished. His wish was that everything he touched should turn into gold. He was to find out that this applied to his food and drink.

[37] The gigantic, courageous, stable "bulwark of the Achaeans" in the Trojan war. Alan is probably referring to his enormous size (Il. 3.226 ff.) and to the fact that he bore more than his share of the fighting. In *Od.* 11.543 ff., his death is attributed to the arms of Achilles having been given to Odysseus rather than to him. Later sources, the best known of which is the *Ajax* of Sophocles, state that the loss of the arms drove him to madness and suicide.

[38] Son of Priam. His abduction of Helen led to the Trojan war. Alan is referring to two separate episodes. Antenor proposed to end the war by returning Helen and all her property to Agamemnon and Menelaus. Paris replied that he would give up all the property but not Helen (*Il.* 7.356 ff.). On another occasion, Paris offered to meet any one of the enemy in single combat. Menelaus accepted the challenge and Paris ran back in fear to the Trojan ranks. Taunted by Hector, he agreed to the combat and was on the verge of being killed when Aphrodite (the Roman Venus) rescued him and transported him to his bedroom. She brought Helen to him and there he spent part of one of the grimmest days of the war for the Trojans. Hector came to reproach him and even Helen expressed her disgust (*Il.* 3.15 ff.).

he lays aside the soldier's role, to his reproach he makes up with her for what he is losing in battle. The owl is surprised to see the form peculiar to herself in Davus[39] and finds in him consolation for the blemishes in her own appearance. Whatever, then, receives in full the gifts of Nature or avoids her moderating art the painting's story shows drawn by the pen. Nature, which decrees every single thing with profound wisdom, has its own ordinances for these abodes and with far-seeing eye shapes the laws which it promulgates throughout the wide world. She examines the causes[40] of things and the seeds of the universe. She sees who reformed ancient chaos with a fairer aspect when matter,[41] as it bemoaned its disorder, sought the aid of improving form and a fair mien; who, seeking to check by a trustworthy bond civil wars and fraternal quarrels, imparted to the elements the kiss of peace and bound them together with the more effective knot of number; who beholds with unimpaired judgement earthquakes, the crash of the thunderbolt, the sea's raging tempests, the battling gales and skilfully restrains the weather's vagaries within an effective enclosure; why Winter, saddened by hoar-frost, grieves; why Spring smiles; why Summer pulses with heat; why Autumm pours out a great torrent of fruit; why the earth is stationary; why water flows; why air circulates; why flame leaps upwards and ungrudgingly keeps faith with the other elements; why water in liquid form, not daring to

[39] Davus is a stock name for a slave in the Comedies of Plautus and Terence. The owl's face has something clownish about it. *Tyll Eulenspiegel* is a mischievous clown, hero of a very old German folk-tale.

[40] For causality in Alan, see De Lage, 59 ff.

[41] Alan explains the word in *Dist:,* 944C as meaning, among other things, *primordial matter.* ὕλη in Greek means both a *forest* and *raw material.* From the second meaning it easily came to mean *primordial matter. Silva* strictly means a *forest* in Latin. The meaning, *primordial matter*, seems to be a development of its use by Cicero (often with a palliative, e.g. *quasi*) to translate the *raw material* meaning of ὕλη.See J. R. O'Donnell, "The meaning of 'Silva' in the Commentary on the *Timaeus* of Plato by Chalcidius", *Mediaeval Studies* 7 (1945) 1-20.

break faith, keeps its covenant with earth and restricts itself to a definite course.[42]

When the heavenly band had filled the gilded seats and the house itself shone with the effulgence of so much divinity and was astonished at the light of a day so great, Nature stood up in the centre of the council-chamber. Keeping her head somewhat inclined towards the ground, showing her thoughts by her serious expression, with her right hand she commanded silence and holding their rapt attention, she proceeded to speak as follows:[43]

> "Long and frequently and with a mind ingenious in many fields, have I reconsidered each and everything that the skill of our right hand has fashioned. Yet I find no living thing that is perfect in every way and could not bring many complaints against us, should it choose to attack our art. Since, however, we regret the mistakes our hands have made, these errors do little harm and blacken less the record of what we have done. I cannot, however, wipe out ingrained stains: the law of prescription in favour of a condition deep-set and long established protects them. For medicine has nothing to suggest when the source of the disease is chronic and longstanding illnesses look not for slow-working treatment. I imagine that there is but one relief for so great a pestilence but I refuse to give a detailed

[42] *unda labilis* is difficult to translate. It means "water capable of flowing". *Genesis*, 1. 6-8, tells of God's separation of the waters beneath the firmament from those above. *Aer* came to be regarded as the means of separation. The water beneath *aer* was called *aqua labilis*, the water above, *aqua vaporaliter suspensa*. See Thierry of Chartres, *Tractatus de Sex Dierum Operibus*, ed. N. M. Häring, *Commentary on Boethius by Thierry of Chartres and his School* (Toronto 1971) 558-559. Cf. Clarembald of Arras, *Tractatus super Boetii Librum de Trinitate*, 18, and *Tractulus super Librum Genesis*, 41, ed. N. M. Häring, *Life and Works of Clarembald of Arras* (Toronto 1965) 114, 244. In Bk. 1. 194, Alan speaks of the covenant arranged by Nature between the four elements. He here speaks of "keeping the convenant". If the fire's flame spread laterally or water did not collect in wells and streams, earth would be destroyed.

[43] Nature's address. Cf. Claud., *In Ruf.* 1. 86-115.

description of how this would be accomplished until my intention receives the approval of your expressed judgement. Long has this idea lain impressed upon my mind that all of us together, with zeal, care and skill, should exert ourselves on one work: that each should pour on it so many gifts that, when these gifts are given, she may seem herself to be in need: that the faults of our work be redeemed in one work: that the perfection of that one make up for the faults of many and that one washing remove so many blots. Through our efforts let a man[44] not just human but divine, inhabit the earth, a man with no odour of earthly dregs and let him console us for the damage we have done. Through his soul let him dwell in heaven through his body on earth. On earth he will be human, in heaven divine.[45] Thus he will become God and man, so becoming both that he is not just either and he will tread with perfect safety the road between the two.[46] In him let our skill and our gifts find expression. Let him be for us a mirror that we may see ourselves in him, see our trustworthiness, our power, our strength and the extent to which that strength can improve. If the difficulty of the labour points an accusing finger at our inadequacies for a task so great and maintains that our skill is unequal to the work we undertake, the nobility of the project is our defence and it answers the objections arising from our sense of modesty. If Nature does not admit our inadequacy, then courage of soul should lend its aid and bring our desires to fulfilment. For what no one can do by herself, our efforts combined for a single project will effect, so that where individual efforts are of no avail, the combined efforts of many working at the same time

[44] For concept of perfect man, see Introduction, p. 29ff.

[45] Bern. Silv., 2.10.15 ff.

[46] *Ib.* 2.10.19. Cf. *De Arte Praed.*, 161C; Ovid, *Met.* 2.137.

may prove helpful. For many rivulets gushing forth make a stream, many sparks produce a flame and a number of stones makes a heap.[47] Alas! let us feel shame that our work so often missed the mark and that the result was so often a poor return for our effort. Alas! let us feel shame that our decrees for the earth get no hearing because love for us grows cold, our waning reputation loses its power, we are exiled from the whole world as useless, Tisiphone[48] looses the reins of crime, hands them over to the world, rejoices as she triumphs over our race and sucks her joy from our grief. We are suffering defeat; Erinys[49] puts the defeated beneath her heel and punishes our necks with heavy chains."

Thus Nature expresses her thoughts in words, brings her discourse to an end and her speech to its conclusion. The Council rejoices and agrees with Nature; it praises her desire and the Sister's desires do not differ from hers.

Here Prudence, set apart by the restraint shown in her quiet mien and reserved manner, arises. Her golden tresses fall around her neck but a hair-pin parts them and checks the struggling locks[50] and a comb imposes its rule upon them. Her well-ordered brows, in proper balance arranged, neither too light nor beclouded with luxuriant growth,[51] resemble twin crescents.[52]

[47] A reference to the *sorites*, the sophistical puzzle: "how many stones make a heap ?"

[48] One of the Furies; the other two were Allecto and Megaera.

[49] Strictly speaking, *Erinyes* in the Greek equivalent of the Latin *Furiae*. Alan uses *Herinis (= Erinys)* to mean *one of the Furies*. This is standard usage in Latin. Cf. Vir., *Aen.* 7.447; 7.570; Ovid.« *Met.* 1.241; 4.90. Alan's use of *one of the Furies*, after he had mentioned Tisiphone by name, is somewhat clumsy.

[50] *litigium crinis, litigation between locks.* Alan liked this odd phrase to describe unruly locks. Cf. *De Pl. Nat.*, 432B: W. 431; 472A; W. 502; 475B; W. 509.

[51] Cf. *De Pl. Nat.*, 432B: W. 431.

[52] *sese geminos exemplat in arcus.* Alan probably got this phrase from Propertius 4.6.25. It is a pity that he did not use some form of *lunarat*, the word that gives some distinction to Propertius' line.

Her radiant eyes give forth starlight, her forehead stands forth lily-like, her nose gives balsam-odour, her teeth rival ivory, her mouth, the rose. Living colour glows upon her face and no adventitious lustre makes its disgraceful contribution to the image of a beauty so great.[53] Lilies wedded to roses have chastened the face's brightened glow and a rosy tint prevents a cloak of paleness from overshadowing its fair hue. The smooth chin, brighter than silver, more striking than yellow gold, clearer than ice, more delicate than any crystal, does not lessen the beauty of the roseate lips.[54] The neck sits beautifully, its nape not extending far from its seat on the shoulders but rising with the distinction of due length. The apple-like breasts,[55] descending in gentle swell, hang not flaccid and broken-down but by their very firmness give proof of personal chastity. She extends her arms in a wide sweep before folding them and you would think that they sought what they might duly embrace.[56] Her curved flanks, yielding to fit restraint, unite the upper and lower parts of her body, the head and the feet.[57] Who does not know that beneath these other and better things lie hidden to which the quiet exterior serves but as an introduction?[58] No space, marked off with set measurements, impedes the movement of her body or checks it with definite limits. Now going further away, she strikes the heavens with her head; now leaving us gazing in vain, she takes up abode among the heavenly bodies; now she returns to us and submits to the discipline of our restraints.

Her robe was woven of fine thread; it does not fake its colour and by no trick does it deceive our eyes: rather its native red

[53] Alan follows the tradition of denouncing cosmetics. Cf. *De Pl. Nat.*, 472D: W. 502.

[54] *De Pl. Nat.*, 432C: W. 432.

[55] *De Pl. Nat.*, 432D: W. 432.

[56] *Ib.*

[57] *Ib.*

[58] *De Pl. Nat.*, 432A: W. 432.

permeates it.[59] There the material does not seek the support of beauty nor do defects in beauty seek to cloak themselves. Neither element is deficient; neither yields precedence to its counterpart; both face on equal terms the contest to determine which will win. The image[60] that emerges shows, as in a dream, the beauty of things, which, however, old age bids die to some extent and few traces of the old beauty remain: yet she unclasps this robe to rend it apart in various places: the robe seems to mourn and bewail the insults heaped upon it. In her right hand she balances a scale which weighs each and every thing — its number, form, measure, weight, cause. Thus adorned, gay in this clothing, wise Prudence prepares to speak and the council hangs on her words. Eyes and ears turn quickly and intently toward her but their differing desires conflict. The eyes seek to feast on beauty so great, the ears to draw honeyed words from her lips. In the following words, then, Prudence speaks her mind while rapt attention holds her sisters spell-bound.

"This opinion, envisaging a project so great, has no flavour that is not divine: it is so refined by the fire of reason that no trace of foreign dregs remains. It does not bespeak slackness of mind nor the lethargy of a dulled intellect. It is not based on sudden impulses nor is it spat out from the tip of the lips; it comes from the depths of the mind and offers healing for our ills. That mind has a wisdom beyond man; it is flavoured with the relish of divine intellect, from whose deep fount a river flows that gives your minds

[59] Reading *illam.*

[60] Lines 310-314 do not give an account of things actually happening but of a dream or vision that comes to the viewer. The unclasping and rending of the robe signify the indignities to which Prudentia will be subjected. The description of Prudentia resembles the description of *Philosophia* in Boeth., *De Cons.* Pr. 1 (Stewart-Rand 130 ff.). In Boethius violent hands had cut off parts of Philosophy's robe and carried them off. The violent hands represent the philosophical sects.

discernment. Nature's mind, then, supported by a patron so great[61] does not lie inactive, is not short of virtue nor devoid of reason, does not wander abroad unbridled, is not tossed about by chance. What biting attack could hurt that great mind? What sting of envy could urge it on? What spite or hatred could bring confusion's cloud upon it? Why should a royal path guide it and lead it along the right road in its travels? It is to guarantee[62] that what you have conceived may not be aborted, that so great a project may not collapse, that light may not come to its end in shadow but may be brought out and flash forth. Let this plan go forth to enjoy the common good;[63] under the light it will have a better development. What lies hidden and shut off[64] from the influence of this good grows weaker from insufficient light, but it is a more shining success if it enjoys the light. Thus the flower will turn to fruit, the overflowing stream will return to its regular channel and the rich corn-ear will advance to the harvest. What better than this can the concept of a noble mind hope for? What more beyond this will it be able to desire? If the idea is a good one, if it is permitted to go so far, let the idea take a firm stand on this project and seek not to wander farther afield. But there remains this consideration which upsets my mind, puts an obstacle in the plan's way and slows my designs. It is the fact that our skill, which is thus bringing the man towards existence and yearns to perform this task, does not realise the strength required for a work so great, the burden of its

[61] *tanto suffulta patrono* could mean *modelled on so great an exemplar.*

[62] I am putting a period after *praefulguret* (1.345). If "It is to guarantee ... flash" is not an answer to "Why should a royal path ... travels ?", the question is pointless.

[63] *in commune bonum*, in the context of what follows, must mean *into the sunlight.*

[64] *sepe* is best understood as the ablative of *sepis, an enclosure.* It is difficult to grow crops in a small enclosure where trees of high hedges deprive them of sunlight.

many parts, the great labour involved. In so far as our skill does not bring him into being, it but works on him but does not complete him. It ever moves him closer to being but never brings him all the way. It can work towards his being but has not the power to bring about his birth. The two constituents of this man's being, though different in nature and substance and unlike in formation,[65] come together to give him being. One has the flavour of earth, the other of heaven; the latter's home is in heaven, the former's on earth; one is compelled to pay its debt to death, death's law holds the other exempt; one is permanent, the other transitory; one endures, the other passes away; one has the name of being, the other has divinity. The body possesses the earth, the spirit the heavens: earth then, holds earthly things, heaven keeps heavenly things. The mortal body recognizes our anvil, calls for our artisans and our art; the birth of a soul demands other artisans:[66] a heavenly origin demands the aid of a higher artisan and its form is beyond our mint. Showing the wonders of a divine product, it spurns our work and it smiles at the ordinariness of our art. The Wisdom of God alone, from the depth of whose breast comes everything that comes into being, knows how it comes forth from nothingness, without form, seed, cause, matter, movement, feeling, guide, helper, ungenerated, simple, living, moving, pure and without the aid of a supervisor. Here the elements are silent, the seeds of things lose their power, the stars grow faint, nature holds its peace, the planetary power fails and is surprised that its ordinances are stilled. Since then, the norm of

[65] *forma*. This cannot mean *form* as in *matter* and *form*. For the body and soul and their relationship, see Baumgartner 102-106.

[66] Alan constantly reminds us that the soul is directly created by God. See 1.388; 2.60; 5.215; 6.353; 7.34.

things knows no such power of creation on our part and the canvas is aghast at a figure so large and our hand suffers failure at the very beginning of such a work. I do not see, do not understand, do not judge that I know the manner, causes, principles, seeds, forms or instruments by which, with the intervention of our wisdom, the birth of a heavenly soul may be started on its way. I cannot, then, bring the scales of counsel to bear on this thing. I have no power, I hesitate, I stop, I am slowed down. Bereft of advice, argument and credibility, my suit will fail and my wish will not be crowned with a definite fulfilment unless Reason[67] weigh each and every thing on better scales. With her nothing is obscure, unstable, changeable, futile, unknown, deceptive; to her each and everything is clear, all is obvious, nothing in doubt. To her the stars do not seem high, the clouds dark or the sea deep. As the sun of the mind, the eye of the intellect, the light of the wayfarer, the homeland for the exiled, consolation in death, the rule of virtue, the path of right, let her replace doubt with certainty, falsehood with truth; let her consolidate the mind in certainty, cut out doubts, wipe away the darkness of error, make the mind's day clear with the light of truth and drive out the clouds of falsehood. Let a fairer breeze favour the mind, tossed by the waves of doubt, soothing by the gentle breath of Reason the mind's heaving tides and checking its surges. The great burden of work involved cannot bring an accusation of indolence against me. I do not give up, defeated by toil so great nor do I beg for the sanctuary of slothful rest. I will attempt whatever Reasons orders, nay, whatever she desires, and I shall not prove delinquent in

[67] Lines 399-413 are a magnificent tribute to reason. Cf. *De Pl. Nat.*, 443B-444A; W. 451; *Sent.* 251B.

anything touching me but shall work towards the objective as far as in me lies. But since it is considered disgraceful, unreliable, unstable and foolish not to bring what is begun to a finish or to give it a finish borrowed from something else so that the middle is not in keeping with the beginning nor the end with the middle,[68] I should prefer to give up in the beginning rather than fail at the end."

Thus she speaks and the entire council is shaken by a great whirlwind of doubt. The troubled troop of sisters waver in uncertainties, staying their turbulent thoughts as well as their deep voices and only a whisper runs around the place. Just as the wind roars, clouds whirl, the waves, which Zephyrus with gentle breath first smoothed, toss, if the wild North-wind shakes the sleeping deep or with force wakes up the hovering sea-storms, so too their spirits toss and mind conflicts with mind. The minds that Nature has previously blown over with gentle breath, Prudence blows over with stronger breeze.

Reason rises to her feet and with nod, voice, hand and face asks for silence. Her countenance rightly secures her peace and quiet and at the nod of the maiden's head, the waning whispers fade away. In her face there is a strong resemblance to Prudence and Prudence follows the lines of the countenance she copies.[69] The faces show relationship. Each has the contour of the other and within it fashions a face in conformity with herself. For

[68] Hor., *A.P.* 152. Cf. Arist., *Poet.* 6.1450b25.

[69] *Prudencia plurima vultu/paret.* This somewhat odd turn of phrase seems to go back to Statius, *Achilleid*, 164-165: *plurima vultu/mater inest,* "there is much of his [Parthenopaeus] mother [Atalanta] in his looks." Alan certainly kept the resemblance of Parthenopaeus and Atalanta in mind. References to it are to be found in *Regulae*, 641A and in *Dist.* 816D. His contemporary, Hugh of Honau, treats of the significance of facial resemblance in *Liber de Homoysion et Homoeysion*, 31.2, ed. N. M. Häring, *Archives* 34 (1967) 202 and in his *De Divinitate Naturae et Personae* 31.21, ed. N. M. Häring, *Archives* 27 (1962) 180.

either, one face calls both faces to mind. The two countenances are different from each other; their faces show differences, but, as sisters' faces should, not opposites. In them were matching faces, matching dress, matching bearing, matching restraint and matching grace but their countenances differed with their years. Reason more powerful carried the banner of seniority: she is greater in age, more mature in the fullness of years. Her right hand is resplendent, aflame with the brightness of a threefold mirror,[70] The delicate glass, which rejects as alien to it any rough handling and scarce can bear the light touch of a finger, has a triple reflection in the threefold mirror. Reason devotes her close attention to the use of one of the mirrors. In this mirror she sees the system of causes;[71] she examines the primordial element of things. She sees the marriage of matter and form; she sees the kisses which the union shares;[72] she sees what this temporary union toasts as it weds matter to form.[73] She sees which form gives matter existence, which completes that existence; which sets a thing on the road to existence, which brings it to the end of the road, which produces it, which changes it, which preserves it in being. She sees what a thing is or how large, of what kind, how it is and she discovers its other conditions. The surface of silver which covers the beautiful second mirror has rid itself of the alloy in the ore and flashes forth with a brightness surpassing the light of day and the stars.

[70] Lines 450-510. The three mirrors correspond to the four spheres in the *Sermo de Sphaera Intelligibili.* See Marie Therese d'Alverny, *Textes Inédits*, 168-169, 299-301. Cf. the *speculum Providentiae* in Bern. Silv., 2.11.16 ff. The same lines show the effects of the neo-platonism of the school of Chartres, particularly that of William of Conch, Gilbert of Poitiers, John of Salisbury and Thierry of Chartres.

[71] For the system of causes under a first cause, cf. 6.181; *Reg.,* 55-56, 647A-B, 654A.

[72] For *concrecio* referring to the union of matter and form, see Gilbert of Poitiers, ed. N. M. Häring, 84.

[73] *Nativa* in Gilbert of Poitiers means "what begins and ends in time", "what is corruptible". To this is opposed *genuina* "what is eternal". See ed. N. M. Häring, 256.

Here she sees matter divorced from form return to primordial chaos and pure form seek again her own source, regain her youth in her proper state and no longer have to bemoan her disgust with degenerate matter. She sees how form joyfully finds rest in her own being and no longer suffers,[74] like one shipwrecked, the changing tides of matter but how, like a wanderer, she returns to her place of origin, escapes the destruction of matter and avoids sharing its death. The youth of form, not ravished by aged matter, keeps form forever a fair maid. With unruffled countenance and profound mind, she perceives how the composite is simple; the heavenly, mortal; the different, identical; the heavy, light; the moving, stationary; the dark, bright; the dear, cheap; the jocose, tearsome; the eternal, temporal; the revolving, fixed.[75] The excellence of gold, more refined than any known gold, and scarcely deigning to recognise its own genus and species, lends its reflection to a mirror, the third one, which cannot counterfeit the shadow of things but shows every thing with more definiteness and reflects the whole with greater clarity. Here she sees the fount of things, the genus of the universe,[76] the idea, exemplar, species, cause, first beginning and ultimate end of the world and she measures each and every thing by definite boundaries. She sees by what plan, by what causes, why, how, when, this unstable, generated, unsteady, changing universe got its shape, being, condition, species, life and origin from the ungenerated, stable and fixed; how the heavenly idea begets the earthly form, transforms chaos into the species we know and sends abroad the forms which it

[74] Reading *sentit.*

[75] Cf. *Ser. de Sph. Int.*, M. T. d'Alverny, *Textes Inédits*, 301; *De Pl. Nat.*, 453C: W: 479.

[76] For some contemporary ideas on the Creator and creation, see N. M. Häring, "The Creation and Creator of the world according to Thierry of Chartres and Clarenbaldus of Arras," *Archives* 22 (1955) 137-216.

destines for earth; how the child[77] degenerates from the father,[78] lays aside her father's face and forgets the mien of her parent of old. Here it was possible to see how the image of the idea is reflected in the universe and the idea's pure splendour is sensed in its copy;[79] how the river, winding its way from the fount of forms, loses its native sparkle through corruption by matter; what fate determines; what comes to pass by chance; what the power of free-will, keeping its place between the two, can do. Reason devotes herself entirely to these mirrors. For the present she gives freer rein to her eyes, racks her brain, gives her soul free-play that she may draw from within the mirrors something approved by Reason that would be well worth bringing to ears so important.

[77] Form.

[78] God.

[79] This shows the influence of Plato. The *form* of hylemorphism, the *idea* of Plato, is joined with matter but its divine origin can still be sensed.

BOOK II

The entire hall falls silent. The murmuring dies away. The members of the council turn their eyes and unruffled countenances on high. Their minds keep pace with the eyes and the will, charioteer of the eyes, wishes to outstrip fleet-travelling sight. Reason's teeming eloquence pours forth her ideas and an address as follows gets under way:

> "You bid me to show a power greater than I have when I untaught am forced to teach your Minerva.[1] Thus myrtle takes a place above laurel, oleaster above olive, Celtic nard above roses. Thus worthless seaweed is given preference over hyacinth, clay over precious stones, hemlock over violets. Thus the sheep begs a fleece from the goat, the swollen torrent begs water from the rivulet. Thus Narcissus[2] is wont to ask Davus[3] for beauty. Thus the candle's flame adds to the light of day. In so far, however, as your desire urges, orders and insists that the aid of my counsel, which you beg, be given in regard to these questions which your good judgement has brought up, I am unwilling to resist your pleas entirely and thus my will begins to coincide with your wishes and finally to desire whatever is necessary for their accomplishment. I prefer to give expression to inward thoughts that are insufficiently refined and call for another form rather than rebuff your prayers with boorish mien or have my silence give grounds for a

[1] Goddess of wisdom, arts and crafts and poetry.

[2] A beautiful youth, son of Cephesius and Liriope. He fell in love with his own reflection, pined away, died and was turned into the flower of the same name. For a different version, see Ovid, *Met.* 3.342.

[3] See Bk. 1, n. 39.

suspicion of pride. I crave your indulgence, then: let your kind pardon follow hard upon the fault and your sympathy ease the sickness, should my words serve up a fare of principles that are underdone:[4] or my address struggle on, barren of reason and spiritless. Do not let amazement break down the bulwarks of your mind, if my address should host the blemish of errors. Error roams abroad, the tireless companion of human affairs. A mass of ferment discolours everything with which human speech or the human mind busies itself. However, if the pursuit of the end is commensurable with the obligations of one's office, someone else, not the one trying to plead, will be in error, someone else, not the one trying to apply remedies, will be at fault if the original purpose is brought to naught by a subsequent one. The javelin does not always strike the object it threatens; the physician does not always heal; the orator himself does not always persuade; the logician does not always reach his goal, nay, indeed, often lying on the ground, he gasps tired out at mid-course.[5] I account Nature's plan wise, prudent, careful, praiseworthy, safe, useful. I approve her desire; I praise her project; I honour her effort, directed to the end that a new Lucifer, over whose pure-bright rising no future setting would cast a cloud, should leave home to live on earth; that at the sun's setting a new sun should signal his rising; that a new sun should rise for earth and that at his rising, the sun of old should be thought to bewail his defects; that he alone should possess what all of us together possess.[6] Thus this

[4] *minus excoctas.* The metaphor is from cooking and the meaning is that of the colloquial *half-baked.*

[5] If the one undertakes a task is qualified and does his best, he cannot be blamed if he fails. Cf. Hor., *A.P.* 350; Boethius, *De Trin.* Prol. 26-29 (Stewart-Rand 4).

[6] Cf. Bern. Silv., 2.10.17. The perfect man will have body and soul, matter and form, united in one. He will be the perfect type of all creation. Cf. St. Gregory's statement that

one man shall be all men; thus he shall be everything because he will be the one. He shall be one in being but all in virtues. Let him be the protector, defender, judge, champion, advocate against the vices that seek to dethrone us. When the world dislodges us from our abodes, let our home and our refuge be fixed firm with him. I do not, however, contradict the statements of my blood-sister. They convey the impression of extensive re-examination, rather these same statements could be more truly said to set us an examination,[7] since the wavering frame of the human structure recognises our work and calls for our anvil. Our customary art brings man's body into being: it does not extend to the soul of man which is ever exempted from these laws of yours and is fashioned by a higher hand. Yet, this urgent proposal should not be diverted from a project so great, nor should it admit defeat without a fight, even though Nature's task sighs at the prospect of troubles so great and toil so great and sinks down inactive at the prospect of them. However, the hand of God Himself will make good what the norm of Nature leaves below the standard of perfection. What nature makes, the divine Artist will perfect. The Divine creates from nothing. Nature makes mortal things from some material; God commands, she serves; He directs, she acts; He instructs, she accepts instruction. If God, then, is kindly disposed to desires of ours that do not deserve His favour and eases even our sighs, He will give fuller approval to prayers that are simple petitions and seek to be clothed in nothing better than

man typifies all creation, even the angels, *iuxta aliquid omnis creatura est homo*, In Evang. Hom. 2.29.2, *PL* 76.1214B; Claud. *In Ruf.* 1.111 (Platnauer 34).

[7] Alan is playing on the different meanings of *examen*. Its most common meaning in antiquity was a *swarm of bees*. Could Alan mean that Reason is claiming that Nature's words are "stirring up a hornets' nest?"

the sincerity of the entreaties. Desires, however, sweetened by our prayers, can merit more when they are the better seasoned with this relish. Let us then pour forth our desires, prayers and souls to Him so that He, who alone can bring them to fulfilment, may favour and aid our desires. The divine mind will not be slow to answer prayers if the created mind sends out an ambassador. Neither a speech varied with the figures of rhetoric, nor a hoarded heap of wealth, nor the muse of Maro nor hypocritical love nor preferment that chases after[8] love delights that divine mind: only the sweetness of prayers wins it over, if they are drawn moistened from the fount of the heart.

It remains doubtful and is not quite clear which of us, with what help, by what pathway carried to the abodes on high, would be accorded an ambassador's reception, could recommend our desires to God and urging them with a shower of entreaties, could drench the divine ears with prayers. And yet, as the thought in my own mind suggests, no one can better undertake the work of this post[9] than our sister, Prudence, whose courage no multitude of toils can vanquish, whose journey no obstacles on the way can slow — no din, no sea's rage, no valley's depth, no mountain ridges, no challenge from sheer lofty peaks, no rough road ridged with rocks nor the very obscurity of the winding path and the wastes that know not travellers, no wind's rage, no clouds soaked with rain, no dread pest of thunder, no lowering sky: none of these can prevent her from approaching the heavenly beings, from visiting the stars and imbibing the secret of God. Watered from the divine fount,

[8] *honor venator amoris*. This seems to mean promotion or honours given to someone to gain his love.

[9] *muneris usum*. Hilary of Poitiers uses the term *usus muneris* to indicate the Holy Spirit, *De Trin.*, 2.1, *PL* 10.51A.

she sees in the secrets of the Gods above who is the creator of the world, what God himself wills, what He is preparing for the world, what He foresees for it, what provision He is making for it, what He has in store for it, what power the mysteries of the heavens have, what the stars say, why the course of the heavens, ever veering towards the West, plays a trick on us by that same motion when the planets struggle against it, going the opposite direction[10] and hold the heavens in check. She sees what the unwholesome planet, Saturn[11], threatens the earth with, what help to health kind Juppiter announces to the world, what wars Mars foretells, under whose direction, why, with what material, through whose protection, the sun, the eye of the world,[12] the source of life, the candle of the Universe provides for and favours, soothes and looks to the interests of the earth by its gentle heat, movement, gift of life, light and course. She sees what allurements, what gloomy joys, what sad rejoicings, what dangerous delights, what bitter draughts Venus offers earth and drenches the world with honeyed poison. She sees by what bond, law and covenant Lucifer[13] and Cyllenius,[14] the attendants of our Sun, are

[10] The speed of earth is greather than the speed of the outer planets. Thus, for example, Earth overtakes and passes Mars. As one views this from Earth, Mars seems to slow down as Earth approaches it, stop momentarily as Earth passes it, reverse its course as Earth leaves it behind and finally resume its regular motion. The apparent reversal of course is known as *retrograde* motion. Cf. Bk. 4.36-38. The apparent reversal is not over the exact course that Mars has travelled but in a narrowish loop. The explanation of the illusion was first given by Kepler.

[11] With Saturn, Jupiter, Mars and Venus, Alan is in the realm of astrology. Belief in the influences of the planets on man continued through the Middle Ages. Planetary influences did not determine a man's actions. It disposed him in certain directions and could be nullified by will-power.

[12] Bern. Silv., 2.14.41.

[13] Usually Venus as morning-star, but see n. 15 infra.

[14] Mercury, so called from Mt. Cyllene in Thrace, his birthplace.

joined as they follow their courses. They carry his standards at his rising, tend him at his setting and alternate the roles which each shares with the other: each transfers himself to the other's function: one is shining at sunrise, the other at sunset and by turns they interchange names with each other: Hesperus accompanies the setting sun, Lucifer the rising sun.[15] She sees how the moon begs light from somewhere else: why Phoebe deprived to a small extent of light bewails her loss of brightness, and later drained further complains of the extensive loss of all her light, but glowing again from her brother's fire, she nurses the injuries to her damaged beauty and finally being at full, revolves with perfect lustre.[16] She sees who binds the rain in the clouds, why the air rumbles, who fathers the winds, who plants in them the seeds of rage, why the cloud-substance takes on so many appearances — now dense with tear-drops of rain, now white with frost, now clothed with the appearance of snow; again it takes up the arms of hail and earth is amazed at the heaven's darts. Who, then, will undertake the office of ambassador more effectively than Phronesis to whom all the secrets of God speak?[17] If she is willing, then, to defer to our prayers, everything will go forward as law demands and order requires and each detail will reach a fixed goal. I do not think that she could wish to frustrate so great a struggle for an objective, such great efforts of mind, the urgings of an inclination so great

[15] In classical times Venus, when west of the sun, was called *Lucifer, the morning-star*; when east of the sun, it was called *Hesperus, the evening-star* (Cic., *De Nat. Deor.* 2.20.53). The same terminology is used to-day. Alan shares the rôle between Venus and Mercury. Astronomically this is quite feasible as Mercury, when visible, trails the setting sun down the sky or rises before it in the morning.

[16] A poetic description of an eclipse, somewhat spoiled by the *nutrit attriti damna decoris* of line 138.

[17] The *secrets of God* is a favourite phrase of Alan. Cf. 2.106; 5.114, 167.

and to gainsay advantages so great. No doubt remains if those here co-operate. Let us all set about the work; a happier fate will attend us. The one who has made a beginning has half the work done; the favour of a happy ending ever waits on a worthy beginning."

Thus Reason seeks to capture their souls and to win over her sisters' minds and she forces the willing band to be more willing. However, Prudence alone shows less agreement and claims that she is not equal to a labour so great. Pressure is brought to bear upon her, she persists in her refusal, and the refusal was rightly subjected to pressure. She wavers, she denies that she is unwilling but will not say that she is willing; she hovers between the two: she does not agree and she is afraid to refuse.

While thus her mind hangs in doubt, wavers, hesitates, Concord, a mediatrix in all things, steps to the centre. In her face the image of divinity shines and gives rise to distaste for the boring human countenance. Her hair, more glittering than gold, keeps its place of its own accord, arranges itself and does not look for the comb's aid but able to look after itself, lies in such order that the breath of Boreas blowing through cannot disturb it or cause a tangling disorder in it. Its contour, arrangement, style, thickness and length well suit her body-structure and perform their due office.[18] The parts of her body,[19] joined in har-

[18] Lines 174-175. I have taken these lines as a further description of Concord's hair. Bossuat's punctuation indicates that this is his opinion. These lines could be a general description of Concord and the *sic* of line 176 gives some reason for thinking so. Alan, however, uses *sic* in much the same way as conversational English uses *so*, with little attention to its real meaning. If the words refer to Concord in general, they would mean: "her form, figure, manner, dignity and height fit well her body-structure and perform their due offices." This gives *numerus* a rather odd meaning, but in *Dist.*, 877D, Alan gives *dignity* as one meaning of *numerus*.

[19] *Membrum* can be used for any part of the body, even the beard (Cic., *De. Fin.* 3.5.18).

monious peace, are in keeping with one another so that on none of them is an unsightly ligature to be seen.

Her dress, of uniform appearance and satisfied with a single colour, serves to set off her limbs and is so closely fitted to them on the outside that it seems painted on them. There a painting by its art gives a second life to those whom chaste love, uncomplicated friendship, unclouded trust, true affection have joined together and in whose case an association of purified love has made one out of two. For David and Jonathan[20] are two there but yet are one; although they are separate individuals, they are not two in soul but one; they halve their souls and each gives part to the other. Theseus, returned to earth, faces the abodes, monsters, dangers of the lower world that Pirithous[21] may be restored to him. He insists that he can have no life by himself unless he has a life in Pirithous. Tydeus rushes to arms that his other self may be king. He identifies with his friend Polynices[22] in the battle and when he wishes his second self to be king he feels that he is seeking kingship for himself. Another Nisus appears in Euryalus[23] and another Euryalus flourishes in

[20] I Samuel 18.1 ff.: "The soul of Jonatham was knit to the soul of David and Jonatham loved him as his own soul".

[21] Theseus, the national hero of Athens, and Pirithous, a Lapith, were close friends and shared many exploits. When Pirithous' wife, Hippodamia, died, Theseus accompanied him to the under-world to carry off Persephone and make her Pirithous' wife. They were captured: the usual tradition is that Theseus escaped or was freed by Hercules, while Pirithous never escaped. In Alan's version Theseus has escaped but returns to the underworld. This probably comes from Hyginus, *Fab.* 251.3.

[22] The sons of Oedipus, Polynices and Etiocles, agreed to rule Thebes in alternate years, Etiocles, the elder, taking the first year. At the end of the year. Etiocles would not hand the kingdom over to Polynices. Polynices, accompanied by his friend, Tydeus, father of Diomedes, set out to recruit an army (*Il.* 4.376). They attacked Thebes and both were killed in the battle as was Etiocles.

[23] Euryalus and Nisus were close friends. Nisus' rather unsportsmanlike aid to Euryalus is to be found in the account of the foot-race in Vir., *Aen.* 5.286-361. Their daring raid against the Rutulians and their death together are described in *Aen.* 9.176-445.

Nisus; thus either one of them reflects the other and from one of these companions a judgment can be made on both. The descendant of Atreus rages in madness and Pylades[24] considers the madness his own and submits to Megaera to save his friend and *alter ego*, his other identity, from the same fate. The painting speaks its hidden secrets in symbols. The object itself does not give a fuller, nor an oral description a more faithful, presentation of such things and the painting encloses such things in the shadow of things, beguiling the sight of our eyes by this type of artifice.[25] An olive branch, which is usually the herald of good and the emblem of peace, matures in Concord's right hand, tressed with hair of leaves, pregnant with flowers, looking forward to fruit and seeking not the tender aid of mother-earth. By means of this olive branch, Concord entwines interchanges, bonds, ties, pacts, friendship, peace. With a dip of the wand she asks for quiet and reinforcing her verbal requests with these dips, she proceeds as follows, her feelings dictating the tone of the speech:

> "If the world of old had observed my laws, my covenants, or if it were now observing the obligations of the bonds of love, earth would not be groaning beneath disasters so great.
>
> Phoebus would not have wept for the feast served by brother to brother, that travesty of a feast, and would not have sent on earth a darkness out of its time as he bemoaned the crimes of errant Nature.[26] The King of

[24] Orestes and his constant companion, Pylades. Clytemnestra murdered her husband, Agamemnon. Orestes, her son, took revenge by killing his mother. The Furies drove him mad. A gloss bears witness to a tradition that when Megaera, one of the Furies, was approaching Orestes, Pylades stood between them and tried to divert the attack to himself.

[25] See Bk. 1. n. 17.

[26] An ever-recurring story in antiquity. The brothers, Atreus and Thyestes, disagreed. Atreus banished Thyestes but later offered to be reconciled with him. At a banquet, celebrating the reconciliation, Atreus served Thyestes the flesh of the latter's children.

Thebes, Polynices' brother and enemy, would not have changed into an enemy, divesting himself of the role of brother.[27] Progne would not have devised her wiles, divesting herself of the role of mother, smelling of crime rather than maternal affection, of a stepmother rather than of a mother and she should not have turned her degenerate right hand against the fruit of her womb, nor would rage have armed the mother against her own child.[28] Noble Troy, glorious Troy, Troy renowned in fame, would still be flourishing and would not lack the bloom of glory,[29] Crassus,[30] drunk from gold and thirsting for a drink of gold, would not have taken it when he was already dangerously tipsy from gold. Magnus[31] would not have long ago experimented with crime between citizens, the arms of Caesar, the attitude of the boy-king,[32] the kingdom's

The sun, Phoebus, turned back on its course in horror. See Eur., *El.* 699 ff., *Or.* 995 ff.; Appolod., *Ep.* 2.12; Hyg. *Fab.* 86-88; Seneca, *Thyestes*.

[27] See n. 22 supra.

[28] Tereus, king of Thrace, pretended that his wife, Progne, was dead and sent for her sister, Philomela. When she came, he raped her and cut out her tongue to insure silence. She wove the story into a piece of embroidery and sent it to Progne. Progne killed Itys, her son by Tereus, and served his flesh to her husband. See Appolod. *Ep.*, 3.193 ff.; Ovid, *Met.* 6.424 ff.

[29] Vir., *Aen.* 2.56.

[30] Crassus, one of the first to realise the power of money in politics, increased his wealth by every means at his disposal. If Alan means that Crassus' trust in money without the support of an army proved his undoing, he is making a very shrewd assessment of the situation. Crassus met his death fighting against the Parthians at Carrhae in 53 B.C. Alan probably had Bern. Silv., 1.3.237-238 in mind. Bernardus is referring to the gold poured down Crassus' throat after his death at Carrhae. Alan either misunderstood the reference or is trying to be witty.

[31] Pompey. The title *Magnus* was given to him in 81 B.C. From 80 B.C. he was a power to be reckoned with on the Roman political and military scene. He was allied with Caesar and Crassus in the First Triumvirate. He later broke with Caesar and was defeated at the battle of Pharsalus in 48 B.C. He fled to Egypt but was murdered as he came ashore.

[32] The "boy-king" is mentioned in Luc. 8.537: the reference there is to Ptolemy XIII of Egypt who was only fifteen at the time of Pompey's death. He was well-disposed

treaties, the dread Servile War[33] and the slaves. He would not have lain forsaken on the bare beach, dead, mutilated, denied the honour of a funeral. Caesar, after the din of so many campaigns, after deaths in war, after the fury of the sword, after so many crises, would not have experienced treachery and the cowardly thrust of steel.[34] Antony[35] would long ago have easily avoided insults from Caesar,[36] the disturbances of war, the fury of Fortune, the vicissitudes of chance and his wife would not have mothered serpents at her bosom, suckled snakes and carrying them at her breasts, have carried death there.

If I had not bound the elements[37] with a stable bond, a covenant of harmony, unending peace and my alternations, internal crashes would shatter the clashing first elements of things and internal warfare would agitate them. The elements would lie dormant, removed from their alloted work, knowing nothing of motion, rough-rusted

towards Pompey but his ministers presuaded him to agree to his assassination. Cf. *puero principe* of Bern. Silv., 1.3.240. The other young king that Pompey aided was Pharnaces II of Pontus. Pompey defeated his father, Mithridates VI, put Pharnaces on the throne and hoped that he would be a faithful ally of Rome. When opportunity offered, he reinstituted his father's expansionist policies. He was finally defeated by Caesar at Gela in 47 B.C. It was after this victory that the famous *veni, vidi, vici* dispatch was sent.

[33] 73-71 B.C. Pompey helped Sulla crush the revolt. *nortis servile genus:* that could refer to the slave-like manner of Pompey's death but it is difficult to construe it in this sense after *probasset.*

[34] Caesar was stabbed to death on March 15, 44 B.C.

[35] Marc Antony supported Caesar and became leader of the party after his death. After defeating Brutus and Cassius at Philippi in 42 B.C., he was sent to reorganise the East. He fell under the influence of Cleopatra. Rome finally declared war on Cleopatra and Antony was defeated at Actium in 31 B.C. He committed suicide before Octavian's troops entered Alexandria. Cleopatra committed suicide by the sting of an asp to avoid being led in Octavian's triumphal procession.

[36] The Caesar here is Octavian, who received the title of *Augustus* in 27 B.C.

[37] Lines 242-255. Cf. Boeth., *De Cons.* M. 8.1-4, 16-19 (Stewart-Rand 222); Bern. Silv., 1.2.34-146. See Baumgartner 51 ff.

from inactivity, jumbled together in space, confused in shape, tossed about by chance. If the stars in the sky, the alternations in the heavens and the seven planets[38] were not the willing subjects of my laws and were not bound together by ties of order, peace, faithfulness, harmony and restraint, all of them without fixed direction would perish by chance crashes. If my bond had not united soul to body, the spirit, refusing to live in a hovel, a penitentiary of flesh, would leave and return to its place of origin. Reason proves, proclaims, states, teaches, insists and demonstrates this, that nothing is kept in existence if it refuses to observe my laws and ordinances. Let one love, then, one will, one policy to do, one policy not to do bind us sisters together.

If the rest of creation is obliged to keep the rule of peace, all the more are we at whose nod earth in set in order, in whose power lie the decisions, laws and rules for the universe.[39] What bond, what real love, what covenant of love, what sense of duty, what unadulterated faithfulness, what path of right will preserve even the traces of peace in the rest of creation if our concord stays discordant?[40] The damage from the ailing head will flow down into the limbs, the defects of the soured root will soak its way up to the branches, the pollution inherent in the river will flow into the streams.[41] What splendour has the moon if the sun's light goes awry? What flow has the stream if the river's supply dries up? What fruit from grain is there, if the ear droops and withers? If discord unstitches, or rather, rends,

[38] Sun, Moon, Mercury, Venus, Mars, Jupiter, Saturn.

[39] Cf. Hor., *A.P.* 263.

[40] In line 267 there should be a comma after *servabit* and a note of interrogation after *discors*.

[41] *Rivus* is frequently used by Alan to indicate a channel of water diverted from a river.

the garment of our peace, our power disappears, for it is said that a power divided against itself cannot stand but suffers a fall.[42] Since it is unanimity that gives us matured strength, disagreement between us will drain its power. Medicine in half doses refuses to produce its effects. The river is less in flood when streams have diverted part of its water to themselves. The fire in the forge glows less if part of it has been taken away. A keener onslaught from vice and a tougher battle lies ahead of us, should error divide our ranks. When disagreement has wrecked the stone outworks, it exposes the undefended walls to the enemy's attack.[43] The sword thrusts more sharply and vents its rage more widely when there are no close-packed ranks to offer a defence or no close succession of these to counter the sword's attack. Jove's winged bird[44] more keenly makes his lightning swoop on a fowl when the terror of his approach has scattered the flock. The torrent spreads more widely when no obstacle bars its way and refuses its flood a passage. One in heart, then, let us hasten to join in one prayer for what Nature seeks, Reason recommends, Honesty approves, nay, desires, Piety prays for and longs for. Nor will Phronesis by herself, keeping her distance, opposing, disagreeing, separate us into factions, to the extent of loosing the bonds of love between all of us who are united under a uniform law of peace, but rather taking her place with us, sharing our joy, in harmony with us, one in heart with us, she will come to our way of thinking lest it may be thought that she is overcome by the prospect of the struggle and is giving up before the preliminary skirmishes, or that pride with swollen breath blows over her mind or that biting envy gnaws the depths of her soul. Or will she

[42] Luke, 11.15 ff.

[43] Alan is thinking of a castle with its courtyard surrounded by walls for defence.

[44] The eagle.

who, above all others, is wont to seek for the good, be the only one to wipe out this good common to all, this honour for us, this beneficial quest, she who, above all others, should gladly and of her own accord urge all of us on to this great work and this great service, should our determination become less ardent and sluggish and our spirit refuse to scale such heights?"

Further fired by these words, Prudence checks her inclinations and in her heart takes a firm and definite stand.[45] The storm in her mind dies down and the waves recede. She brings her will into unison with the will of her sisters. Accordingly she considers, investigates, studies, tries to discover, seeks to choose which road, which trail, which path will bring her more directly to the upper world and the secret kingdoms of the Thunderer.[46] So that the roughness of the path may less plague the traveller's steps and her feet be free from stumbling blocks — in a word, that she may more quickly complete the task she is intent on, Wisdom orders a chariot to be fashioned in which she may traverse the heavens, the sea, the stars. With no slow step, result follows desire: rather they press on their way together: result begins its existence when the will for it is born. Thus a simultaneous beginning is granted to mother and offspring.

There are seven maidens,[47] cautious, prudent, beautiful,

[45] Literally — "fixed her mind's feet firmly on a definite spot", an odd and strained metaphor.

[46] Cf. Ovid, *Met.* 1.170.

[47] The seven Liberal Arts — Grammar, Logic, Rhetoric, Arithmetic, Music, Geometry, Astronomy. The first three constituted the Trivium, the other four the Quadrivium. *Art* in this context means "branch of learning". In dealing with the Seven Liberal Arts Alan borrows from or adapts various authorities. An attempt will be made to indicate these authorities. Practically everything found in Peter of Compostella's treatment of the Liberal Arts is to be found also in Alan. The text of Peter of Compostella is edited by P. B. Soto: *Petri Compostellani, De Consolatione Rationis Libri duo* in Beiträge 8.4 (Münster 1912), 61-151. So much of the terminology and so many phrases are iden-

resembling one another: under seven countenances they reflect one countenance: one faith and one will guide those whom one face, one family, one age, one form, one power encompass. They come to Phronesis' aid and carry out her orders, ever ready to show fervour in her service. The gifts of Sophia lavish so many endowments on them that Prudence pours her entire self into them. She shares herself with them and builds up her treasure in them. Thus though divided, she yet remains whole; though scattered, she is in the end concentrated; though diversified, she returns with high interest. Turning their faces towards her and towards the hidden depths of her mind, in her countenance as in a mirror, the band of sisters sees, considers, learns, notes and is instructed in whatever parchments contain, the mind conceives, the tongue dares say and it absorbs from this limitless wisdom whatever the artisan's hand, the painter's charm, the carpenter's skill, the tireless application of the sculptor can do. This band[48] paints like Zeuxis,[49] shapes like Milo,[50] speaks like Fabius,[51]

tical that it seemed best to put the complete text of Peter of Compostella on the Liberal Arts and the parallel passages of Alan side by side in an Appendix.

[48] Lines 343-362. These lines, in which name is piled on name, are an example of the influence of degenerate rhetoric on poetry. This list is based on Sidonius Apollinaris, *Ep.* 4.3.5 ff. He adds several names to Sidonius' list but omits all his references to Christian writers. Alan has double references to Caesar, Ovid and Virgil, making in all a list of forty-one names. He outdoes Sidonius in pedantry and this is not easily done.

[49] Greek painter. He is mentioned as a young man in Plato's *Protagoras* (318B). The dramatic date of the *Protagoras* is 430 B.C. Cf. Cic., *Brut.* 18, *De Inv.* 2.1.

[50] A gloss of William of Auxerre says that this Milo was a worker in marble and an excellent geometrician. Alan was probably misled by the "cow of Milo" in Ovid, *Pon.* 4.1.34. The man in question is Myro(n), a sculptor who flourished in Athens around 450 B.C. One of his famous sculptures was of a cow. See Bern. Silv., 1.3.47. Cf. Cic., *Brut.* 18.70, *De Or.* 3.3.26, *In Verr.* 2.4.60; Pliny, 34.58; Juv. 8.102.

[51] This is certainly an odd statement. Sidonius has *moratur ut Fabius, he delays like Fabius*, a clear reference to Fabius Cunctator whose policy of avoiding a pitched battle wore Hannibal down in the Second Punic War (218-201 B.C.). If Alan is referring to him, he may be accepting the tradition (probably incorrect) that it was this Fabius who delivered Rome's ultimatum to Carthage in 218 B.C. The fact that the tribute to Fabius' power as a speaker is followed by a reference to Cicero's success in his perorations might

perorates like Tullius,[52] gives opinions like the Samian,[53] philosophizes like Plato, catechises like Hermes,[54] makes distinctions like Socrates,[55] draws conclusions like Zeno,[56] perseveres like Brisso,[57] studies like Critias,[58] sees like Argus,[59] corrects time discrepancies like Caesar,[60] investigates the stars like Atlas,[61] balances like Zethus,[62] deals with numbers like Crissipus,[63] measures like another Euclid,[64] sings like

indicate that the Fabius here is Quintilian — M. Fabius Quintilianus. However, the *loquacem ... Fabium* of Hor., *Ser.*, 1.13-14 is a more likely candidate. Nothing is known of him beyond a few questionable statements by the Scholiasts, Porphyry and Acron.

52 Cicero.

53 Pythagoras, born in Samos. Cf. Cic., *De Fin.* 5.27.

54 William of Auxerre identifies him as Hermes Trismegistus. *Hermes Trismegistus* (*τρίς μέγιστος*) is a clumsy translation of the Egyptian "Thoth the very great". He is the reputed author of the works known as *Hermetica.* His *Asclepius* is in question-and-answer form. See A. D. Nock-Festugière, *Corpus Hermeticum* (Paris 1945) 2.259-404.

55 The famous Greek philosopher, who figures in the Dialogues of Plato.

56 Zeno of Elea. Aristotle calls him the inventor of dialectic (fr. 65). His practice was to draw contradictory conclusions from the premises of his opponents (Plato, *Parmen.* 128C).

57 Bryson of Heraclea Pontica, a sophist, who worked hard but unsuccessfully in his attempts to square a circle. See Arist., *An. Post.* 75b, *Sophist. El.* 171b, 172a.

58 Critias, a somewhat violent and unscrupulous political intriguer. He wrote Elegiacs and Tragedies. Cicero praises his speeches in *De Or.* 2.22. As a participant in the dialogue in the *Timaeus* he would be well known to the Middle Ages. For his devotion to study see R. Bossuat, "Quelques Personnages cités par Alain de Lille", in: *Mélanges dédiés à la mémoire de Louis Halphen* (Paris 1951) 37.

59 The many-eyed monster. He was sent by Zeus to watch Io after she had been turned into a heifer: Aesch., *Prom. Vin.* 678.

60 Julius Caesar. His reformed calendar came into effect on January 1, 45 B.C.

61 Atlas, a Titan, holds the sky up (Hes. *Theo.* 517; Aesch., *Prom. Vin.* 347). His proximity to the stars gave rise to the idea that he was an Astronomer. See Diod. Sic., 3.60.2. Cf. St. Aug., *De Civ. Dei* 18.8 and 39. *CSEL* 40.2, 275 and 330.

62 Zethus and Amphion make their appearance in the lost *Antiope* of Euripides. Pacuvius based his *Antiopa* on Euripides' play. In a fragment of Euripides (188 Dind.), Zethus is trying to persuade Amphion to abandon music and interest himself in war. Apparently in Pacuvius, they are balancing the relative merits of music and philosophy. See Cic., *De Or.* 2.37, *De Inv.* 1.50; Hor., *Ep.* 1.18.41: Hyg., *Fab.* 76 and 155.

63 A Stoic philosopher, who devoted his life to elaborating the Stoic system and wrote so much on it that his name ultimately became identified with Stoic orthodoxy. The Stoics had a deep influence on the growth of ancient mathematics.

64 His name has become synonymous with geometry, although he wrote on other things, e.g. astronomy and music.

Phoebus,[65] plays the harp like Orpheus,[66] draws circles like Perdix,[67] constructs citadels like Daedalus,[68] forges like Cyclops,[69] fashions arms like the Lemnian,[70] teaches like Seneca,[71] flatters like Appius,[72] insists like Cato,[73] inflames like Curio,[74] conceals like a second Perseus,[75] pretends like Crassus,[76] disguises like a

[65] Apollo, patron of music.

[66] A Thracian singer and musician who could charm even animals and inanimate objects.

[67] Nephew of Daedalus and inventor of the compass. Ovid., *Met.* 8.247.

[68] Legendary artist, craftsman and inventor. He was the inventor or perfecter of a host of things — artificial wings, steam-baths, reservoirs, the axe, the saw, the auger, etc. He is said to have built a fortress near Agrigentum. This seems to be what Alan is referring to here.

[69] Earlier traditions about the Cyclopes can be found in Hom. *Od.* 9.106 ff. and Hes., *Theog.* 149. In Call., *Dian.* 46 ff., they are Hephaestus' workmen in his forge under Aetna. Cf. Vir., *Geor.* 4.170, *Aen.* 8.416.

[70] Vulcan, so named from Lemnos, an island in the Aegean where he had his abode.

[71] For Seneca, see Bk. 1, n. 20.

[72] According to William of Auxerre, *Ms Paris, BN Lat. 8299,* this is Appius Claudius, who was "one of those who brought the law of the XII Tables to Rome and was by his flattery an effective speaker". Appius Claudius was one of the decemvirs in 451 B.C., when the Twelve Tables were most probably introduced. The flattery might refer to his flattering treatment of the plebeians. Bossuat (216) confuses him with Appius Claudius Caecus, consul in 307 and 296 B.C., who had the Appian way built. If we ignore William of Auxerre, there is no reason why Alan should not be referring to this Appius Claudius.

[73] Cato is probably Cato, the Censor, upholder of Roman traditions, opponent of Greek influence, agriculturist, historian, and stern moralist. The *Catonis Disticha*, attributed to him by Bossuat (215), belongs to a much later date. It is possible that the reference is to this Cato's great-grandson, Cato Uticensis. He was a determined supporter of Pompey and of the Pompeians after Pompey's death. He was an intransigent, uncompromising individual and his suicide is mentioned often and with approval by later writers.

[74] G. Scribonius Curio, a stormy character, was first an enemy, later an ally of Julius Caesar. He was defeated and killed by Juba in 49 B.C.

[75] William of Auxerre says that this is either the "Perseus who, covered with a crystal shield given him by Pallas, slew Medusa of Persius who wrote obscure satire (*occulte satiram scripsit*)". If the reference is to the satirist, there may also be an allusion to *Satires* 1 and 5 which seem to be veiled references to Nero.

[76] See n. 30 supra.

second Julius,[77] condenses like Soldius,[78] explains like Naso,[79] blooms like Statius,[80] composes like Maro,[81] understands, explains, imitates, assumes, completes the capacities of Mercury,[82] the rage of our own Demosthenes,[83] the flow of Ovid, the flash of Lucan,[84] the depth of Virgil,[81] the sting of Satire,[85] the refuge of Solon.[86]

Minerva, then, seeing that the sisters are shining with the splendour of Sophia and with so many great gifts and endowments, arranges, charges, bids, commands, begs that each of these companions, accompanied by Sophia, should immediately, in body, mind and faithfulness, show zeal, sweat, pant, press on and see to it that the chariot races towards existence, the chariot in which Prudence could cross the extent of earth, the sea, the

[77] Julius Caesar.

[78] Manuscripts vary between Soldius, Solidius, Solidus. One gloss has Solinus. The reference is most probably to Sidonius Apollinaris whose full name was Gaius Sollius Apollinaris Sidonius. Alan borrows heavily from him in this section. The reference could possibly be to Gaius Julius Solinus, whose *Collectanea Rerum Memorabilium* is a survey of the geography, history, customs and products of the known world. He was the first to use the term *Mare Mediterraneum* (Mediterranean Sea) and apparently the first to use the word *inspiratio* for poetic inspiration.

[79] Ovid. Reference is to his etiological works, the *Metamorphoses* and *Fasti.*

[80] Apt though it would be, *vernat, blooms,* cannot refer to Statius' *Silvae.* It was not available in medieval times. The manuscript was discovered by Poggio at Constance in 1417. The reference is to the florid and rhetorical episodes in the *Thebais.*

[81] Virgil. The *abyssum Virgilii* is mentioned in lines 361-362. *In. Dist.* 689D, *cor hominis profundum et inscrutabile* is given as one meaning of *abyssus.*

[82] God of traders and commercial ventures.

[83] The most famous of Greek orators; *nostri Demostenis* means Cicero.

[84] Author of the *Pharsalia.* Reference is to the striking epigrammatical utterances that abound in Lucan.

[85] Probably refers to Juvenal.

[86] Greek statesman and poet. Athenians, who had contracted debts with no security to offer but their persons, became the slaves of the nobles (Eupatridae) if they could not repay. The Eupatridae could sell them in Attica or overseas. Attica seemed on the verge of a dangerous economic revolt. Solon's reforms prevented this. He cancelled all debts for which land or liberty had been pledged as security and prohibited all borrowings where the person would be pledged as security.

stars, the clouds, the heavens and passing the pole of the triple heavens,[87] investigate the secrets of Noys,[88] draw on her deep meaning and inquire into the will of the supreme master. Scarcely has she expressed her wish when her sisters show zeal and rivalry in fulfilling the desires of the mistress and they gird themselves for the task. Their heart is not in opposition to the work, nor their hands to their heart; rather the heart's desire sets the hand to work, the hand's work proclaims without what the heart holds dear within. Thus the hand becomes the faithful interpreter of the heart and in its work lays the heart before us.

The first of these enthusiastically sets about having the pole produced,[89] so that it may be the first part of the great work, the pole which is ahead of the axle and is a kind of preface, so to speak, to the coming chariot. This maiden, wakeful, enthusiastic, willing, attentive, energetic, delighting in her task, turns her attention to work. Her dress is not mean nor her face smeared nor her carriage ignoble nor her language unadorned nor her actions barbarous. Yet pallor draws on her face the lines of toil, but it is a modest pallor which does not obliterate the rosy-red glow of her face or the beauty of the snow-white skin, since the bloom of virginity is not deflowered in her nor does the cleft of Venus ruin her chastity. Her breasts, however, float in a deep flood of milk and give the appearance of the ravages that come from lost

[87] The account of the journey in 4.245-5.39 describes the triple heavens — the Air (haunted by evil spirits), the Ether (region of the Sun, Moon and Planets) and the Firmament (region of the Signs of the Zodiac and the Constellations). For a very detailed description of the heavens, see Bern. Silv., 2.7.10-110.

[88] Noûs, Divine Wisdom. Prudentia or Phronesis is human Wisdom, understood as the soul's highest cognitive power. See R. H. Green, "Alan of Lille's Anticlaudianus, Ascensus Mentis in Deum," *Annuale Medievale* 8 (1967) 3-16.

[89] The first maiden is Grammar. Grammar included poetics and metrics. See Stephen of Tournai, *Rythmus* 113-116, ed. M. Auvray, *Mélanges Paul Fabre* (Paris 1902) 288; Walter of Châtillon, 3.7, ed. K. Strecker, *Moralisch-satirische Gedichte Walters von Chàtillon* (Heidelberg 1929) 41.

nulliparity.[90] While the child still sighs at the breasts of his nursing mother, this food feeds him and the one who cannot yet take solids is nourished by liquid. While at this milk-white age, he enjoys draughts of milk and, in one and the same draught, there are food and drink coming from milk alone. She increases the severity of one of her hands[91] with a whip with which she punishes the faults which youth in its way absorbs. Thus by blows she makes the milk more bitter, by the milk she makes the blows more mild. In one and the same action she is father and mother. By the blows she makes up for a father, by the milk she fills the rôle of mother. Her other hand fulfills its function with a file; it clears the tartar from the teeth as she changes the teeth's boxwood tint to an ivory gleam and beautifies them by her whitening process. If, however, one tooth strays from the rest of the row, she cuts the outgrowth back to normal.[92] This maiden teaches infants to speak, looses tied tongues and shapes words in the proper mould. A white garment, woven from Egyptian papyrus, clothes her. She does not impair its beauty and its beauty does her no disservice. Raiment and beauty unite in a charming marriage and each pays its own homage to the other. On the garment the following are inscribed and show forth their description:[93] the force, nature, power, order, matter, divisions,

[90] Cf. 1.289-291. There Alan seems to identify loss of virginity with pregnancy or motherhood. Here Grammatica is a virgin but has some of the physical signs of a mother. Cf. the definition of *virgo* and *virginitas* in *Dist.*, 1006B-C.

[91] *Asperat illa manum scutica.* The obvious meaning of this would be that she roughens or wrinkles the boy's hand with marks from the whip. However, in line 404 he refers to her *manus altera.* This indicates that the *manum* of line 399 belongs to Grammatica. For the use of the whip and the milk, see Godfrey of St-Victor, *Fons Philosophiae* ed. Michaud-Quantin, 39.131-132: tr E. A. Synan, 44.

[92] Cf. Mart. Cap., 3.226 in reference to the cleaning and evening of teeth. This is a metaphor for correcting mistakes and is not to be taken literally.

[93] See N. M. Häring, "Thierry of Chartres and Dominicus Gundissalinus," *Mediaeval Studies* 26 (1965) 284.

purpose, title and author, function, species, genus, tools and capacity of the art of grammar. There authority is given to the art and rules hold sway; deficiencies suffer exile and know not how to merit pardon. Figure,[94] facing indefinite rejection at grammar's hands, defends itself with its own special method, sleeps outside the doors and craves indulgence. Art admits her, answers her prayer for indulgence but does not cherish her in her bosom but does, however, support her. Here art teaches, reason shows, instruction proclaims why a letter is termed simple and indivisible, why a letter borrows for itself the name "element"[95] or why a letter is usually called "element" by way of metaphor, what formation[96] represents the elements, what names indicate them, what is their total number,[97] what is their right order,[98] what is their pronunciation[99] and what brings all these matters under a definite rule; why the other letters,[100] deprived of even a weak sound, when seeking expression, are mute[101] while the vowel rings clear and gives other letters the

[94] Figures of speech are not nearly as common in Latin as they are in English. Even when found, they are very often accompanied by some softening words like *quasi* or *ut ita dicam.* Quintilian 1.5.5. maintains that it is often difficult to distinguish between a figure of speech and a barbarism or solecism. Cf. n. 103 infra.

[95] *Elementum* is used for a letter of the alphabet. Probus, 4.48.33. The Commentary on Donatus (487.10) quotes a line from Terentianus which shows that *elementa* means the alphabet. Cf. Suet., *Caes.* 56; Priscian, 3.115.20. All references to Grammarians are to Heinrich Keil, *Grammatici Latini* (Lipsiae 1850-1870).

[96] Priscian, 2.6.33 ff. explains the difference between *elementum* and *litera. Elementum* refers to the sound, *litera* to the symbol in writing. He points out, however, that the terms tend to be used interchangeably.

[97] Donatus (4.368.12) mentions the theory that there are only seventeen *Latin* letters. Of the twenty-three in use, one (h) is a note of aspiration, one (x) is a double consonant, two (k, q) are superfluous, two (y, z) are from Greek.

[98] Prisc., 2.37.5

[99] *Ib.* 2.7.5 ff.

[100] The use of *cetera* in line 434 and the fact that there is no reference to the *semivocales* indicate that some lines are missing. The semivocales are f, l, m, n, r, s, x, Don., 4.367.21.

[101] The mutes are b, c, d, g, h, k, p, q, t. *Ib.* 368.5.

breath of expression; what is the explanation of, and what lies behind, the fact that H[102] is not a letter, though it affects a writing-shape, a name and a use, but has only the status of a cipher[103] and maintaining its right to a shape, bears but the shadow of an element. Here was to be seen how in poetry a vowel in conflict with another vowel melts away and loses the honour of being sounded;[104] how in poetry a letter loses its natural strength and its force, banished for a time, languishes;[105] how in poetry one letter claims for itself the force and rights of two, by making good the loss of its fellow-letter;[106] how the same syllable takes on different tones;[107] a grave accent lowers it, an acute raises it, a circumflex rounds it. There could be seen there what the letter can successfully claim as its own;[108] what the syllable can claim;[109] what the word[110] keeps as its own

[102] Quintilian, 1.5.19, says there is some doubt whether H is a letter or merely a breathing. Cf. Don., 4.368.9 and 13; Prob., 4.50.15; Author of *De Ultimis Syllabis* 4.222.4; Servius, 4.424.15. Priscian definitely states that it is not a letter: 2.8.22; 12.20; 13.9; 35.24. Cf. Mart. Cap., 3.252 ff.

[103] *cyphri.* This word comes from the Arabic *cifr,* meaning zero or empty. The word is rare but it appears elsewhere in Alan. He uses it to describe the bat and the value of figures of speech to those who are talking but saying *nothing: De Pl. Nat.*, 436D; W. 439; *Lib. Par.,* 586C. If he means that the only real function of H is to express a number, he could be thinking of the Greek usage, mentioned in Prisc., 3.406.12, of representing a hundred by H (*Ηεκατόν= ἑκατόν*) of the Latin symbol HS (2 1/2). In the later case he would be mistaken as H here is the Roman numeral II crossed.

[104] Refers to elision in poetry: a final vowel is elided when the following word begins with a vowel.

[105] There are three examples of this. Final M is elided when the following word begins with a vowel or H. Donatus (4.308.2) states that *S* in poetry at times loses its power as a consonant. Occasionally a long vowel is shortened in poetry, e.g. unĭus in Vir., *Aen.* 1.45.

[106] Reference is to what Don. (4.396.20) calls episynaliphe: the diaeresis is ignored for metrical purposes, e.g. *Phaethon for Phaëthon, Nerei* for *Nerëi, aeripedem* for *aëripedem.* Cf. Quint., 1.5.17.

[107] Don., 4.371.

[108] Prob., 4.48.33 ff. Cf. Don., 4.368.18 ff.

[109] Don., 4.368.18 ff. Cf. *De Ult. Syll.*, 4.222.18 ff; Prisc., 2.44.1 ff.

[110] Prisc., 2.53.8 ff.

special right; what the noun rightly claims as its own;[111] what the verb appropriates;[112] what the pronoun chooses for itself;[113] what the other parts of speech keep as their special rights; what a noun strictly denotes and what outside implications it takes on;[114] what a verb denotes;[115] what a pronoun indicates;[116] since pronouns point to subjects discussed why do they disdain the aid of declension;[117] why is demonstration[118] their only help and why does it take the place of declension in them. There could be seen on what basis part governs part or is governed by it; why a noun, taking the place of something or portraying something else, performs the function of matter and adds the idea of form; why the voice of a verb is active; why, passive; why nouns enter into a friendly pact with verbs and the noun joined to the verb fulfills its pact; unless noun and verb agree, speech will be mute and silent[119] and the statement cut short will not give complete sense; why a word, formed partly from a noun and partly from a verb, repays each what is owed it and noun and verb together give a meaning that neither could separately, when the word,

[111] Don., 4.355.1 ff. Cf. Prisc., 2.56.27 ff.

[112] Don., 4.359.4 ff.

[113] Don., 4.357.4 ff. Cf. Prisc., 2.577.1 ff.

[114] Prisc. (2.59.4 ff.) speaks of the use of certain common nouns to take the place of proper nouns, e.g. *poeta* for Virgil, *Urbs* for Rome; he mentions the use of *nepos* to mean a grandson (its strict meaning) and *nepos* to mean a spendthrift (an acquired meaning).

[115] Don., 4.381.14 ff.

[116] Don., 4.379.22. Cf. Prisc., 2.577.1.

[117] Priscian (3.144.21 ff.) points out that pronouns have no real declension. Declension in Latin signifies the existence of a root stem to which certain endings are added to denote cases. Thus *mei* is genitive but it cannot be said to be the genitive of *ego*. However, Donatus (4.357.13) accepts without question the delcension of pronouns. For *forma* meaning declension, see Varro, *L.L.* 9.37.

[118] Te term *demonstrative pronoun* as used in English could be misleading. For Priscian (2.577.14) the first and second personal pronouns are always demonstrative because *praesens ostenditur persona*. The other pronouns are demonstrative *simpliciter* if the person or object is present and *relative* if they are not.

[119] Reading *tacebit*.

holding a middle position, effects a union between them.[120] There could be seen why the other parts of speech respect these (noun and verb), submit to them and refuse not to serve them. This series of pictures painted successively drenches the eyes with delight and serve the mind a feast. A very talented painter had painted it or rather, one more powerful than any painter, and the painting proclaims his skill.

The aforementioned maiden, setting about her special task, does not tremble through fear of the burden, is not broken by the prospect of the toil. She exerts herself at her special work. The very refractory material is finally subdued and yields to her will. The tools spoken of before lie inactive and are idle for a time, the tools with which she refines boyhood years. Adopting the role of a craftsman, she uses a craftsman's tools; she overcomes the instability of her material[121] and forces it though unwilling to serve her purposes; she tames the inflexible wood and dresses it to the shape of a pole.

Here a cultural medium gives a place to the artificers of grammar and makes them live with a new birth and a fitting life. There Donatus,[122] grammar's leader, advocate and heir, teaches the rules of grammar, corrects mistakes, ennobles, exalts, enriches, defends, adorns, grammar by scholarship, exhortation, zeal, reasoning, inflection. He earns himself a special name so that he is not called grammarian but emphasis calls him *Mr.*

[120] This is a reference to the participle, which, as Donatus (4.363.13 ff.) points out, takes part from the noun and part from the verb. It gets its gender and case from the noun, its tense and voice from the verb and its number and figure (whether it is simple or compound) from both.

[121] *materie fluxus*. This is a favourite phrase of Thierry of Chartres. See ed. N. M. Häring, 161, 273, 275, 303, 525.

[122] Donatus' *Ars Minor* was the primer in grammar in the Middle Ages and a fairly close translation of it was the basic grammar in many European countries until very recently. A condensed version of his *Ars Major* formed the second section of these grammars.

Grammar, indicating the divinity under the name. Our friend, Aristarchus,[123] heaps offerings on the art of grammar, enlarges her treasures, increases her riches and measures his power in her. Dindimus[124] gathers together the tattered shreds of grammar and assigns each to its proper place in the plan. Our Apostate[125] strings out tracts on grammar and, somewhat tiresome in style, is the victim of sluggish dreams. As he strays far and wide in his writings, he is thought to be drunk or quite insane or to be drowsy. He falters in his faith to prevent the reputation of its book from faltering and he sells his faith not to lose the sales from his book; his faith goes astray to prevent popular fame from straying away from him.

This painting contains only those artificers whose reputation has blessed them with long-standing praise and the glory of whose work has not fallen from fame. It disdains to recognise base grammarians who rejoice in mere husks, whom the richness of the marrow within does not set apart: if they seek chippings from the outside, content with mere shells, they cannot taste the flavour of the nut.

[123] The first scientific scholar in the literary field. He wrote on everything connected with literature. Athenaeus (15.671F) refers to him as the "grammarian par excellence" Cf. Hor., *A.P.* 450.

[124] Didymus belonged to the school founded by Aristarchus. He wrote, among other things, works on grammar. See Prisc., 2.15.4 and 445.14; 3.408.6 and 492.8. Alan may be referring to his attempts to salvage the lost works of Aristarchus.

[125] Several glosses identify Priscian as the person referred to here. In addition one gloss, in rather unintelligible Latin, seems to state that there was a decree from the Roman Emperor that no book by a Christian author could appear under the author's name. It goes on to say that when Priscian heard this, he renounced his faith and his order (?) so that the *liber authenticatus* might bring him undying fame. M. Hertzius' introduction to Priscian (Keil. 2.i-xxiii) has no reference to any such law. What really happened was that Priscian dedicated his *Institutiones Grammaticae* to one "Julianus, Consul and Patricius". This Julian was later confused with Julian the Apostate. The passage of time did not improve Priscian's reputation. Dante (*Inf.* 15.109) saw him condemned to Hell for sodomy. Incidentically he saw Donatus in Heaven: *Par.* 12.137.

BOOK III

Deeper delving, ingenious, assiduous, painstaking, the second maiden shows her zeal, taps the very depths of her mind and activates her hand. The hand incites the mind, sets her native ability in motion and challenges her bodily senses to produce a type of axle and fashion it with so much perfection that, holding second place neither in glory of matter or form, it may challenge its friend, the pole, to a contest, or rather, outshining it in beauty, may cast it into the shade. Comeliness and beauty would have completely suffused the maiden's limbs, as the beautiful arrangement of her parts[1] demands, were it not that the face suffered here and there from a certain leanness. The leanness entrenches it and, entrenched by this leanness, it is deep hollowed and dry skin is wed to fleshless bones.[2] Here by dress, carriage, leanness and pallor she indicates the working of a never-sleeping mind, proclaims that Minerva is sleepless and the lighted lamps ever keep watch with her. Her hair, struggling in a kind of dispute, twists its way far down and unruly strands indulge in a tasteless brawl.[3] No comb restrains it, no clamping buckle holds it fast, no scissors' bite cuts it short. Her eyes rival the stars and seem aglow. The eagle's sight yields her prior place and the lynx's power of vision reverences such eyes, admits that it is surpassed and fears comparison with them.

The gift of flowers decorates her right hand; a scorpion encircling[4] her left threatens with pointed tail. One hand savours

[1] Reading *membrorum.*

[2] The reference is to the effect on Logic of an attempt to cultivate it as a discipline *in se* and segregated from other studies. He has in mind the statement of John of Salisbury that Logic is of great value as an aid to other studies but if it is on its own, it is practically useless, *Metalogicon,* 4.28, ed. Webb 194. Cf. Bk. 2, n. 18.

[3] A veiled reference to eristic dispute, argument for argument's sake.

[4] Reading *incedens.*

of honey, one bears the juice of venom; one promises laughter, the other ends in tears; one attracts, the other repels, one salves, the other stings, one smites, the other soothes; one graces, the other taints.[5] Her clothes were not despicable by filth or dirt nor distinguished by brilliance but kept a middle course, separated from both extremes. There a new painter, with a new art, an imitator of reality, displays the battle of the elenchi[6] and the duel of logic. He shows how the power of logic flashes its two-edged sword and when the face of truth has been maimed, cuts down the false, refusing to allow falsehood to be hidden beneath the appearance of truth;[7] why the pseudo-logician, thief and corrupter of art, liar and hypocrite, clandestine plunderer and sophist, imitates the outer aspect of logic and relying on certain stunts, tries to sell falsehood packaged as truth; what in logic is called a topic,[8] what is suitable for a topic, what is the source of topics,[9] what is a maxim,[10] what is the force of an argument that

[5] Logic defends the good and attacks the evil. However, it may be perverted and used to promote evil.

[6] Elenchus is discussed by Aristotle in *Prior Analytics* 2.20.66b 4 ff. He defines it as a syllogism involving a contradiction of a conclusion, i.e. a syllogism that rebuts a previous invalid syllogism. See Boeth., *PL* 64.705D, 1007D-1040D. Cicero is confused on the nature of the Aristotelian syllogism. In *De Inv.* 1.35.61, he erroneously states that the five-part syllogism was adopted by the followers of Aristotle and Theophrasus. In *Topica* 12.53 ff., where he is supposed to be following Aristotle, he gives the Stoic formulation of syllogisms.

[7] *De Soph. Elen.* 1.164a. Boeth., *PL* 64.1009B.

[8] Arist., in his *Top.* 1.100a 18, states that he is seeking a method to enable us to reason about any problem proposed to us by using generally accepted principles. We would be dealing with the dialectical syllogism based on premises that are merely probable. The *Topica* supply us with these premises. Cicero, keeping close to Aristotle, defines a Topic as an *argument sedem: Top.* 2.8. In fact Topics are files where we have arguments at hand for every occasion. See Boeth., *PL* 64.909D, 1048A.

[9] Arist., in *Top.* 2-7, gives a collection of Topics for Logic. His *Rhet.*, 2.23-24, gives a selection of thirty-eight Topics for Rhetoric. See Boeth., *PL* 64.923B-993B.

[10] *Maxima.* This is the γνώμη of Arist. *Rhet.* 2.21. This is a pity saying dealing with human life or conduct. One of Aristotle's examples is: no man is happy in every respect. Cf. *Rhet. ad Alex.* 11.1430a. Alan would have got this from the *Progymnasmata.* See n. 28 infra.

has its source in a topic, why a topic strengthens an argument, why a maxim, which lends its strength to an elenchus, arms the elenchus; how an elenchus[11] may fail in matter or form and like a mere apparition, produce the ghost of an elenchus; why a conclusion, drawn from premises, by stating what the premises lead to, is stamped with their likeness; why the middle term, acting as an intermediary, joins the extremes and binds all in a tight bond; why there is found a species of shortened elenchus when aphairesis or syncope[12] shortens the elenchus;[13] how induction,[14] trying to usurp the power and strength of the elenchus, goes over particulars and reaches the universal but yet admits its inferiority to the elenchus; how induction brings forth examples, indeed, when part of her has been cut away, the curtailed parent produces little children for herself;[15] how this art of the commonplace[16] is fortified by commonplaces but yet is restricted to no common place since it does not seek common places but a commonplace and accommodates commonplaces,

[11] Alan was very interested in the elenchus. However, he is now changing to the regular syllogism. He cannot use the word *syllogismus* in hexameters and retains *elenchus*.

[12] *Aphairesis* and *Syncope*, as technical terms, refer to Grammar. *Aphairesis* refers to the dropping of the first letter or syllabe of a word, e.g. *temnere* for *contemnere; Syncope* refers to the dropping of a letter or syllable in the middle of a word, e.g. *vixet* for *vixisset*. In Greek logic Aphairesis means abstraction, generally of a mathematical kind (Arist., *On The Heavens* 299a) but it cannot mean that here. Grammar, Logic and Rhetoric are closely allied and Alan crosses and recrosses the boundary lines very frequently.

[13] The shortened syllogism is a *Sign.* Arist., *Pr. An.* 2.27.70a; Boeth., *PL* 64.711B.

[14] Arist. *Pr. An.* 2.23.684b 14; *Top.* 1.12.105a 10; Cic., *De Inv.* 1.55-56, *Top.* 42; Boethius, *PL* 64.708D.

[15] Induction and example, though related, are treated as separate proofs in Aristotle: "It (example) differs from induction in that the latter ... shows from a consideration of *all the parts* that the extreme applies to the middle ... but example *does not use all the individual cases.*" *Pr. An.* 2.24.69a 14; Boeth., *PL* 64.709B-C. Alan regards examples as the children of induction.

[16] Lines 60-63. A series of puns on *loci communes* (topics, commonplaces) and *loca communia* (common places).

though unacquainted with common places; how it defines,[17] divides,[18] collects, unites each and every thing which it embraces to its ample bosom; how definition describing things narrows them down and prevents the term defined from promenading under shifting masks; what divides the genus and separates it into species or what divides the whole into parts and again unites the parts that were previously scattered and collects in one what was divided; how the art of logic, like a road, a gate, a key, points to, unlocks, opens the secrets of Sophia; how she bears arms and serves in every art, makes herself responsible for the suits and damages of her sisters; how she defends the other arts, enriches the needy, strengthens the weak, equips those lacking eloquence, decorates the unadorned, enlivens the languid, arms the unarmed; how she wipes out defects and gets rid of whatever dregs there are, so that defects may not detract from art;[19] how she watches the anvil to prevent the sophist from forging his arms by fraud and stealth. The imprint on the garb makes this clear so that you would think that the art was seeking opponents and a contest for herself. The aforementioned maiden has this dress, form, appearance, bearing: however, she gives up the flower in her right hand for the time being and keeps it free for other purposes. The serpent leaves her left hand and both hands urge her on to a higher commitment. The artisan's tools are at hand so that numbness may not permeate the maiden's hands: these the Lemnian[20] himself fits to her hands and joins her side with his own arms. Devoting herself, then, entirely to her toil, the maiden tries to soften the steel's hardness, to bend its stiffness,

[17] Arist., *Post. An.* 1.2.72a, 75b; 2.3-8; *Top.* 1.5.101b; 4.102b. Boeth., *PL* 64.745B, 754D; 891B-910B.

[18] Boeth., *PL* 64.875D-892D.

[19] Once again he insists on the value of Logic to other disciplines and the need for integration.

[20] Vulcan, the smith-god.

to wipe out its deadness, drive out its dulness, so that she may overcome the steel's refractoriness and fashion it into an axle. Shaping the basic steel into a better form, now the fire softens it, now the hammer bends it and both sigh as they long to put the finishing touches[21] on the steel. Thus steel meets steel to mould it, to honour its confederate and be honoured in it. After much sweat and toil, after the bouts of the contest, relentless toil overcomes the warring steel, wipes out its dull resistance, confines its ploys and pounds back its forays. It strikes the shapeless material and clothes it with shape; the material, which was just now unharmonious, crude, rough, inert, becomes tempered, shaped, moulded, changed and when thus refashioned, has the shape of an axle.

A series of pictures there gloriously displays the logicians of renown to whom fame grants unending life when it does not bury those whom earth covers in their graves but revivifying the dead, raises them up for the world's benefit. There Porphyry constructs an unwinding bridge and points out the path by which the reader may enter the depths of Aristotle and make his way to the heart of the book. There Porphyry solves mysteries like a second Oedipus, solving the riddle of our Sphinx. Our friend, Aristotle, the disturber of words, is here; he disturbs many of us by his turbulence and rejoices that he is obscure. He treats logic in such a way that he gives the impression of not having treated it: it is not that he does this unintentionally here but because he so veils everything with the veil of words that scarce any toil can unveil it. He drapes his words with such covers so as not to prostitute his secrets and by passing on his mysteries, make them finally grow cheap and common.[22] The

[21] Reading cultum.

[22] Reference to the often postulated esoteric nature of Aristotle's works. Porphyry solves the riddles of the latter-day Sphinx, Aristotle, as Oedipus solved the riddle of the Sphinx of old. Reference is to Porphyry's *Introduction to the Categories of Aristotle*.

dignity of something secret is cheapened and loses all its glory, if it be made public, for whoever publicizes things mystic decreases their dignity and what the public knows is no longer a mystery. Things noised abroad ever give rise to disgust: from such arise loathing and contempt. Zeno,[23] logic's protagonist, logic's champion, Sophia's king and leader, is here, seeking to do battle in logic's camp. He strips off its covering and lays bare its innermost recesses. He brings the dark back to light; he brings new things into use. He defends tropes and brings figures under a rule.[24] Severinus[25] clarifies the doubtful: under his guidance, logic with its power, abandoning its native tongue, leaves home to serve us and enriches Latin.

No way inferior in refinement and appearance, taking second place to none among the arts, the third maiden does not defraud the chariot of her service. She calls her mind into action; when it has answered the call, she fixes it on the projected work and directs her hand under the guidance of her mind. She applies those hands which give the finishing touch, brings the work of her sisters to perfection and adds embellishment to the thing just produced. She raises to the superlative degree what on its production was in the positive degree and did not attain the glory of the upper limits but was restricted to a secondary position. It is no wonder that, in giving added embellishment to things previously produced, she perfects them and gives the charm of further refinement, since beauty and grace of form smile on her, because she outstrips her peers in many of the

[23] See Bk. 2, n. 56.

[24] These are the *σχήματα* of Arist., *Pr. An.* 1.7.29a; 1.26.42b; 1.45.50b. Treatment of the various types of Figures is to be found in *Pr. An.* 1.4.25b; 1.9.30a; 1.15.33b; 1.16.35b; 2.2.53b; 2.5.57b; 2.8.58b. Boeth., *PL* 64.641C-665A. Cf. *Scemata in consequentiam ... reducimus*, Gilbert of Poitiers, ed. N. M. Häring, 55.

[25] Boethius.

painter's skills and enfolds in her bosom the complete art of the painter.[26]

Her locks reflecting the gloss of gold lie adorned with wondrous artistry: her hair falls down to cover her neck. Her countenance is steeped in radiant colour:[27] a brilliant red glow tints her face with roseate lustre but a foreign glitter haunts her face to some extent and tries to combine with the native hue.[28] Now a many-streamed flood of tears bedews her face; now the oft-changing smile of dawn makes it fair, as it chases away the tears of sorrow; now the maid adopts a countenance stern with a dignified inflexibility; now her eyes turn their gaze on high; now this high gaze is lowered; now turning her full keen glance to the side, she seeks the shade of digression.[29] In her right hand she

[26] Arist., *Rhet.* 1.1.1354a: "Rhetoric is a counterpart of Dialectic; for both treat of such matters as are in some manner within the cognizance of all men and they are not restricted to any special science". Rhetoric will not produce any particular part of the chariot but will ornament the parts already produced. In the twelfth century, the idea, dating back to Cicero, of rhetoric as the integrating factor of all education was prominent at Chartres. See John of Salisbury, *Metalogicon* 1.1. Webb, 7 *Entheticus* 363-368, *PL* 199.973A-B. According to Plutarch, *Glory of the Athenians* 346F, Simonides defined poetry as vocal painting, painting as silent poetry. Painters based their work on material found in literature and for Alan all literature, prose and verse, is essentially rhetoric.

[27] Colours and colouring are frequently used to describe style in Rhetoric.

[28] *candor peregrinus inheret.* This comes from Peter of Compostella, ed. P. B. Soto, 62.25. Formal rhetoric (as opposed to oratory) was regarded as peculiarly Greek. It was resented and distrusted in Rome. Attempts to expel rhetoricians or curtail their influence were made in 161 and 92 B.C. Finally the type of rhetoric, advocated by Cicero and Quintilian, became the accepted standard for Roman rhetoric. It was Greek in origin and format. Rhetoric, strongly influenced by Greek, also came to the Middle Ages through the *Progymnasmata.* These were preliminary exercises for the elementary stage of instruction in the schools of rhetoric. Several collections of them are extant. There is another way in which rhetoric was foreign. Arist., *Rhet.* 3.2.1. advises the orator to give his style elevation and increase its power to draw attention by avoiding the unrelieved use of everyday language. He goes on to say: "men react to style as they do to foreigners and citizens. Therefore we should give our language a foreign element".

[29] Alan summarizes the various facial expressions and gestures of the orator. The final reference is to the part of a speech called *digressio.* In this the orator speaks of something only very vaguely connected with the case, e.g. reference to some other cases that might emphasize a point for himself. It came just before the peroration, Cic., *De Inv.,* 1.97.

bears a trumpet, her left she decks with a horn and on it she gives the signal for the preliminary exercises[30] of the war. A garment covers her: painted in various colours, it rejoices that it is overlaid with various hues. Here with the painter's aid gleams a picture of Rhetoric's power of colour and thus a picture adds colour to a picture. Here, as in a book, one reads:[31] what is the end in view; who is the orator; what are Rhetoric's species; what is its role; what is a lawsuit; what is arrangement; what is the special domain of Rhetoric; what is its special excellence; how at one time it thunders over us with threats, again flashes with the light of words, now pours forth prayers, now fills the ear with praise, what establishes the genera in Rhetoric; what the aim of Rhetoric is; to what terminal point it is making its way when it discusses the useful, decides what is just, confirms the right, designates the honourable; what are the parts of the art, by what

[30] A word-play: *preludia* = progymnasmata.

[31] Alan tends to leave a point and come back to it later. This can be confusing. The following outline might help:

(a) Rhetoric is the faculty of discovering the available means of persuasion in reference to any subject, or, the art of giving effectiveness to truth.

(b) Rhetoric deals with a theoretical issue, not restricted to a particular person or occasion (*quaestio infinita*), or with a particular person or occasion (*quaestio finita*).

(c) The Rhetoric dealing with a *quaestio finita* is divided into three classes (*genera*): deliberative (*deliberativum*), dealing with political issues and emphasizing what is advantageous (*utile*); forensic (*iudiciale*), dealing with lawsuits and concentrating on justice and right (*iustum, rectum*); epideictic (*demonstrativum*), display pieces, such as panegyrics, funeral orations, where the honourable (*honestum*) is the theme. Cicero (*De Orat.,* 1.31.141) and Quintilian (3.3.15; 4.1-14) accept this division with reluctance. Cicero (*De Inv.* 2.156 ff.) regards the just as a subdivision of the honourable and would add the honourable to the domain of deliberative Rhetoric.

(d) The Art of Rhetoric is divided into: Finding of arguments (*Inventio*), Arrangement (*Dispositio*), Style (*Elocutio*), Memorization (*Memoria*), Delivery (*Pronuntiatio*).

(e) The orator is a good man who has mastered this Art. He attains the ends of Rhetoric by a speech. He should be able to teach, to delight, to move, to defend.

(f) The subdivisions of a speech are: Exordium, Narrative (*Narratio*), Summation (*Partitio*), Proof (*Confirmatio*), Refutation (*Refutatio*), Digression (*Digressio*), Peroration (*Peroratio*).

arrangement they are connected; how at first the art discovers arguments, then arranges them, gets the fitting style, memorises them, delivers them, so that in the regular scheme of arrangement, arrangement may make a fitting arrangement for itself;[32] what and how many parts the orator's speech has and by what sequence they are knit together; how the exordium stirs the judge's mind, makes him prick his ears, sharpens his attention, conditions his heart so that the auditor becomes more attentive, more tractable, more kindly disposed and devotes his attention to what he hears; how the narrative is a brief exposition of the truth or of the falsehood lurking beneath the guise of truth; how the partition brings together in summary fashion all that is to follow, collecting together what is scattered, compressing what is prolix; how a statement favouring our side[33] high-lights the arguments, establishes them, sets them forth, structures them, draws inferences from them; how a refutation[34] is a blow to the opposite side, ruins them, weakens them, breaks them up, puts pressure on them; in what way the peroration, rounding out the several parts, brings the speech to a close with a regular end and reins in the discourse; which deed or type of deed or alleged deed[35] does a point at issue look for when it is supported by several lines of argument,[36] which suit involves a dispute about a fact,[37] which a question of law,[38] what and how many kinds of issues are there, which issue is simple, which has a connection

[32] Even after reading Boethius' *Int. Pr. An. Arist.* and *Int. Elench. Sophist.*, Alan cannot keep away from this type of scholastic joke. From note 31 supra, it can be seen that Arrangement is the second of the subdivisions of Rhetoric. Alan's witticism is that Arrangement arranges that it will be in second place.

[33] This refers to *confirmatio,* the positive side of proof. Cf. Cic., *De Or.* 1.31.143.

[34] *Infirmacio.* This refers to *refutatio,* the negative side of proof. *Cf. Cic., ibid.*

[35] Cic., *De Inv.* 2.17.52; Mart. Cap., 5.449.

[36] Cic., *Top.* 25.95 ff.; Quint. 3.6 ff.

[37] Cic., *De Inv.* 2.4.14; Mart. Cap. 5.549.

[38] Cic., *Top.* 25.95 ff.

with something else and what are the constituents of this connection,[39] why this aspect intensifies the charges in the accusation, that calls for a change of court,[40] another rebuts, still another, weighing advantages and disadvantages, finds them equal;[41] how a case on either side gains strength when a law clashes with and opposes a kindred law[42] or the intent disagrees with and conflicts with the letter of the law[43] or an ambiguous sentence in the written law gives rise to a doubt[44] or when a word can be so defined that the undisputed definition removes the ambiguity[45] or when by a judicial point of place, person, time, the case itself is changed to another court[46] and will cause confusion elsewhere or if a claim, covered by no definite law, is being urged and obtains support by an argument from analogy;[47] in what way a person's character arms and strengthens the arguments, while arguments based on name,[48] disposition, mode of life, fortune showing harassed face, habit, feeling, plan that miscarried, interests, accident, speeches, achievements, fail as

[39] Cic., *De Inv.* 1.12.17: Quint., 3.10.1 ff.

[40] Cic., *De Inv.* 2.19.57.

[41] Cic., *De Inv.* 1.52.78; Quint., 4.2.26. This is one of the few instances where he is following. Quintilian. Note use of *repellere* and *transferre* in both.

[42] Cic. *De Inv.* 2.49.144; Quint., 3.6.84, 3.7.7 ff; Mart. Cap., 5.464.

[43] Cic. *De Inv.* 2.42.121 ff., *De Ov.* 1.31.140 Quint., 7.6.1 ff.

[44] Cic., *De Inv.* 2.40.116; Quint., 7.10.1 ff.; Mart. Cap. 5.466.

[45] Cic., *De Inv.* 2.5.153 ff.; Quint., 7.10.3 ff. It is strange that Alan did not make some use of the example given by Cicero. It has all the earmarks of scholastic rhetoric.

[46] Cic., *De Inv.* 2.19.57 ff.; Quint., 3.6.46.

[47] Cic., *De Inv.* 2.50.148; Quint., 3.6.87.

[48] Cic., *De Inv.* 1.24.34 ff., gives the attributes of persons as name, nature, manner of life, fortune, habit (acquired), feeling, interests, purposes, achievements, accidents, speeches. Cf. *De Inv.* 2.9.28 ff.; Quint., 5.10.24 ff., lists eighteen attributes and states that he is giving just a short selection. Only name (*nomen*) needs explanation. Is a man named *Caldus (calidus* = hot)likely to have a violent temper (*De Inv.* 2.9.28) ? Is a man named *Pius* likely to be an admirable citizen (Quint., 5.10.30) ? They agree that the name is significant only if it has been given to this individual because of his personal traits. Alan's list is Cicero's with a few changes to suit the metre.

they have only the appearance of strength; what things[49] have sequels, what does a question of fact include, what are inseparable adjuncts of a deed or what, as circumstances demand, follows it in the normal course of events; what is the manner of performing the deed, what are the constituents of the deed, what is the place, time, occasion, motive, opportunity.

One part of the garment has this representation of the art of Rhetoric, the other, however, shows the outlines of its artificers. There Marcus[50] makes Rhetoric a child adopted by him alone or rather fathers it: thus this art will rightly be called Cicero's daughter since Tullius begets her and the art tracing its origin to him may well be called Tullia.[51] There Ennodius[52] bedecks his poems with many a flower and smoothes out all rough edges from his discourse. Quintilian[53] is here, cloaking fictitious cases with the appearance of real ones; he sets forth a new type of hypothetical lawsuit and forces us into the courts with no actual issue at stake. Symmachus,[54] sparing of words, profound in mind, expansive in intellect, restricted in diction, rich in intelligence, somewhat poor in expression, happy in his fruit rather than his foliage, compresses richness of intellect by con-

[49] Alan turns now to attributes of the action. Cic., *De Inv.* 1.26.38 ff. and 2.12.38 ff., lists time, place occasion, manner, facilities, opportunity, inseparable adjuncts, actual performance, concrete result, resultant feelings. Occasion means conditions without which the deed could not have been done. Quint., 5.10.32 makes a long and scientific analysis of the attributes of actions. Alan's list is from Cicero.

[50] Marcus Tullius Cicero.

[51] Cicero's only daughter was named Tullia; Alan is attempting another of his many word-plays.

[52] Ennodius, Bishop of Pavia, wrote, amongst other things, model speeches. He was extremely preoccupied with style. His attempts to combine pagan and Christian elements would appeal to Alan. Some notion of his literary ideas can be got from his *Opusculum* VI, *Ambrosio et Beato, CSEL* 6.401-410.

[53] Reference to the specimen cases that abound in Quintilian.

[54] Symmachus was a cultured and sincere pagan of the fourth century. Ten books of letters and some fragments of speeches are extant. He is best remembered for his attempt, when he was City Prefect in the reign of Valentinian II, to have the Altar of Victory restored to the *Curia Julii.*

ciseness of language. The discourses of Sidonius,[55] in ceremonial dress,[56] gleaming with many a star, flash forth and glitter with gems of colour and the painted peacock finds an echo in his words. Now he exercises his delicate Muse on a slender reed; yet it is not an anaemic discourse bewailing its hunger. Now he holds a middle course, neither falling to the depths nor swelling to the heights; now he thunders, as he treats serious matters in high-sounding words; now in bombast he rumbles with loud, windy noise. Gay in this attire, the maiden does not refuse the aid of her art but rather her skill in production is given in abundance to the chariot's formation. She bespangles the pole with the beauty of gems and sets it in a class apart;[57] she clothes it liberally in silver and the highest decoration is brought in to supplement the wooden material, which has less distinction and this decoration compensates for the wood's inferior status. An adoptive splendour hides wood's primeval origin from sight and removes every basis for complaint; the old age of wood disappears and thus it forgets its primeval origins.[58] A star-cluster of gems, then, gilds the pole; in fact its light restores true day and the actual day grows dull for the natural light of day sinks down in admiration before an adoptive light so great. The maiden in like manner traces many a flower on the axle and with fresh blooms makes the steel grow young again. Though steel is usually rigid with the stiffness of cold and reminds one of deep Winter's frost, this steel knows no Winter, leaves behind its congenital cold, establishes its claim to the smiling joys of Spring and with its pattern of flowers sets before

[55] Sidonius Apollinaris, a man with a penchant for backing losers, held various public offices, including that of City Prefect. Finally he became bishop of Auvergne. Twenty-four *Carmina* and nine books of letters written by him are extant. His works are poisoned with pedantry and rhetoric.

[56] *trabeatus*, wearing a *trabea*. The *trabea* was a robe of state of augurs, knights, etc.

[57] Reading *insignit*.

[58] Cf. Bern. Silv., 1.1.1.-1.2.35.

us a view of meadow. While the maiden thus enlivens the pole with gems and flowers, giving it the ultimate in ornament, the trumpet gives place to the painter's reed, the horn makes way for an engraver's burin and thus these two assume the rights of the other pair.

The fourth sister comes next. The first wheel is the fourth sister's work. She gives her attention to this with all her energy. Although she is the fourth sister, she refuses to admit that she is second to any, maintaining in fact that she should be called the first. Proper, decorous, graceful, precise, keen, she shows her power and her mental ability shows itself in her countenance. For our countenance is a book and is written with the words of our heart; it is the messenger, truthful reporter and portrayer of the soul. This maiden shows the countenance of a careful person, the mind of a prudent one, the culture of an honourable one, the appearance of an attentive one and she bears the stamp of a person of restraint and with her man-like mind she transcends her sex.[59] No foreign tint finds a home on her roseate cheeks; rather, native hue holds sway and no reddish dye is on her face to suffer the disintegration that comes to purloined colour. She bends her head towards the ground but her senses do not hunt for things that slip the catch. Her eyes rest as they allow her mind to take over. One hand holds aloft the Table of Pythagoras,[60] which offers food for the mind and savours of delights for the soul, not nourishment for the body. The other

[59] Alan must have been irked by the fact that all the *Virtutes* and the seven Liberal Arts were feminine. He tries here and there to inject a masculine element. The quaintest example is in *De Pl. Nat.* (439D: W. 445). His beloved and almost omnipotent Nature is coming from the heavens in a car drawn by Juno's birds. A man looking over her shoulder, supplies what is here wanting to the fair sex and meekly offering directions, tries to guide the car's course: *homo vero virginis capiti supereminens ... impotentiam sexus supplendo feminae, modesto directionis ordine, currus aurigabat incessum.* Here Arithmetic has a woman's form but a man's mind. Masculine elements will appear also in Music and Geometry in lines 410 and 513 infra.

[60] The *abacus*. See Boethius, *PL* 63.1333C.

hand displays fights, arranges the marching line of numbers,[61] depicts battles, shows various charges and numbers in rebellion.[62] Finally, she brings the war to an end in subtle triumph. A dress of cotton, clothed with its native colour, covers the maiden's shining limbs. The material was finely spun; the workmanship, finer still, excels the material. Thus skill from practice outstrips the power of nature and nature is surpassed by art. Here a painting, though silent, indicates by its lines and proclaims by its figures the whole art of numbers. It shows: what is the power of numbers, what is their law, their bond and order, their knot, their love, their proportion, their league, their harmony, their limit; in what way number binds all things with a harmonious bond, arranges individual things, directs the universe, sets the world in order, moving the stars, uniting the elements, wedding souls to bodies, earth to heaven, the celestial to the transitory; in what way number was the beginning, end, exemplar, form and image for the birth of the world and the creation of things, when according to its pattern, the idea in the divine mind imprinted form on things and shape on the universe;[63] in what way the beginning, source, mother, origin of numbers is the monad[64] and by itself it begets a host of numbers

[61] *Numeri* means *numbers*; it also can mean *army divisions* (Tac., *Agr.* 18, *Hist.* 1.6; Amm. Mar., 14.7.19). Alan plays on these two meanings in the section on Arithmetic.

[62] As can be seen from Nicholas of Gerasa, the Greeks were forever trying to arrange numbers in series or ranks. They resented any sequence of numbers that could not be brought into line and looked on them as mutinous — the *numeros rebelles* of line 292.

[63] Nic., *Introd. to Arith.* 1.4.2; Boeth., *PL* 63.1083B. Nicomachus states: "It existed ... in the mind of the creating God like some universal and exemplary plan, relying on which as a design and archetypal example, the creator of the universe sets in order his material creations and makes them attain to their proper ends".

[64] Nicomachus did not formally treat of the monad in the works we have. He has a few references to it: 1.16.8; 2.8.3; 2.9.2; 2.10.2; 2.11.1-2; 2.13.8; 2.14.1. These are found in Boethius, *PL* 63.1099B, 1123B-C, 1124A, 1131A, 1131C. Cf. Macrobius, *Comm.* 1.6.7.

from itself; in what way the maiden[65] gives birth and giving birth, remains intact: though single, she multiplies herself, begets from herself and remains virginal, merely counterfeiting the birth-process of a mother; which number is classed as a mere numeral, which is a number connected with objects;[66] which number repeats, which distributes, which collects, subtracts, adds;[67] which reduces a number to its prime root; by what just ordinance or what process of reasoning is an even number styled feminine, an odd number, masculine;[68] the virgin Minerva;[69] why the teaching of the wise denotes the soul, the heavens, reason, joys, life by an odd number; why an even number designates body, earth, the senses, the sorrowful, death and indicates the worse fate; which number is a point,[70] which is a

[65] Nicomachus, according to *Theologumena* (Ast.) 4, had a theory connecting the monad with God. Outlandish powers are attributed to it. For the idea of *monas parit*, see Thierry of Chartres, ed. N. M. Haring, 297-298.

[66] Cf. Dist. 877C; *Quoniam Homines*, ed. P. Glorieux, 187. Despite the statement in *Dist.* 877C, Boethius does not seem to have used the terms *numerus numerans* and *numerus numeratus*, although he discusses the ideas they were later used to convey: *De Trin.* 3 (Stewart-Rand 12 ff.). The words seem to have been first used by Thierry of Chartres or a member of his school, ed. N. M. Häring, 488. Cf. St. Thomas, 1. q 30 ad 4.

[67] Alan here takes his material from the various kinds of enumeration mentioned in an abstruse and difficult section of the Commentary on Boethius' *De Trinitate* by Gilbert of Poitiers, 3.12 ff., ed. N. M. Häring, 104 ff.

[68] The odd number could not be broken into equal parts and was considered indestructible. Cf. Macrob., *Comm.*, 2.2.17; Mart. Cap., 7.736.

[69] The *virgo* is seven. Seven is a virgin because, within the sacred decade, i.e. one to ten inclusive, she alone cannot be broken into factors and is not herself a factor of any number there. She is called Minerva because she is produced by the monad alone as Minerva (Athena) sprang from the head of Zeus: Macrob., *Comm.* 1.6.11; Mart. Cap., 7.738. The preoccupation with the number seven seems to have arisen from superstitious beliefs about the influence of the moon's phases on gestation, birth, disease, mental stability, etc. See W. H. Roscher, *Hebdomadenlehren der griechischen Philosophen und Ärzte* (Leipzig 1906).

[70] Unity. "The point itself is the beginning of dimension but not itself a dimension". Nic., 2.7.1; Boeth., *PL* 63.1121B.

line,[71] which a plane figure of equal sides,[72] which is termed spherical,[73] which, square,[74] which, cubic,[75] which, pyramidal,[76] which is cyclic[73] and makes the round trip from itself back to itself; which number is equal to its own factors, which is greater than its factors or which, being superabundant, is exceeded by its factors;[77] what harmony binds number to number and how does it happen that extremes are connected by means; why are two squares connected by one mean,[78] while two means unite cubes.[79] With this refinement the highly refined maiden, then, did not try to escape the heavy work, lest through fear of its weight, she run away from its weighty honours and shunning the onerous, miss the honourable. A man by intelligence, a woman

[71] 2.3.4.5.6. etc.: Nic., 2.7.3; Boeth., *PL* 63.1121C.

[72] An equilateral triangle. Triangular numbers are 1.3.6.10.15.21.28 etc.: Nic., 2.8.1; Boeth., *PL* 63.1122C.

[73] The numbers 1, 5 and 6 have the property that whatever power they are raised to, the resultant number ends in 1, 5, or 6. Thus $5^2 = 25$; $5^3 = 125$; $6^2 = 36$; $6^3 = 216$. If they are raised to the second power, they are called cyclic; if they are raised to a higher power, they are called spherical. Nic., 2.17.7; Boeth., *PL* 63.1137B; Mart. Cap., 7.735.

[74] Square numbers are: 1.4.9.16.25 etc. Nic., 2.9.1: Boeth., *PL* 63.1123D.

[75] Cubic numbers are: 1.8.27.64.125 etc. Nic., 2.15.1; Boeth., *PL* 63.1133D.

[76] Pyramidal numbers vary according to which polygonal plane figure forms the base of the pyramid. Alan mentions only triangles and squares. The numbers for a pyramid with a triangular base are: 1.4.10.20.35.56.84.120 etc.; for pyramids witha square base the numbers are: 1.5.14.30.55.91.140.204 etc.: Nic., 2.13-14; Boeth., *PL* 63.1129B-1132A.

[77] A perfect number is equal to the sum of its factors, e.g. 6 has factors 1.2.3. A deficient number is greater than the sum of its factors, e.g. 8 has factors 1.2.4. A superabundant number is less than the sum of its factors, e.g. 12 has factors 1.2.3.4.6. Mathematicians pointed out that perfect numbers, like perfection itself, are rare. There are only four under 10,000: 6.28.496.8128. Nic., 1.14-16; Boeth., *PL* 63.1097A-1099C. Cf. Euc., 7. Def. 22.

[78] Algebraically: between a^2 and b^2 there is one mean, ab, and a^2: ab:: ab: b^2, Arithmetically: between 36 (6^2) and 81 (9^2) there is one mean, 54 (6×9) and 36: 54:: 54: 81.

[79] Algebraically: between a^3 and b^3 there are two means, a^2b and ab^2, and a^3: a^2b::ab^2: b^3. Arithmetically: between 27 (3^3) and 512 (8^3) there are two means, 72 ($3^2 \times 8$) and 192 (3×8^2) and 27: 72:: 192: 512. Plato, *Tim.* 31C.

by sex, she surpasses a maiden in strength by a superabundance of power and by her skill. In one way a woman, in one way a man, in mental capacity she is not a "she" but a "he". She does not give her thoughts expression by any sudden move to action nor commit the offspring of her mind to hasty deeds. If the mind itself brings forth an idea before the idea has undergone a process of formation in its womb and has taken on a definite image from the parent mind and before that image has come to life and been long fed by nourishment from reason, the foetus will suddenly come to an untimely birth: unfitted for life, it will die at its birth or living it will at all events bewail its defects of form. To prevent the mind's conception from straying from the road leading to normal birth and having any cause for complaint against its mother, the mind conceives and then reason nourishes what the act of conception produces, and fashions the intellect's foetus in the bridal bed of the mind before she delivers the material product. Thus with mental labour, helped by the artisan's spirit and enthusiasm, the idea of a wheel is formed; later she combines this with matter to form a copy of itself. Thus she conceived the original in her mind with a view to birth; in the actual product she gave it its second birth. First laying aside the objects that dominated her hands, she directs her enthusiastic attention to the work of stone-cutter; by her art she subdues the hard marble and first planes the sections to the test of the nail.[80] The jagged points are planed down to give a level surface, the hollows come up to be level with the rest, the edges are rounded to curves, a rim encloses the flat surface and turns it into a circle. A protuberance, rising at the centre, projects upwards but stretching upwards does not separate itself from the part below.[81]

[80] *ad unguem.* The close-cut nail was run over a sculptured surface to detect uneveness. *Ad unguem* came to mean a stringent test. See Hor. *A.P.*, 294.

[81] This refers to the nave on which the rest of the wheel would be hung.

When the parts had been curved with the help of the steel, the maiden took out parts and marking off the marble by openings, divides the entire circle into sections.[82] She places the nave in the centre and surrounds it with many a spoke which the rimside encloses in a circle. Here a picture tells us what authors discovered the ways of numbers, taught this art, brought it out of its hiding place, sang its praise when it fell on evil days. Here Nicomachus[83] sports in the art we mentioned and, as it were, by numbers foretells things secret. There Gilbertus[84] has his camp and, as a soldier in the same discipline, skips part of the course by a deceptive progress. Pythagoras, feasting his mind, not his flesh, satisfying minds, not sating bodies, ascribes to the fixed laws of numbers birth, existence, change, causality, motion, and the connection between things. Chrysippus devotes himself to numbers with such love that number finds an echo in his words and deeds and you would think that he was counting in his sleep.

[82] Wind-resistance would cause trouble if a wheel were solid: so would water-resistance if the vehicle had to be taken over the bed of even a shallow stream. For this reason perforations of some kind must be made.

[83] Nicomachus of Gerasa. Alan got most of his material from an adaptation of Nicomachus' *Introduction to Arithmetic*.

[84] This refers to Gerbertus. He was a brilliant scholar and an inventive genius. He was successively Archbishop of Rheims, Archbishop of Ravenna and Pope with the title of Silvester II. He was an extremely fine mathematician. His mathematical works have been published: *Gerberti postea Sylvestri II Papae Opera Mathematica,* Nicolaus Bubnov (Berlin 1889). Stories about him must have been common in his lifetime as his pupil, Richerus, felt called on to defend him: *Richeri Historiarum Libri IIII*, ed. Georgius Waitz, MGH, SrG 3.99-109. Even the gentle Hermannus Contractus felt that he had devoted too much attention to secular studies: *PL* 143.227A. A host of bizarre stories were soon to appear. Benno II of Osnabrück speaks of his trafficking with the devil, deceiving many and being finally deceived himself about the time of his death. The deception about his death appears in all the stories. He asked the devil, in different form in different stories, when he would die. He was told that he would not die until he had visited Jerusalem. He felt that he could postpone his death indefinitely by avoiding the trip to Jerusalem. He did not advert to the fact that there was a church in Rome called "Jerusalem". He went there to say Mass, realised that he had been deceived and fell fatally ill. Benno maintains

The fifth sister is like the fourth and shows her resemblance to her predecessor in her face. She reproduces her in appearance, traces her work back to her, is engaged in a similar pursuit and succeeds her sister. In her work she makes the fourth sister her exemplar and, with her eyes on her sister's work, she puts the stamp of Arithmetic on her own work. The one whom long ago Nature made Arithmetic's sister becomes her sister in action and perfects everything that falls within Arithmetic's scope. For reason teaches, law demands, order requires that their work should proclaim what is made evident by their native character.[85] This renowned maiden turns her countenance into a mirror for the viewer; whoever gazes at her face sees himself reflected in it and the eye feasts on her mirror-like countenance.[86] One hand holds a cithara, the other plucks its chords and produces a sweet

that Gerbert's disciples carried on his nefarious practices and that there was a succession of magician Popes: K. Francke, *Benonis aliorumque Cardinalium Scripta* in *Libelli de Lite Imperatorum, MGH* 2, 377. William of Malmesbury, with the stock excuse that he is only recording what everyone is saying, gives an account of love affairs, pacts with the devil, speaking statues, etc.: *De Gestis Regum Anglorum Libri Quinque*, in Rolls Series 90.1 by W. Stubbs (London 1887) 193-203. Walter Map outdoes his predecessors with his details of Gerbert's love for the provost's daughter of Rheims, his meeting with Meridiana, a woman not of his world, who supplied him with money and advice and finally deceived him: M. R. James, *Walter Map's De Nugis Curialium* (English Version, London 1923) 192-201. Alan felt that Gerbert's life left much to be desired but that he died in grace, a point on which the majority of the tales agree. He attributes the *Prosa de Angelis* to him: M. T. d'Alverny, *Textes Inédits*, 195. The gloss on Alan by Ralph of Longchamps is of a piece with the other stories. According to it Gerbert had the devil shut in a skull. He consulted him about a point in mathematics, got a poor answer and had to skip that part in his work. This omission is the *saltus fallax* of line 378. Attempts to identify the particular problem have not been too convincing. See Bubnov. *op. cit.*, 972; cf. his *Accedunt aliorum Opera ad Gerberti libellos aestimandos intelligendosque necessaria* (Berlin 1899) 31 ff., 391.

[85] Lines 386-394 emphasize the kinship between Music and Arithmetic. Alan's ideas can be traced back through Boethius to Nicomachus of Gerasa, who stated that Music and Arithmetic both deal with quantity — Arithmetic with absolute quantity and Music with relative quantity. Nic., 1.3.1; Boeth., *PL* 63.1081B.

[86] Music can represent every feeling and every mood, indeed can produce them.

delight of sound that is a feast for the ears and a prelude to slumber for the eyes. With such music did the Thracian bard[87] bid the stones become tractable, the woods to run, the rivers to stop, the wild beasts to grow tame, disputes to cease. By his laments he overcame the inflexibility of the Eumenides, made them yield to pressure, made Dis show a fatherly kindness and the Furies forget their fury. With such music Amphion[88] converted the Tyrian rocks into walls, thus taming stones which the music of the harp alone could tame, since no axe could overcome the hard, rough crags and its steel was silent. Dressed in a striking cloak,[89] the maiden shows that she is the foster-child of peace and seeks not the thunderbolts of war. There a gay and smiling picture disports itself, showing under various forms: what music can do,[90] what are its bonds, with what ties it joins all things together, what are the species of the art, which music joins the parts of the day together, separates the months, establishes the seasons of the year, restricts their vagaries, unites the elements, links the planets, gives the stars motion,[91] which music sets afoot the various alternations; which music sets in order the parts of the body of man, that little cosmos, and so adorns him with the form of the greater cosmos that the pygmy deserves to be the little brother of the giant,[92] the smaller to be represented as an image of the greater; which music harmonises

[87] Orpheus. According to various myths, he could attract trees, wild beasts, stones. He could charm whomsoever he wished. He went to Hades and persuaded its lord. Dis (Pluto), to release Eurydice.

[88] He was given a magical lyre by Hermes. With it he drew stones after him and used them to wall Thebes.

[89] The *toga* is a man's garment. See note 59 supra.

[90] Music shares in the phantastic powers attributed to numbers.

[91] Lines 415-418 deal with *musica mundana*, the music of the universe; 418-424 with *musica humana*, music relating to man and 424-445 with *musica instrumentalis*, instrumental music.

[92] Juvenal, 4.98. See Baumgartner 88.

the faculties of the soul, allies the soul with the body, strengthens this mutual alliance; which music distinguishes pitches and marks the intervals by numbers; why every melody and sweet-sounding song is the product not of one note but of a union of pitches, a sound that is like and unlike, different and the same, one and simple, double, two-formed and different; in what way music by changing the melody, brings about a change in itself, weaving laughter with tears, the serious with the sportive: now it swells forth in enharmonic;[93] now recording things sad, it wails in diatonic;[94] now it sports in chromatic;[95] which pitch makes a double proportion to another so that the note sounds at the octave, or which has a sesquialter proportion to it and the concord sounds at the fifth; what combination of voices produces the fourth[96], in which one voice contends, or rather sports, with three others; why one part of a tone always overflows encroaching on the remaining part so that the entire tone cannot be divided into equal parts, but rather that one part exceeds and is greater to some extent than the lesser part and the other part is greater than a limma[97] by its comma,[98] but yet that the comma, divided into two diastemata,[99] does not reject equally divided parts.

Resplendent in this dress and shining with this beautiful appearance, the maiden abandons her harp-playing for a time,

[93] Mart. Cap., 9.930, 942; Boeth. *PL* 63.1188D. Enharmonic, diatonic and chromatic represent three Greek *genera* of music. Their meaning has changed somewhat in modern usage.

[94] Mart. Cap., 9.942, 954, 956.

[95] *Ib.* 956, 959, 964.

[96] *Ib.* 950, 951.

[97] *Ib.* 1.11; Boeth., *PL* 63.1218B.

[98] Boeth., *PL* 63.1222C.

[99] *Diasymata.* The word is not to be found in any lexicon. Probably it is used for *diastemata*. See Mart. Cap., 9.948, 950. *Diaschismata* is a possibility: see Boethius, *De Musica*, 3.8, ed. G. Friedlein, 278.20 *PL* 63.1232B.

while she undertakes the work of a tradesman. By the power of her passion she turns the stone into bronze; from the bronze she builds the second wheel which, evidencing the beauty of form of its predecessor, proclaims that it is its sister. Although the material which adorns them is different, the form makes them twins. There a painting preserves the fame of the artificers whom music wishes to have as her associates or whom she deigns the honour of being designated by her name. The Milesian[100] makes use of his honey-sweet voice and, so to speak, gives the ears a festival of song and enervates the mind with that art of his. Another,[101] at the opposite extreme, discovers the distasteful protracted song, the brawl of thick voices and refractory chants, which assail our ears with their sounds rather than hail them and he offends our ears. Our friend Gregory[102] steers a middle course, avoids either extreme and shuns the dangers arising from voices. Music, avoiding the song of the Sirens and Charybdis,[103] is amused at Michalus[104] as a teacher and corrects its errors under such instruction.

[100] Timotheus. He was from Miletus, which had a reputation for wanton, lascivious songs.

[101] A gloss in one Manuscript gives this man's name as Philoades. This seems to be the only mention of him. The name is suspect. Someone probably contrived it from the Greek **φίλος ἀοιδῆς**, *lover of song.*

[102] Pope Gregory I. The invention of Gregorian Chant is attributed to him, although the first source for connecting the chant with him seems to be a life of Gregory written by John the Deacon more than two-hundred years after his death.

[103] The Sirens are the irresistible but destructive singers in Hom. *Od.*, 12.39, 184. Charybdis was a whirlpool in a narrow sea-channel. Opposite her was Scylla, a sea-monster in Homer but later a dangerous rock. It required expert seamanship to navigate the channel. The channel was later identified with the Straits of Messina, but there is no whirlpool there.

[104] Arist., *Pr. An.* 1.47b, uses the name *μουσικὸς Μίκκαλὸς* in an example of a syllogism. *μουσικός* most probably means "cultured". Boeth., *PL* 64.677A, translates this *Michalus musicus.* Alan is using some fine irony here. The *Michalus musicus* of Boeth. and its Greek original are part of the middle term or mean in a syllogism. It is a defective and unsatisfactory example of a mean and Alan is saying that Music which loves the mean will be only too happy to accept correction from an imperfect mean.

The sixth sister sets about her task; she directs all her energy to her chosen work, clinging to her devotion more devotedly than the others. Carriage, dress, beauty vie equally in increasing the honour due her and in sounding her praises. She keeps her head inclined though she is subject to no defect of body but is directing her gaze to one spot that this concentration may indicate on what she is fixing her attention. Her face reveals her mind and manifests her spirit. The maiden carries a wand with which she encircles the whole earth, measures the expanse of land, encloses the sea within set limits, circles the heights of heaven. Although her cloak is sprinkled with a shower of fine dust, the beauty of the material and the grace of the pattern are not obscured, but embroidered with many a pen-stroke, it shines and prides itself on many a decoration. Here in the language of painting the whole art is reviewed, the art which spreads abroad the knowledge of mensuration and teaches its use,[105] confines the boundless, restrains the wide-spreading, reaches the small, measures the great, examines the deep, dwells in valleys, scales heights. Here one may read[106]: what is a point, a curved line, a straight or even-lying line; what is called a semi-circle; what surface, knowing not depth and lacking height, lies evenly within a plane; what is a quadrilateral, what forms a triangle, what is enclosed in a threefold measure;[107] what is a cube, what is a line drawn around a centre of its own,[108] why the centre has its place in the middle; why every angle droops as an obtuse an-

[105] Plato, *Rep.*, 10.602-603, maintains that mensuration is par excellence the faculty of reason given us to check on the aberrations of the senses, particularly sight.

[106] Most of the questions in geometry that are mentioned are very elementary. They do not go beyond Euclid, 1.26. Boeth., *PL* 63.1307A. The Middle Ages had a somewhat awesome reverence for Geometry. See Godfrey of St. Victor, *Fons Philosophiae* 369-380, 449-452, ed. Michaud Quantin 47, 50: tr. E. A. Synan 23, 53, 56.

[107] An irregular cube. Boethius shows some confusion in his use of *solids* and *cubes*. Alan uses *solidus* or *sterion* for a cube.

[108] An attempt to compress the definition of a circle found in Boeth., *PL* 63.1308A.

gle or is an erect acute or a right angle, less than an obtuse but greater than an acute;[109] why, according to the laws of the art and the norm of the data, an equilateral triangle is directly constructed on a given line and the given line, forming the base, contributes a part;[110] how from a point a line is drawn equal to a given line and repeating the given line;[111] why a longer line, with a part at its end cut off, produces a shorter line;[112] why the Eleufuga[113] terrifies the beginners in this discipline and drives

[109] A common method (but not in Boethius) of showing the three types of angles was: L, ∠, ∟.

[110] Euc., I, 1.

[111] *Ib.* 1.2.

[112] *Jb.* 1.3.

[113] *Eleufuga.* Du Cange lists only the use of the word here in Alan. Bossuat (203) mentions its use by Roger Bacon and Philip of Bury. To these can be added two examples of its use by Peter of Compostella: ed. P. Soto, 67. We find there: *cur eleufuga sano/ vis intellectu capitur* and *cur urget eleufuga datura/ arte sub hac dociles.* The vagueness of *capitur* makes it difficult to give an entirely reliable rendering of the first reference. "Why the strength of a sound mind is overcome by the *eleufuga*" involves two difficulties: it interferes with the metre and it forces a strained meaning on *sano intellectu.* Any other rendering retaining *vis* will involve the metrical difficulty. It is always hazardous to suggest emendation without Mss. authority but a reading of *vix* for *vis* would give: "why the *eleufuga* can be understood with difficulty by a sound mind", or, more idiomatically: "why even a sound mind has difficulty in understanding the *eleufuga*". This would be consistent with the second reference which means: "why the *eleufuga* puts on pressure with a view to forcing pupils into this discipline". In Alan *eleufuga* terrifies the pupils and causes them to abandon geometry before they come face to face with more difficult problems. Roger Bacon states that students who could not see the value of geometry would abandon it after, at the most, three or four propositions, with the exception of small boys who were compelled by the cane to continue. For him *eleufuga* meant the fifth proposition of Euclid. He offers an etymological explanation for the word: *elegia* in Greek means the same as *miseria* in Latin and *elegi* in Greek is the equivalent of *miseri* in Latin. *Eleufuga* means, then, the flight of the unfortunate ones who do not appreciate geometry. His etymology is not correct; *elegia* and *elegos* both mean an elegiac poem. For Philip of Bury the *eleufuga* drives pupils away from geometry like a high, sheer rock that cannot be scaled even with ladders. The fifth proposition of Euclid, dealing with the angles at the base of an isosceles triangle, poses the first real difficulty for the beginner in geometry. He is faced with common angles and almost completely overlapping triangles. Many primers in geometry now give a simple but non-Euclidean proof of the theorem.

them to abandon it before they face deep problems and to give up before they get into difficulties in the discipline; by what rational process a triangle finds another equal to itself;[114] why a line is bisected by equal parts[115] or an angle divided by a similar method[116] and one bisection divides what was one into two. The maiden is resplendent in this garb, or, rather, the warrior-maiden[117] explains in it the nature of her mind. Giving her wand a rest, she adopts the craftsman's role and concentrates her far-ranging mind on a single object. She attacks the task with mind, hands and zeal; she puts the material, the lead, in order and many a hammer-blow falls upon it. She fashions it into the form she desires: the old form leaves and the new form, coming to the lead, frees it from its former defects. The third wheel is produced from the lead and when produced is a copy of its predecessor and has its shape and appearance. There the painter's mark proclaims the artificers who enclose within set limits the expanse, measurements, weights and boundaries of things and, with a like process of reason, examine the air, sky, stars, seas, lands. Here the geometrician, Thales,[118] without moving, crosses the circle of the aerial region: without wings he flies over the sea; without oars he crosses the expanse of ocean; without a lad-

The *Eleufuga* refers to this proposition. It comes from the Greek ἐλέου φυγή meaning the flight or banishment or abandonment of pity and refers to the difficulty of the theorem and the pressure that the teacher had to put on the pupils here and its results — the departure of some and the suffering of others who had to continue. *Fr. Rogeri Bacon Opera Quaedam Hactenus Inedita,* by J. S. Brewer (London 1859) 21; Philip of Bury, *Philobiblion,* 13.26, ed. A. Altamura (Naples 1954) 116.

[114] Euclid, 1.4.8. and 26.

[115] Euclid, 1.10.

[116] Euclid, 1.9.

[117] See note 59 supra.

[118] Thales is credited with the foundation of geometry by a study and development of Egyptian land-measurements. Other traditions speak of his ability in astronomy, geography, mathematics, etc. There is an old, but not too well-founded, tradition that he foretold to within a year the solar elipse of May 28, 585 B.C.

der he climbs to the stars; he touches Olympus without laying hands on it. Euclid,[119] uniting his theorems and problems in a sequence and reweaving the science, places its parts in proper order. He joins them, so to speak, with the rope of reason, connects them together and one would think that the subsequent parts followed from just one original.

[119] See Bk. 2. n. 64.

BOOK IV

Last in the line comes the maiden[1] who, first in beauty, first in style, has a first-rate mind within her breast.[2] No disease nor gloom nor dependence on another intellect lowers her head to earth. Her gaze is fixed on the stars, her eyes leading the way for the mind, track down the secrets of the heavens and their elusive causes and report back to the mind and the mind's pupil often proves its master. Bright light gleams on her face and when lightning flashes from it, it strikes our gazing eyes, and shunning the full-blown lightning, they fear to open their lids. A ball[3] equips her hand; it could give the impression of being just the shade of a ball, since it keeps ever in the shade and does not, in keeping with the special nature of a ball, float upwards but lies below and is lifted by no inflation. Her dress, glowing with gems and proud with gold, seems to rival the stars in splendour. Here a teaching body, qualified by a painting, holds forth, lectures, instructs — nay orders its students. It teaches the laws of the stars, their locations, times, movements, signs, powers, wanderings, names, causes. Here one may read: what is the celestial sphere, what axis divides the sphere in parts, what pole, rising high above or sinking deep below, marks the end of the axis;[4] why the shape of the world is round and why the earth is bound

[1] Astronomy. Alan's mixture of astronomy and astrology shows the influence of many theories. There are elements from Plato, Ptolemy, Macrobius, Albumasar, Gerard of Cremona's translations from the Arabic, Al Fergani. For an analysis see P. Duhem, *Le Système du Monde,* vol. 3 (Paris 1954) 223-230.

[2] The use of *prima* here does not mean that Astronomy is a more basic science than Arithmetic. See Nic. 1.5.2; Boeth., *PL* 63.1082D-1083A.

[3] Alan plays on the two meanings of *sphera*, a globe (especially one made to represent the heavenly bodies) and a ball for play (in strict Latin, *follis*).

[4] The celestial axis is found by producing the axis of the earth at either end until it reaches the heavens. The celestial poles are at the ends of the axis.

by five parallels that go around it and is cut into a number of what one might call belts;[5] why it is frozen at its extremes, along its middle roasts with heat and keeps the two zones along this central zone temperate and by extending them on either side, checks the expanding heat by the cold; why a truncated circle marks the end of both colures[6] and neither colure can return to its former point[7] and the truncation gives each its name;[8] why the zodiacal belt, crossing (the heavens) slantwise and stretching in a downward direction, enriches the heavens with twelve signs and generously offers free lodging to the pilgrim planets and shares what it owns with them; according to what plan the stars go on their way; by which law the planets proceed on a forward course, by what law they rush into retrograde motion or hesitating stop at a fixed point;[9] why the Signs follow a slantwise course; why the sun comes to its rising with more dispatch than it sets; it steals time at its rising but loses at its setting the extra time it puts aside at its rising;[10] what is the path along which the moon moves, what is the orbit of the sun, the orbit of Mercury, the path of Venus, the route of Mars, what delay slows

[5] The five zones (zona = belt): the torrid, two temperate, two frigid. Mart. Cap., 6.602; Bern. Silv., 1.3.61.

[6] The Colures are two great circles of the celestial sphere, passing through the celestial poles. The equinoctial Colure passes through the equinoctial points of Aries and Libra and the pole of the equator. The solstitial Colure passes through the solstitial points of Cancer and Capricorn and the poles of the ecliptic and equator. Mart. Cap., 8.823 and 832; Bern., 1.3.65.

[7] As a result of precession, the points through which they pass are ever changing. Only at the completion of the Great Year will the heavens return to its original position. Plato, *Tim.* 39D; Macr., *Comm.*, 2.11; Mart. Cap., 8.868; Bern. Silv., 1.3.66.

[8] Colure comes from the Greek *κόλος docked*, and *οὐρά a tail*. The names were given to them because part of the circles was always invisible in Greece.

[9] See Bk. 2. n. 10.

[10] Because of the uplifting effect of the refraction of light, the sun is visible before it has theoretically risen and after it has theoretically set. For Alan it is a traveller who makes very good time at the beginning of his journey but loses his advantage at the end.

Saturn,[11] on what path Jupiter travels and what circle equalises his irregularity of motion;[12] what eccentric circle rises up and passes beyond the earth and cannot locate its centre at that of the earth.[13]

A maiden, then, weighted with the solemnity of a discipline so important, does not entomb her mind, not distract or enervate it by idleness or leisure. Rather she plies her pursuits with her whole mind and body. The globe passes from her hand, since this hand is called to do new work and in fashioning this work, it establishes its claim to the forger's art. As her hand moulds the gold and gives its mass a shape, the fourth wheel emerges from the gold. This wheel, by the charm of its beauty, surpasses its fellows and makes the first wheels take second place. An inscribed surface rings forth her praise and in the script gathers together those who, launched in the mind's bark, sailed off to the abodes above, examined the secrets of the heavens and merited thus a godlike honour. There Albumazar[14] consults the stars, the poles, the heavens and the seven planets and brings their advice back to earth, arming the earth and

[11] Saturn's sidereal period is 29 1/2 years. Its mean synodic period is only 378 days as opposed to 780 days for Mars. See n. 62 infra.

[12] Ptolemy's system seemed simple and logical at the beginning. Later observations either had to be explained away or new hypotheses had to be added to the original theories. It ultimately became so complicated that Alfonso X of Castile is supposed to have said that if he had been around at creation, he could have given some good advice. Among observations made was that the heavenly motions were not uniform: acceleration and retardation were noticed. This was first declared to be an illusion. Later an explanation was offered by way of equants and epicycles.

[13] The fixed stars seemed to move in concentric circles around the pole. They would be concentric with the earth. The planets moved in such a way that they obviously were not concentric with the earth.

[14] Albumasar was an Arab astronomer. He lived in Baghdad and wrote some fifty books on astronomy. Three of his works have been translated into Latin: *Flores Astrologici* (1488), *Introductorium in Astronomiam* (1489), *De Magnis Coniunctionibus* (1499). He contributed some valable information on the law of tides.

strengthening the tottering against the rages of the heavens and the fury of the powers above. The strength of Atlas[15] supports the stars, while he gets his support from them; he bears the weight of the heavens without finding it an unprofitable burden. He keeps up the heavens, while he gets his upkeep from it; he yields first place to the interests of the stars as he bears them and they bear him interest in his secondary position.

As rule requires, order demands, reason requests, Prudence orders, the aforementioned band of sisters, working together with finer file, moulds and remoulds, fashions and refashions, decks and bedecks the parts of the chariot. They remove from them every appearance of irregularity of form and every flaw that would invite criticism. Concord, with the touch of the finest hand, brings the work to a happy end, unites the scattered parts in order, binds them by law and fits them in place. With their articulations, nails and connections to unite them, they make a chariot which, as it gleams forth with the light of beauty, shows by its very appearance that a divine hand and Minerva[16] from the gods above have toiled over it. Then Reason, reminded and instructed by mistress Nature, presents her with five horses.[17] Nature leagues them in an acceptable link, a harmonius peace, a reliable bond and forces the untamed team to submit to the yoke. These horses bounteous Nature has nurtured from their earliest years and giving them some traces of intellect,[18] so fashioned

[15] Atlas was, among other things, an astronomer (Diod. Sicul. 3.60.2.). Astronomy was a profession and means of livelihood. Alan has a series of puns on what Atlas does for the stars and what the stars do for Atlas. Aristotle, *On the Heavens* 2.1.284a, says that the myth of Atlas arose from the belief that the heavenly bodies were earthlike and had weight. Alan may be thinking of this in the *sine pondere pondus* of line 67.

[16] Goddess of arts and crafts.

[17] The five horses are the five senses through which all knowledge comes to man. Bern. Silv., 2.14.9-10.

[18] See Plato, Tim. 45B-C, where the senses are called "organs for all the forethought of the soul".

the horses' traits that, beasts though they are, they nevertheless revere the one who reared them. Moreover, in so far as Nature allows, each horse boasts his own natural gifts. No training or grooming that could fully crown a horse's beauty is a stranger to them.

The first horse[19] surpasses his mates in training, grooming and speed and makes the others yield him pride of place. Training, grooming, colour, appearance, spirit and speed enhance him nor is he subject to a defect from the fact that[20] a reddish[21] colour tinged with white gives him a golden sheen. He does not walk, rather he flies; he does not leave a distinct impression on the ground by separate hoofmarks nor bend the grass as he goes but with swift flight, his passing hooves flick the ground but leave no tracks there. Light air is amazed that he has obtained its fleetness and Boreas is astonished when his speed lags behind. The breeze falls behind, the birds are slow, the winged arrow's flight slackens; everything lags behind the horse in speed. He does not wait for the spur's reminder but of his own accord, launches himself on his course and yet is guided by a light touch of rein. Moreover, the very nobility of his pedigree crowns his native qualities for he proudly lays claim to Pyrois[22] as his sire and the sire himself, mirrored in his progeny, shows forth his image. Jupiter's generosity gave this horse as a gift to Mother Nature and the value of the gift increases her gratitude and the favour of the donor: no greater gift could a father so great have bestowed on so great a mother. By these

[19] Plato, speaking of the power and value of sight, says that it distributes the motions of every object it touches or is touched by throughout the body even to the soul. *Tim.* 45C-D, 47A-B. Cf. Bern. Silv., 2.14.41-48.

[20] Reading *hoc.*

[21] Red, being a sign of war and passion, was a dangerous colour. In *Dist.* 928B-C, Alan says that it is on record that a red (*rufus*) horse symbolises a concentration of evils.

[22] Pyrois was one of the horses of the Sun.

gifts, then, as his nature demands, is the beauty of this horse ennobled.

The second horse[23] is of lesser worth, ranks lower in beauty, with less grooming rates lower in appearance and is slower of pace than the first. Although he is inferior to the first and rates lower in appearance, he is superior to the others and first among them by his quality of beauty: surpassing the rest, he is surpassed by only one. Although he cannot challenge the first horse with matching speed, the fleet breeze cannot outdistance the second horse, indeed he races it with equal speed. Ever changing he restricts himself to no one colour but often counterfeits the appearance of an appropriate hue. He snorts in rage, rends the air with frequent neighs and inflicts a scarless wound on the volatile breeze. Bells, hanging from his neck, render sweet sounds and drench the air with a flood of music. In appearance this horse bears his father's image, for he reproduces Eous[24] in his capers and his beauty proves that he was his sire. Lavish in her gifts, Juno[25] crowned Nature's wealth with this gift, merited the goodwill of this supranormal power and by her gift showed her love.

The third horse[26] is placed somewhat aslant the rays of this bright beauty and does not lay claim to the gifts of the previous ones; indeed, holding a lower place he heaves a yearning sigh

[23] Hearing, Plato, *Tim.* 67A-B; Bern. Silv., 2.14.49-86.

[24] Eous was one of the horses of the Sun.

[25] *Juno*, found in some Mss., is undoubtedly the correct reading where *vivo* appears. See G. J. Engelhardt, "An Emendation in Anticlaudianus," *Speculum* 23 (1948), 110-111.

[26] Smell. Plato, *Tim.* 66D, mentions the indefiniteness of odours. "Smells ... are all smoke or mist". He states that, beyond "pleasant" and "painful", there is no classification of them. Alan may be thinking of this when he states that it is impossible to pinpoint the colour of this horse. However, he goes on to mention various aromas, but this is not a classification of them. Smell is in Bern. Silv., 2.14.99-102. For this horse's pedigree, cf. Hom. *Iliad* 20.219 ff.

in their direction. Although his beauty is dimmed in comparison with them, nevertheless, compared with the others he reveals his lustre and is not cheated out of his own special beauty. Although he may be left behind in the fast race by those we have discussed, nevertheless a victor over the others, he shows a winner's joy, surpasses the others in speed and with his own movement puts them in their place. He is dappled with a subtle mixture of hues, but his colour, eluding the eyes, defies the power of sight. A sequence of entwined flowers clothes him, so to speak, with a comely robe and each flower breathes its special aroma on him. The odour of violet drenches him, the rose intoxicates the breezes around him and the nose is sated with the fragrance of thyme. A mare, with no experience of natural mating, bore him: she knew no stallion but satisfied with the gust of conjugal air, was impregnated by the coital Zephyrus. With the gift of this horse Zephyrus purchased Nature's love and paid her a fitting price.

The fourth horse[27] is of lower class and less power and has a plentiful lack of speed; he fails in beauty and lags in fleetness. Serving the others we have mentioned, he, as it were, sinks down in adoration before them. He waits on them and does not deny that he is their dependent but like a household slave, ministers to his masters. However, he does not find Nature a complete niggard; indeed he is well supplied with the endowments with which to protect himself and, in keeping with Nature's practice of favouring her subjects, is made to suffer no flaw in any aspect of these gifts. The violet does not fade, however much the rose may shine in her place of honour among the flowers and bright beauty set off the lily. Not everyone who lacks Ulysses'[28] cunning will prove insane nor will everyone be

[27] Taste. Bern. Silv., 2.14.87-98.

[28] Odysseus, the wily hero of Homer's Epic. See Bk. 1. n. 25.

dumb whom Maro's[29] Muse ignores. The gleam of silver does not darken even if gold flashes. Hector's[30] rush to arms is not lessened, if Ajax shows more of the lightning's flash. In the same way not every claim to renown forsakes the fourth horse, even if he is denied that pace that brings the definite place of honour in which Nature has confirmed the previous horses. He has not, however, to complain that he has been degraded from every honour of Nature but rejoices in that good fortune with which plentiful Nature has blessed him. A grayish colour favours this horse, the rain sprinkles him and the dew falls on him in a moist shower. This particular trait he reserves to himself and maintains as his own — that, though quick to drink, he does not forget food. He is devoted to drink; all by himself he rushes to eat for the benefit of all the others and in drink makes good the defects of his team-mates.[31] The horse of Triton sired him and establishing an heir to a father's rights, produced his own image in him. Triton,[32] offering a sign of mutual goodwill, bestowed him on Nature and accompanied the gift with his goodwill.

The fifth horse[33] will scarce make good his claim to the appearance and form of a horse, should one try to compare him with the previous ones. For he will lay aside a horse's nature and wearing a horse's mask, will give a performance smacking of

[29] Virgil.

[30] Hector, Priam's eldest son, was the most prominent of the defenders of Troy. He challenged any Greek to single combat. Ajax took up the challenge and Hector had the worse of it. He was finally killed by Achilles. His funeral is the final episode of the *Iliad*. For Ajax see Bk. 1. n. 37.

[31] Reading *pro cunctis*. Taste has to do with food and drink. This food and drink, taken into the body, benefit the other senses. See Plato, *Tim.* 75E, 78E. Cf. Apuleius, *De Dogmate Platonis*, 1.14.

[32] Triton was a merman. The Triton's do not figure very prominently in mythology. Vir., *Aen.* 6.171, relates that a Triton slew Misenus.

[33] Touch. Bern. Silv., 103-108.

an ass, held back by an ass's slowness and divested of a horse's traits. If, however, the comparison of this horse with the previous ones leaves us nothing significant and we examine him in himself, his style will not stand deprived of its own excellences and he will show himself subject to no defects of form. The fifth horse reminds us of the fourth and partly resembles him in shape, but yet he is downgraded a little in that beauty smiles somewhat more grudgingly on the horse in question and he droops his head more to earth as he goes. He does not raise his head sufficiently to show a full face but rather, as he turns his lowered face aside, his eyes look down to the ground. A coat of dusky colour covers him in which black predominates and will allow no shading. His standing by pedigree is no mean one. Aethon[34] sired him and he rejoices in having the horses of the Sun as his brothers and maintains his standing by his brothers' rank. Ops,[35] Mother of the gods, made a gift of this horse to Nature as a pledge of alliance and from this the knot of love, made tighter, united their aspirations.

Reason, with her own intellect as guide, brings the above horses beneath the yoke, hitches them to the pole, bears down upon those that fight the bit, harnesses the untamed ones, reins in the unruly. She saddles the first horse, mounts him when saddled, with the reins checks his twistings, applies the crop, plies him with blows, words and threats. She can scarcely quiet him but finally he is overcome and subdued; he obeys her and tired out, pants at Reason's nod.[36] Thus does the charioteer of Sophia

[34] Aethon appears variously as a horse in the chariot of Pallas, Aurora, Pluto.

[35] Ops was a somewhat obscure Roman deity. One of her feasts, the *Opalia*, was on December 19 and coincided with the *Saturnalia*. This associated Ops with Saturn. He was identified with Kronos and she with Rhea. This would make her mother of the gods. Cf. Ovid, *Met.* 9.498.

[36] Reason must establish control over the senses. The most powerful and probably the most refractory of these is Sight. If Reason subdues it, the others will easily fall in line. Alan's analogy is not a happy one. No one could successfully use this treatment on a spirited horse, hitched to a chariot-pole with four spirited companions.

bring the first horse into line, lest if Phronesis should mount the chariot while the horses are unsubdued, they would run awry, leave the appointed course, follow byways, shake the yoke loose, undo the fastenings and the whole structure become unstable, the chariot totter, the joints fail, the girths slacken, the articulations grow loose, the reins be dropped and the entire framework of the chariot collapse. When order has been established and Reason has quickly gone over every item and put each in place, Phronesis decides to mount the chariot and makes ready to use it as it is. She takes her seat in it. The entire band together applauds, rejoices, shows its satisfaction with her, cheers her departure with expressions of great goodwill, begs for an omen of a happy outcome, prays for a peaceful outward journey with an even better return trip. They seek kiss after kiss, multiply them, impress them deeply, leaving their imprint on her face. Entwining their arms in embraces, they enfold her neck, wish her well with their hearts as well as their words, double, repeat and reiterate their good wishes. Then, at Reason's call, Prudence presents herself. She mounts the chariot and the chariot's beauty, given the finishing touch, excels itself and is afire with the roseate glow of her countenance. Reason urges on the horses; obedient to the whip, the horses launch themselves on the journey. The chariot is raised, leaves the ground and in its flight departs into the subtle air. As she passes through the regions of Air, Prudence carefully turns her mind to an investigation of each and every thing to which Air lays successful claim; she examines and makes a deep analysis of the elusive element. She asks herself: what is the material and origin of the clouds; in what way the earth, damp with its own moisture, sends exudations to form clouds and arranges a mantle for itself in the heavens; why Phoebus, thirsty and panting from the heat of fire, draws draughts from Oceanus,[37] turns his cup to spill on

[37] Oceanus was the son of Sky and Earth and the father of River Gods and Oceanids (nymphs).

the clouds, hangs in dense air pails of rain-storms, goblets of various showers, bottles of rain; how fire grows dull and dies in the clouds and while dying causes lightning[38] and thus in death is a more serious threat than in life; for in life it cannot inflict on us what it does at death; from what source the winds arise, what seeds of things breathe motion and the power of causing motion into them; why Auster, the butler of rain, pours rain for earth and lavishly serves draughts to the world; how thirsty Boreas drinks up Auster's showers and, like a street-brush, clears the streets of water;[39] how Zephyrus, the husbandman, cultivates the land without ploughshare and beautifies the beds of flowers in the garden;[40] why a bird, safe with fast oarage of wings, fashioning its feathers into oars and its wings into sails, crosses the aerial sea like a phantom ship and safe from shipwreck, makes its way in safety over such an abyss and fears no Charybdis[41] in such a sea.

Phronesis examines in more detail the hidden approaches of Air, its secret places and coverts and pursuing her investigation with keen perception, sees with clearer vision the wandering denizens[42] of Air, for whom Air is a prison, the abyss a punishment, joy is sorrow, life is death, triumph is failure. Their

[38] Sen., *Quaest. Nat.* 2.12 says that some think that the fire which produces lightning is resident in the clouds, while others think that it is produced for the occasion and does not exist until it comes forth. Aristotle holds the second opinion. *Meteor.* 369a-b.

[39] Auster, the south-wind, brings rain; Boreas, the dry north-wind, quickly removes the dampness from hard surfaces.

[40] Reading *in hortis*. Zephyrus, the prevailing, gentle westwind of Spring, accompanied and fostered growth. *Extollere* can hardly be used of raising flowers. Even if it could, it is hard to see what meaning there would be in the *in ortus* of Bossuat or the *in ortis* of some Mss. *Extollere* is used with the meaning of *to adorn* or *to beautify*. Indeed, Tacitus used it in the sense of beautifying a garden (*An.* 11.1). *In hortis* is found in a number of Mss. and seems best.

[41] See Bk. 3. n. 103.

[42] See Ephesians 2.2. Bern. Silv. has a strange collection of "angels" in the regions between earth and heaven. For those in the lower air, see 2.7.92.

minds, impaired by the degrading poison of envy, cause this venom to overflow on the human race so that it may suffer from a like illness and the same disease. They are the ones who ever arm themselves against us, lay low the unarmed, overcome the armed, rarely do they themselves surrender but once defeated they cannot renew the battle.[43] These confounders of truth with falsehood, equipped with a kind of aerial body, counterfeit a likeness to us and with many phantoms delude dull man. They feign light in darkness, agreement in contention; they conceal treachery under the mantle of peace; they represent the bitter as sweet; they give noxious draughts under the pretext of doing good. God created these as divine beings; the true day bathed them in true light and from their very beginning divine honour enveloped them. They abandoned the light and went off to their darkness. They left the fountainhead and sought the pools of hell. They stripped off the robe of glory and put on the garment of mourning and the sackcloth of grief. They despised the divine majesty and merited eternal ruin. Oh grievous outcome, piteous fall, one and only destruction ! The one who was free is a slave, the one who had plenty is a beggar, the one who was the chief power in the palace suffers exile, the one who held next place to the king suffers punishment. By this fall gems become clay, purple becomes sackcloth, light darkness, clarity confusion, glory misfortune, joy sadness, rest toil, the hyacinth a seaweed. Thus the star of heaven falls; thus Lucifer,[44] who knew no rising, is overwhelmed at his setting; thus the citizen of Olympus is driven out to exile and no hope of return softens the exile's

[43] Apuleius speaks of "daimones" between men and gods. They share immortality with the gods but are subject to every other human affliction: *De Deo Socratis* 13 and *passim.* Michael Psellos insists that a spirit, if cut in two, will suffer a little but will redintegrate: *De Daemonorum Operatione* 23, *PG* 122, 871B ff. Alan thinks that a defeated spirit is put permanently out of action.

[44] Literally the morning star, figuratively the prince of the rebellious angels.

prospects; all hope is gone and gives place to fear. Oh stain of pride that is to be shunned, Charybdis that is to be avoided, grievous fault, universal affliction, general pestilence, gateway to sin, mother of vices, fount of iniquity, seed of hatred, hunter of strife. Oh pride that is falling as it rises, that is dying at its full bloom, that is being doomed as it is being set up, that collapses when it has reached an advanced stage, that is puffed up on the verge of its fall, that cannot abide itself and reaching above itself, suffers a fall beneath itself: it cannot support itself, indeed it is overthrown by its own mass and falls by its own weight. It drives man to seek himself outside himself; man goes outside himself and set in opposition to himself, is at variance with himself: forgetting himself he fails to recognise himself; passing the limit, he still keeps on his way, trying to be more than he may be and not content with his stock, he wishes to be greater than himself and strains to surpass himself.[45] Missing what he seeks, losing what he longs for, desiring what deceives him, he chases after false honour. This pestilence flaws the good, disfigures the upright, breaks down character, puts justice to flight, ruins what is useful. This valerian obscures the roses, this cloud blacks out the stars of virtue, for by its darkness they suffer eclipse. By this stain an Angel, barred from the hall of the heavenly kingdom, dethroned from his seat, broken by his vaunting, cast down by his pride, ruined by his envy, pays for his sin by exile and for his guilt by suffering.[46]

Having traversed the expanse of Air to the place where the cloud-formations of heaven in their own night weave their mantle of darkness, where the hanging clouds collect water, where

[45] His image of himself contains excellencies that he has not got. There is a continual struggle between his real self and his imagined self.

[46] The essential suffering of the damned is the loss of God (*poena damni*); the pain of sense (*poena sensus*) is secondary.

the hail hardens for a shower, where the winds contend, where the rage of the lightning swells, Phronesis passes on to Ether where the charm of ultimate peace prevails, where pleasing quiet and a breeze more pleasing still caress everything, where all is silence, where a clearer atmosphere smiles and banishes tears, where the veiled air sighs and shines throughout with a mystic light.

Crossing the tracts of Ether's light, the maiden enters the higher realm where brightness and fire hold sway. A pleasant light sparkles here but the power of the heat, which is wed to the light, undoes its charms. Here the novelty of things, their beauty, their singular form, the elegance of this region soothe the maiden's eyes as she passes and a new kind of song intoxicates her ears, but from its low audibility she perceives the sound in fainter tone, yet gladly listens with unerring ear. It is as when the sound of the celestial harp breathes forth in subtle notes when the moon's sphere, its music less tense, sighs low, nay almost falls silent, and slows in tempo.[47] It functions like a lower string, produces a lesser chord and scarcely deserves its place on the lyre. Here with widened vision Prudence sees the moon's wanings, changes, course, movements, difficulties: how it happens that Phoebus, though her partner, robs her of light while she, on the other hand, steals his prerogative of brightness and producing a false night drives men to fear and creates the appearance of night when there is no night;[48] why the moon causes humours; why the sea pays the penalty for the moon's

[47] The music of the spheres. Arist. *On the Heavens*, 2.9.290b criticizes the Pythagorean theories on the Harmony of the Spheres.

[48] Total eclipses of the sun have caused anything from panic to unease depending on the viewer's knowledge. Alan is referring to a total eclipse of the sun when stars would become visible. As the zone on earth from which the eclipse could be total cannot exceed a width of 167 miles, few people ever witness a total eclipse. What is popularly referred to as a total eclipse is in reality an annular eclipse.

deficits and rejoices when she is rich;[49] what is the meaning of the mark on the moon or what does it signify by its spot: the moon's high concentration of light cannot wipe off this faint smear and the small stain clings to the source of brightness, refuses to yield to the adversary with whom it contends and the dark patch becomes more clearly outlined from the rays of light.

Going aloft the maiden ascends still to the heights, where the Sun holds sway, where his candle burns, where the living fount of light gushes forth, where the vein of heat originates and there is an abundant store of unused brightness. There the maiden sees: what is the way, the path, the course of the sun; whence the father, fount, mother, origin of Ether's light draws the sustenance to support his energy; how the sun, reigning among the stars and pressing the planets into his service, now compels them to stop in their course, now by sheer majesty bids these haughty bodies follow bypaths, now granting them freedom of movement, confers his own prerogatives on them;[50] how the sun changing his appearance becomes, at the beginning of his course, a boy, at midday a young adult, finally plays a man's role and is a complete old man by evening: thus he displays a different age-appearance hour by hour and in one day covers an entire life. By now the maiden's ear becomes disenchanted with the music of the moon since a sweet and finer sound attracts her, feasting her ears and preventing her from remembering the

[49] The twelfth century was the heir to a great deal of confusion arising from the disagreements between those who maintained that the tides are caused by the moon and those who attributed them to other causes. Alan is an advocate of the moon's influence. Cf. Bern. Silv., 1.3.141-142, 2.5.216-219, 2.6.22-23. See Duhem, *Le Système du Monde* 3.112-135. For the effect of the moon on moods, see Giraldus Cambrensis, *Topographia Hibernica*, 2.3, ed. J. F. Dimock, *Giraldi Cambrensis Opera 5,* Rolls Series 21.5 (London 1867) 78.

[50] See Bk. 2. n. 10. The bypaths (*devia*) here refer to the apparent movement of the planets in a loop.

previous sound. This sound is produced by a Siren[51] who is closely associated with the sun's movements and who by her sweet singing intimates the harp. Every voice admires her and bends in admiration before her and the entire music of the harp sighs longingly in her direction.

Passing beyond the realm of the sun, the maiden hastens her steps ahigh but her progress is impeded by the curving crosspaths in the terrain and the confusion of countless winding ways. Finally negotiating the steep trail by heavy toil, precaution and persistence, she reached the region where Venus and Stilbons[52] cling in close embrace. There, Lucifer, herald of the sun and harbinger of day, shines forth: he ushers in the blessings of light for earth, at his own rising sets the stage for the rising of the sun and in his rising foretells the dawn. Stilbons clings, an inseparable companion, to the sun's steps, accompanying his master on his journey like a personal slave.[53] Veiling his locks with the sun's rays, he controls its heat and with his halo from the sun obscures his position.[54] The sphere of Lucifer is light of movement; its breeze is fresher. Producing sound as it moves, it sports with a treble voice; nor is the Muse of Venus' harp considered common but rightly deserves the ear's attention.[55] With like voice and measure and kindred song. Mercury's Siren sings, answers Venus' song and harps to her friend with equal sound.

[51] Macrobius, *Comm.*, 2.3.1 ff., refers to Plato's statement that a Siren sits on each of the spheres. He adds that the divinities are thus provided with song. Cf. Plato, *Rep.*, 10.617B.

[52] Stilbons is Mercury. Mercury and Venus were said to be bound together by chains fashioned by Vulcan.

[53] Mercury is the planet closest to the sun. When visible it can be seen for a short time before dawn or after sunset.

[54] *solis obnubilat astra galero.* It is difficult to get a satisfactory meaning here, if one understands *astra* as *star* or *stars. Astrum* is found with the same meaning as *atrium*, a house: see Du Cange, s.v. That meaning suits here.

[55] Reading *auditus.*

Phronesis proceeds on her way,[56] and entering the blazing palace of Mars,[57] is stunned by the impact and vehemence of the heat which the place produces: steaming from end to end with fire, it knows only the rage and storm of fire. There Winter does not moan nor Spring's charm smile; Autumn shows not its fullness: there is ever Summer's blast. Mars, glowing with fire, here holds sway, prolific in wrath, sowing the seeds of war, thirsty for disputes, thirstier still for our blood, banishing peace, wiping out treaties. Decked in a fiery comet's tail, it is his joy to do violence to a country's loyalty and to upset the fortunes of the mighty. He prepares arms for men, leads fanatics to entertain hopes, sows the seeds of insolence, fathers rage, weakens love. His very face shows what his heart is planning and by its redness proclaims the pestilential rage of internal fury. By his corruptive influence he affects his companion and neighbouring planet and in his malice teaches the violent to show more violence or the mild to turn savage and he wounds with his venom. Like Jupiter his rushing sphere roars with thunder and in its roar resounds with deep bellows. The Siren of thundering Mars sounds louder than the others but the sweetness of its song is dulled as it grows faint in a storm of sound, a harsh tone lessens its appeal and roughness of voice damages it.

By now the maiden's toil is carrying her past Vulcan's disgorgement and its fiery vapours, and the flame did not approach her

[56] With Mars, Jupiter and Saturn we are in the realm of astrology. Astrology had had a rational basis. Men had noticed the effects of the Sun and Moon (planets for them) on Earth and its inhabitants. They had a basis for concluding that the other five planets had each its own influence. When succeeding ages began to detail these influences, wild imaginings took over from reasoned observation. Then by a not uncommon reversion, the planet itself was described in terms of its supposed effects. The *Tetrabiblos* of Ptolemy is the best handbook for astrology in Alan's time. Page references are to the Loeb edition of 1940 by F. E. Robbins.

[57] Mars' strong red colour naturally connected it with war and strife. See Ptol., *Tetr.* 3.163-165, pp. 353-357; Bern. Silv., 2.5.101-114.

on her journey or dare touch her hair. Then she succeeds in making her way to the undamaging fires of Jupiter,[58] the joy of its calm peace and the smiling regions of the (celestial) pole. Here the entire region shines with light from the star of Jupiter and rejoices in the happiness of unending Spring. Here the star of Jupiter glows, brings tidings of safety to the world, checks Mars' rage and fury and opposes his madness with serene peace. Even if a star that is a herald of evil and a precursor of misfortune is joined to him, Jupiter makes friends with the unfriendly star and brings about a change in him, turning gloom to laughter, lament to applause, bitter tears to joy. Should it happen, though, that a star that heralds safety is allied with Jupiter, the star of Jupiter, with its more propitious aspect, further guarantees its protection and doubles the omen for greater success, since it loves agreement, cultivates peace, fosters love, uproots resentment, outlaws wars, restrains rage, terminates disputes and curbs Mars. The sound which he produces in his motion does not strike the air with dull note but beguiles the ears with sweet song and Jove's delightful Muse echoes sweet Philomena,[59] and music, having the treasure of her own art increased, delights in a patron with sound so sweet.

Proceeding still further, Prudence directs her steps towards the dwellers on high, passing in her course beyond the halls of Jupiter. She enters the abodes of Saturn[60] that are spread over a

[58] The friendly planet. Ptol., *Tetr.* 3.161-163, pp. 347-353; Bern. Silv., 2.5.73-101.

[59] Philomela, daughter of Pandion, king of Athens. The gods turned her into a nightingale (or in the Greek tradition, a swallow) to help her escape the vengeance of Tereus. See Bk. 2. n. 28.

[60] For Saturn see Ptol., *Tetr.* 3.157 ff., pp. -347; Bern. Silv., 2.5.45-73. For Ptolemy Saturn is connected with homosexuality and bestiality. Bernardus Silvestris states that he devours his own children and gives a revolting picture of him forever keeping close to his wife awaiting her delivery. He further represents him as a hater of everything beautiful and an enemy of the human race. In ancient religion Saturn's cult-partner was Lua and this title was connected with *lues, pestilence*, a word used especially for anything that blighted growing things. Saturn is a planet displaying many contrary-to-nature aspects.

wider area. She shudders at the cold of Winter and the frost of Winter's solstice: she is amazed at the paralysing chill combined with a high temperature. There Winter is feverish, Summer catches cold, heat shivers and when the temperature is beginning to fall, there is derangement of light.[61] Here darkness shines, light darkens: there night shines with light and the dawn-light brings darkness. There Saturn ranges over the territory with greedy tread, with slow progress and lengthy stopovers.[62] Here by his cold be robs spring of its joys, ravishes the charms of the meadow and the glory of the flowers. He freezes as he heats, heats as he cools; though dry, he floods; though dark, he shines; though a youth, he is an old man. Yet his music does not stray outside the family of song: rather his voice surpasses the voices of his companions in matured harmony and no dulled song makes the harmony insipid since the sweetness of the voice gives it a flavour. Here grief, groans, tears, discord, terror, sadness, wanness, mourning, injustice hold sway.

[61] See William of Conches, *De Phil. Mundi* 2. 17, *PL* 172, 62B.

[62] Saturn's mean synodic period is 378 days. This means that when Earth passes Saturn and makes a complete orbit, Saturn has orbited so small a distance that Earth will overtake it again in approximately thirteen days. When the Earth passes Mars, it will make two full orbits, plus approximately fifty days, before it passes it again. The mean synodic period of Jupiter in 399 days. Apparent slow-downs, stoppages and retrograde motions could be observed more frequently in Saturn than in the other planets.

BOOK V

Her burden of the toil duly borne, the maiden joyfully enters the realm of the unrestricted light and the source of brightness, where the stars twinkle, where the constellations of the pole vie with one another in deep brightness and make for themselves their own unending light,[1] where the constellations deck the face of heaven and here she rejoices as she is enveloped by the gentle breeze at the pole.[2] There those who have been made gods by renown for deeds done or by stories told of them shine with special brilliance among the stars and enjoy a place in the heavens: they keep their name but not their power. Here the descendant of Alceus in a new life holds a place near the heavens;[3] there Perseus with his sword beheads golden-haired Medusa.[4] There Orion, not being a sword, counterfeits a sword and giving the impression of fighting, ever threatens war without waging it.[5] The old man of Haemonia,[6] as his bow shows, is setting his arrow in motion but it does not speed on its flight or escape the bow's pressure by getting on its way.[7] Here Leda's offspring gleam and do not abandon among the stars the token

[1] Reference is to the Northern Circumpolar Stars. These are always visible. Their number depends on the latitude of the viewer.

[2] Bern. Silv., 1.3.31-38.

[3] Hercules, the constellation.

[4] Perseus, the constellation. The king of Seriphus sent him to fetch the head of the Gorgon, Medusa. With Athena's help he succeeded.

[5] There is an untranslateable pun here. Orion was given the name ξιφήρης sword bearer. In Latin this was rendered *Ensiger or Ensifer.* Finally Orion was called *Ensis,* the *Sword.*

[6] Sagittarius. He was originally the Thessalian Centaur, Chiron. Haemonia is in Thessaly. Astronomers say that the centre of the universe is somewhere in this constellation.

[7] Sagittarius was called *Arcitenens* because of his bow (*arcus*).

of love they formerly shared on earth.[8] He by whose gift the star of healing shone on the sick and gave them the arms of health to fight disease is turned into a constellation and given by it a place in glory.[9] The Parrhasian maiden, transferred to the heavens, is restored her ravished features. Jupiter makes good the flower of her lost virginity and, in return for the bloom of chastity, has bestowed on her the privilege of blooming with eternal brightness.[10] Moreover, the forecourt of heaven is studded with various stars to which the poetic Muse of old, presenting truth in the form of jest, has given various names. The band of twelve constellations, shining with borrowed brightness,[11] stands out among the stars and, leaving the common herd far behind, surpasses the other stars by their position.[12] Here Cancer glows,

[8] Gemini, Castor and Pollux. Zeus, in the shape of a swan, impregnated Leda, the wife of Tyndareus, King of Sparta. Three children were born — Castor, Pollux and Helen. There are varying accounts as to who of the three children had Zeus for father and who had Tyndareus. In one version Pollux was son of Zeus and immortal, Castor was son of Tyndareus and mortal. Castor was killed and Pollux pleaded to be allowed to share his immortality with his twin. Jupiter placed both in the heavens.

[9] The constellation Opiuchus. Aesculapius' progress in medicine was so great that he began to restore the dead to life. Pluto, lord of the Underworld, became alarmed and persuaded Jupiter to kill Aesculapius. Later he repented and placed him in the sky. Ophiuchus means snake-holder. The snake figured prominently in Aesculapius' medical treatment.

[10] The Great Bear. Callisto, daughter of Lycaon, King of Arcadia, where Parrhasia is, bore Zeus a son. Hera or Artemis turned her into a she-bear. Her son pursued her believing that she was a real bear and killed her. Zeus turned him into the constellation Arctophylax and her into the Great Bear. There are variants of every detail of the legend except her bearing Zeus a son.

[11] Reading *excepto fulgore*. The borrowed brightness refers to the Zodiacal Light and/or the Gegenschein.

[12] *duodena cohors ... reliquas (sc. stellas) ... supervenit astro. Astro* can hardly refer to a star or stars in the Signs of the Zodiac. The brightest star in these is Alderbaran in Taurus and its visual magnitude in only 0.86. Only two other stars, Spica in Virgo and Antares in Scorpio, are above the first magnitude. Some of the Signs, e.g. Cancer, Libra, Pisces, are very faint. *Astro* is used here for *atrio*. See Bk. 4. n. 54. The Zodiacal Belt contains the path of the sun, moon and planets and is a privileged part of the heavens. A constellation there is in a favoured position.

Leo burns, Virgo brings the harvest, Libra makes day and night equal, Scorpio becomes violent, Chiron[13] brings cold, Capra[14] brings frost, Urna[15] overflows, Pisces is soaked, Aries gambols, Taurus and the Spartan Twins[16] have a special radiance as they bear the standards of Spring. Phronesis' eye enjoys this view of the heavens which her sight cannot penetrate; she misses the familiar matter and is stunned by the wonder of so much light.[17]

After she left the celestial approaches, traversed the depths of the heavens and the wandering paths of the stars and took up her position at the summit of the world, she hesitated in troubled mood and is drawn in different directions. Her mind is perplexed, her spirit ebbs, her will itself shares the mind's wavering and there is no fixed anchorage for the mind. For she fears and wavers, fearing that she will be led astray by the confusion of directions with which the doubtful road ahead confronts her. This road knows not tracks of men nor flight of birds; it is placed entirely beyond the impact of wordly things and the din of voyagers and is disturbed by no commotion. Here man's faltering steps would stray from the path: even his feet would wander drunkenly and sight, that lights the feet, would grow dull and inactive and refuse its guidance and the eye, faced with the light there, would prove sightless. This would not be because night's darkness holds sway there, for the purified

[13] Sagittarius. See n. 6. supra.

[14] As Alan is dealing with the zodiacal constellations, this must refer to Capricorn, not Capra or Capella in Auriga, although it is a very bright star (visual magnitude 0.05) and is high in the sky in Winter.

[15] Aquarius.

[16] Reading *Lacones*. Castor and Pollux, the Gemini.

[17] William of Conches states that in order to see there must be a ray (*radius*) from the eye, light outside and a material object in the path of the ray: *Philosophia* 4.26, *PL* 172.96. Thierry of Chartres is in agreement with this. He adds that peopole who think that they see the sky on a clear day are mistaken. They just imagine that they see something green: ed. N. M. Häring, 560.43 ff.

splendour of reflected lights sets the night aglow.[18] The ascent to this light is difficult, to slip back is easy; the approach is open to few, mishap awaits all; scarce anyone can cross to it, everyone can deviate from that path which offers passage to few but is closed to many, is very narrow even for the virtuous and teeming with destruction. Not nobility of lineage,[19] not the charm of beauty, not the abandoned love of riches, not glory from accomplishments, not the highest wordly honour, not strength of body, not the presumptuous importunity of men, not unrestrained temerity leads thither but virtue of soul, constancy of mind, nobility attained not by birth but cultivated in the heart, interior beauty, a host of virtues,[20] rule of life, poverty in worldly goods, contempt of position.

Phronesis' mind is in a feverish turmoil since she sees that the approaches are difficult, a fall ever imminent. The horses, overcome with toil, refuse to draw the chariot or to perform their tasks for their mistress and, unacquainted with the road, panic at a path unsuitable for travel, that offers their hooves no foothold. Reason cannot turn them and rein them upwards. Balking they stand firm against the rein and refusing the bridle, fight their mistress and refuse to obey her orders. Meanwhile, conflicting feelings drag Phronesis in different directions and she cannot on her own essay the hidden places with no one to point the way beforehand, escort her and guide her steps on the journey.

Behold, a maiden,[21] with her abode at the summit of the pole,

[18] Reading *inignit.*

[19] Here and in line 67 Alan distinguishes between one who is born a nobleman and one who becomes by his efforts a noble man. See Bk. 1. n. 11.

[20] Virtue here means *habitus bonus operativus*, an acquired facility for doing the right thing.

[21] The maiden is Theology. Alan's idea of theology can be discovered in his *Regulae.* He approaches theology as he would approach one of the Liberal Arts. Theology has its first principles, maxims or axioms. One begins with these and develops them logically. Alan accepts as a basis the Unity and Trinity of God: this basis comes from revelation.

looking down upon the heavens, turning her eyes aloft, searches with every effort of sight for something that lies beyond. She pursues nothing corporeal but passing beyond it, examines the hidden cause of the incorporeal, seeking the beginning and end of things. She presents herself to Phronesis' view; with her bright light she flashes suddenly on Phronesis' vision and with its strangeness, she untensed her mind. This is not surprising, since she stands out in such bright beauty that she is endowed with a resplendence beyond the stars, as she adds brightness to brightness and light to light and has no hesitation in sharing this light, which has made her its daughter, with Olympus itself.[22] She shows nothing of earth in her face; she allows nothing mortal, nothing doomed to die, to creep into her expression. The maiden's face shows her parentage, the maiden's form shows that what she has to offer is exclusively of heaven. Arguments based on beauty prove that she is a goddess. No insistence in denial refutes what this beauty and a face so heaven-like prove. A diadem[23] sets her head aglitter; sparkling with the deep lustre of gems, it is afire with gold and flashing forth, gleams with a cluster of twelve stones. She carries a book in her right hand, a royal sceptre in her left and her eyes frequently seek the book but rarely return to the staff: yet finally they do return to it and cast their gaze around it lest her left hand waver, be overcome by the burden of the rod and relinquish the sceptre.[24]

Then from 623A to 650D he applies philosophical principles to his basic fact. Scripture is seldom used and the Fathers are never quoted as proofs of what he states.

[22] Reading *cesset.* From line 112 it is obvious that Theology draws on both pagan and christian teaching. *Nec ... largiri censet* is odd Latin. *Censet* could easily be written for *cesset* as we find *fonsa* for *fossa.*

[23] See *De Pl. Nat.* 433B. W.433.

[24] In line 181 we are told that the sceptre shows that Theology is a queen, one with power and authority. The fact that her eyes seldom gaze on the sceptre shows that she wishes to use this authority as infrequently as possible, that there are few things that she

She is clothed in a garment steeped in gold, shining with silver, more becoming than any veil, more charming than any regular dress, more gleaming than the pure stars of heaven. The hand of God and Minerva's skilled right hand wove it, as the nobility of its form shows us. Here a fine needle has traced the secrets of God and the depths of the divine mind and with form informs the formless, localises the boundless, reveals the hidden, gives limits to the unlimited, brings the invisible into view. What the tongue cannot tell the picture does: how language, since it fails to reach the essence of God, grows senseless when it tries to express things divine, loses its power of communicating and tries to take refuge in its old meaning. Sounds die into silence, scarce able to lisp, and words stop quarreling about their connotation;[25] how God himself embraces in himself the names of all things which are not repugnant to His Nature; however he conceives everything by means of a trope and by way of a figure and assumes the unadulterated name without the object. He is the just without justice, living without life, beginning without beginning, end without end, measureless without measure, strong without strength, powerful without force, directing all things without movement, filling all places while free of all places, lasting without time, abiding without abode, in possession of all things at once without holding them, speaking

asks us to accept on authority alone and lines 183 ff. show that when we are asked to accept things on authority, it is the authority of God that is in question. The sceptre may also be meant to emphasize the fact that Theology has authority. Canonists were beginning to lay claim to more and more power in the Church and assert their right to determine what should be believed and done by the faithful.

[25] Alan is here following Hilary, *De Trin.* 2.6. ff., *PL* 10.55B ff. There we find: "*language fails to reach the (divine) essence*"; "*all language is inadequate to express what pertains to Him*"; "*language of any kind fails to come forward*"; "*let there be an end to the nuisance of complaints*". *Cf. Quoniam Homines,* ed. P. Glorieux, 119; Boeth. *De Trin.*, 4.1 ff (Stewart-Rand 16 ff.); Gilbert of Poitiers, *Commentary on the Pseudo-Athanasian Creed* 55, ed. N. M. Häring, *Mediaeval Studies* 27 (1965) 40.

without voice, in repose without resting, shining without renewal of brightness, aglow without light. He is not only just in the true sense but is justice itself, not only lightsome but light itself free from night; not only is He called measureless just in name, He is measure itself defining every mortal thing and fitting them with definite limits. He is called strong not only by way of an appellation but He is existing strength itself, reposing in eternal strength: He alone is rightly powerful who, being absolute power, can alone do all things, from whom the power of the powerful comes. Not only does He fill all places but He alone embraces each and every place like a boundary and place of places.[26] Here can be read — but dimly and in a faint figure, how He is the one, abiding, simple, eternal power, the fount, the splendour, the form, the way, the strength, the end, the origin, the unfathered father, living God, one and only creator, one in essence, three in person;[27] how He remains uniquely one in one but a threefold relation[28] makes him triune and He remains one in three, three in one. Here[29] can be seen in what way the Son is the mirror, light, splendour, image of the Father, one and the same God from God the Father, beginning from beginning, light from light, sun shining from sun, glow produced by fire, like from like, true from true, one from one, eternally born from the eternal, equal from equal, good from good, sublime from sublime, how the ardour, love, harmony, form of Father and Son is the Spirit in Whom the Father bestows a kiss on His own Son, finds Himself in the Child in Whom the Parent sees Him-

[26] See Boeth., *De Trin.* 4 (Stewart-Rand 17-28).

[27] The Trinity means three Divine Persons and one Divine Nature.

[28] The threefold relation is Fatherhood, Sonship and Procession. The Holy Spirit proceeds from the Father and the Son.

[29] For line 154, see *Wisdom* 7.26; cf. Ambrose, *De Fide ad Gratianum* 1.49, *PL* 16.562A-B. For lines 155-156, see Augustine, *De Trinitate*, 14.23, *PL* 42.1076.

self while His Other Self is being born of Him, and in the Child shines forth the Father's image.

Touched by the breath of these refinements, the queen of the pole leaves the transitory, seeks her knowledge from the hidden things of God, cleaves to the divine, empties her mind of things human, fills it with draughts of Noys herself, becomes intoxicated with draughts from the divine stream, or more correctly she may be called sober, for intoxication arising from such nectar has the power of complete sobriety: it does not cause the mind to fall below its natural power, rather it raises it to a more noble level, eliminating the effects of contagion from our baseness. With humble tread, bowed head, modest attitude, Phronesis approaches this maiden and first gently greeting her, clothes her thoughts in the following speech:

"O Queen of the pole, goddess of heaven, daughter of the Master above, for your divine face shows that you are no mortal nor need bewail the stain of our race; your countenance proves that you are a goddess, your sceptre proclaims that you are a queen and your glory shows that you are the child of God. To you the abodes of the gods, the ways of the heavens, the path of Olympus, the orb that lies beyond the universe, the entire land of the Thunderer lie open as well as the dominion of God and the destiny that lies beyond. Guide me in my wanderings, direct me in my confusion, steady me in my fears, teach me in my ignorance, take hold of me in my wavering, gladden me in my sorrow, willingly look to the interests of a stranger, complete what is begun, support one tottering, come to the aid of one falling. For I am a wanderer, fearful, confused, untaught, in difficulty, incompetent, unacquainted with the place, a stranger, faint. Trying to cross the poles and enter the abodes above, the inner sanctuary of God, the chamber of the Thunderer and the council of Jupiter, I go along stumbling, straying, alone, losing my way as I essay the hidden ways of heaven. I do not, however, undertake these labours because I am capricious, hasty, improvident, sent on my way by chance. Yielding to prayers and compelled finally to agree by the pressure of Nature, the will of the Virtues and above all by the command of Reason, I am committed to do this task — to present the prayers of Nature herself to the Thunderer on high. Nature, remembering that her work failed in many respects and wishing to undo her failure, obliterate her former errors and atone for ancient blemishes by a new and happy venture, is trying to form a man, to stamp him with happiness, give him complete perfection, create him in virtue in order to cast a veil over her long-standing culpability by giving to the wayward world one man from so many thousands who could make good his claim to righteousness, keep his gaze fixed on virtue, condemn avarice, apportion obligations,[30] remedy excesses, observe the mean, outlaw abuses. Nature is not deciding on this work without the advice, command, guidance and prayers of the Virtues; the entire assembly of her sisters supports the idea with unanimous approval. However, the services of mighty Nature are effective only in regard to things of earth and her power grows weak in things of heaven, where she has no rights and knows not how to create a soul; this only the right hand of the craftsman in heaven fashions and needs no authority in anything from Nature. Bracing myself for a long time now with this argument, I make my way with great reluctance hither, and without a companion earnestly seek the secret haunts of the gods above, so that I may place before God what Nature's mind itself has conceived, what virtue longs

[30] or "portion out offices" or "distribute benefits".

for, so that the will of God may confirm our will, that he may hear our supplications and that His favour may breathe on our prayers. Our prayer is that the hand of God would send down a soul from on high who will be wise in mind, full of virtue, endowed with a sense of reverence, characterised by faith, reflecting piety; who, cloaked in the garment of flesh, will so sojourn on earth that crime will be redeemed by piety, guilt by virtue, incest by modesty, chicanery by justice, failure by glory; that this terrestrial habitation, this earthly power, this covering of the corporeal mass will survive; that this mortal body will be considered a work of mighty Nature, so refreshed with manifold endowments, deprived of no gift of form, so that the spiritual being will no longer disdain to take lodgings in a body nor will a guest so great have to bemoan the hospice's decay, but rather will hold sway in the castle of the flesh. Detail for me, then the course by which the path mounts to the citadel of Jupiter on high and let me not in one place after another be led astray from the path nor let mistaken wanderings bring our project to naught and deprive our toil of its rewards."

Delighted with these words, the queen of the pole with kind address replied that she would offer herself as partner in her journey, a guide on the path, a directress on the course. But she pledges guidance to Phronesis alone and strongly advises her, adding the force of a command to the same advice, that she leave the car behind, give the horses in charge to her companion in the heavens and leave her below to be a reliable guardian of a charge so great, securing the chariot and curbing the horses, lest, if Reason with the chariot and horses should struggle upwards and the celestial path, acquainted with different wayfarers, should not deign to accept such a traveller, the steeds would miss the way, Reason would falter and the chariot reel. The instructions of the goddess are fulfilled and her wishes find favour. Reason remains, the horses are secured, the chariot is stationary. Discarding all the others, the queen grants her companion the second horse[31] alone, as he, trained by a more effective rein and bit, would be less affrighted at that road and would balk but little at that upward journey. Phronesis is borne on the horse, the queen makes her way unaided. The horse proceeds in soaring flight, the goddess vies with the horse, outstrips his fleet pace and keeping the lead, tests the path for her companion.

Thus far my Muse has sung in a gentle whisper; thus far my page has sported in fragile verse to the accompaniment of Phoebus' lyre of tortoise shell. But abandoning things petty, I now pluck a mightier chord and laying aside entirely the role of poet, I appropriate a new speaking part, that of the prophet. The earthly Apollo[32] will yield to the heavenly Muse; the Muse will give place to Jupiter; the language of earth will yield to and wait on the language of heaven and Earth will give place to Olympus. I will be the pen in this poem, not the scribe or author.[33] I will be a sounding brass,[34] the writer's silent page, the singer's pipe, the sculptor's chisel, the orator's muse,[35] the thorn bearing a rose, the reed bringing a potion of new honey, the night with its light from another source, the earthen vase flowing with nectar.

Father on high, eternal God, living power, one and only form of good, way of righteousness, path of virtue, fount of truth, sun of justice,[36] sanctuary of piety, beginning and end, deter-

[31] The second horse is hearing. They are to meet Faith and "faith comes by hearing" (*Rom.* 10.17).

[32] See Verse Prologue, n. 5.

[33] Reading *auctor.*

[34] 1 *Cor.* 13.1.

[35] The orator had no Muse.

[36] For the concept of *sol iustitiae*, see F. J. Dölger, *Die Sonne der Gerechtigkeit und der Schwarze* (Münster 1918); cf. his article, "Das Sonnengleichnis in einer Weihnachtspredigt des Bischofs Zeno von Verona," *Antike und Christentum* 6 (1950) 1-56.

mination, measure, seal, cause of things, abiding reason, kindly Noys, true wisdom, true day, light that knows not darkness, ultimate source,[37] perfect beauty of the universe, eternal life, ruling what exists, sowing the seeds of things to come, preserving what is coming into existence, enclosing all things in numbers, securing each and every thing by balance, encompassing all things within a stable restraint: you, who bring the species of things and the shadow of the sensible world from the exemplar of the conceptual world, fashioning it exteriorly in the image of an earthly form; who clothe the ancient mass, that was complaining of its mournful appearance, in a finer raiment, sealing it with the seal of form and eliminating confusion by a unifying bond: efficient cause, who bring a thing into existence, formal cause while you fashion it, final cause for its existence when you conserve it and confine it within definite limits:[38] direct first on me a ray of divine light; send your rain upon me to bedew still further my mind with heavenly nectar, cleanse me of blemishes of mind, wipe out and dispel the darkness, grant me the clear calm splendour of your light. Refresh my pen, cleanse my mouth of mould, grand the stutterer power to utter your words, supply the dumb with speech, give a spring of water to the parched, direct the wanderer on his path, as mariner, pilot the bark and filling my canvas with a breeze from heaven, vouchsafe a harbour to the fearful.

Now Phronesis, under the direction of the goddess, had succeeded in passing the starry citadels and astonished by the strange path and the tangle of roads, she would complain about the burden of so great a difficulty, were she not feasting her eyes on things strange and were not the queen bearing part of her toil. In her journey she wonders at the water united to fire by

[37] *summa origo*. See Augustine, *De Trin.* 6.10.12, *PL* 42.932.

[38] Cf. Thierry of Chartres, ed. N. M. Häring, 555 ff.

locations side by side without separation, while the flame does not interfere with the water nor the water, a contrary element, contend with the flame but rather they lay aside their battle gear. They no longer seek to remember their natural repugnance: they are bound by a dissenting assent, a concordant discord, a hostile peace, an unreliable reliance, a fictitious bond of love, a deceptive friendship, a shadow covenant. Sophia fixes her mind and eyes on these things, inquiring in her perceptive soul: who caused peace to exist where normally there is no abiding peace; who ordered Mars out of a territory where he holds rights; who arranged a covenant where there is no covenant; who mingled peace and resentment, agreement and dispute; who joined love and strife. Phronesis goes into the inquiry more deeply, pressing her investigation more eagerly: does that liquid flow while the neighbouring fire of the pole shares its bed and does it temper the fire's fierce rage; does the liquid, in the shape of an exhalation and in the form of vapour, spread out to form a cloud, hang at the highest point of the Ether and grant draughts to the thirsty fire; does this liquid contain the species, ice; does it shape itself into crystals and lose its liquidity. Phronesis however, establishes by deductions made on the spot that moisture there cannot in any way wind its way back nor flow away in a stream of its own, since no channel offers it a bed nor does a parent earth open its bosom to it, nor can it, seeking the centre and drawn by its own weight, rush down, favouring its gravity since the fire prevents its descent, compels the water to remain above and holds it fast as though shut up in a prison. For that philosopher who dreams that moisture descends from above by furtive fall, unknown, so to speak, to fire, is devoid of reason, a false prophet, follows idle pursuits, grasps at clouds and emptiness, seeks a knot in a bulrush, smoke in light, feigns a sharp point on a plane surface, darkness in light. By the same reasoning she establishes that no exhalation of vapour in that place causes clouds nor does suspended moisture cover the Ether with water where no earth sends forth exhalations and that the fire does not cause clouds to hang in the Ether. From this Phronensis concludes that the heavenly moisture takes the appearance of a crystal and the form of ice. This type of ice, knowing not frost and unacquainted with Winter, recognises rather Summer and a warm atmosphere and does not in any way deign to melt in the face of fire.[39] This one fact astounds her and she is drawn to a more worthwhile investigation: by the help of what trustworthy bond, by what peace-pact does the cold ally with the hot, the moving with the inactive here where there is no peace-mediator, where a bond is lacking that would unite extremes and, on the establishment of peace, would wipe out hostile contentions and end quarrels.[40] She fails in her investigation and finds herself nonplussed in her inquiry. She is defeated in her investigation and, reduced to complaints, bemoans her own deficiency. Thus the complaint turns into a question that leaves Phronesis with no answer but a sigh.[41] It is no cause for wonder if Prudence withdraws from the lists, faced with matters that are so far beyond the dominion of mother Nature that they rise above her course, cause the mind to fail, the intellect to come to a standstill, the reason to grow numb, wisdom to totter, Tullius[42] himself to be silent, Maro's[43] Muse to

[39] The explanation of hail caused difficulties. It is ice; yet it falls in warmish weather. In *Meteor*, 347b ff., Aristotle deals with Anaxagoras' views on hail and gives his own. Heat and cold have a mutual reaction. In warmer periods the cold is concentrated by the surrounding heat. The cloud descends into warmer air and the frozen water within is released. It falls as hail.

[40] There should be a comma ofter *pigris* (359) and a period after *recidat* (362),

[41] There is an amount of punning between derivatives of *quaerere, to seek* or *investigate* and of *queri, to complain*. They are poor puns but the English without them sounds nonsensical. There does not seem to be any way of transferring the puns to English.

[42] Cicero.

[43] Virgil.

fall dumb, Aristotle to droop, Ptolemy's sense to grow dull.

Prudence proceeds upon her journey, matching step for step with her companion. Finally, with great toil, repeated effort, numerous struggles, she made her way up to the realms of happiness, realms abounding in goodwill, realms dear to God in heaven and to the Thunderer. Here are laughter without sadness, bright sky without cloud, joys unfailing, pleasures unending, peace free from hatred, rest that knows no toil, light ever glowing, sun with true brightness, sunrise that knows no sunset, pleasant morning with no evening to come. Here brightness knows no night, abundance brings no surfeit. Here unadulterated joy flourishes entirely untouched by toil. Here Fortune does not go its unpredictable course, undermining laughter with tears, prosperity with misfortune, joy with sorrow. She does not spoil the honey with vinegar, mingling rough with smooth, dark with bright, joining darkness to light, sad to merry. Rather, rest and tranquillity endure and, as they are unending, there can be no surprise from Fortune to turn them into gloom. Here the very court of the sun in the heavens gleams and rejects man's squalor and earth's contamination. This extramundane world and blessed part of the universe is clearer than clear, purer than pure, brighter than bright, more glittering than gold. It sparkles with soothing light, it gleams with harmless fire; it is free from violent heat, abounds in brightness, possesses the charms of light, is free from injurious heat: it warms with its light, does not harass with waves of heat. This fire is less hot than normal fire but burns more brightly: thus though remaining the same, it is both less and more than the same thing. But since this whole place sparkles with blessed fire and is soothed by the friendly swaying flame, it is identified with the empyrean pole on which the glow of a kindly fire smiles and sets off the court with its lustre. Here dwell the citizens of heaven and the nobles of the Thunderer, the companies of angels and the divine beings, the rulers of the world, the celestial bands, the hosts of heaven, those who guard us. There are different divisions of these by rank, function, duty, varying capacity, perfection of power, difference of station, diversity of work.[44] Here the Seraphim shine, aglow with the warmth of divine light, irradiated with the brightness of the eternal sun. The Cherubim, filled with draughts from the divine spring, excel in knowledge and cling more closely to the mind of God. From the Thrones the impartial judgment of God is echoed; God himself dwelling in them poises his balance. The divine Dominations take their name from their office; as they yield to those above them, so do the others yield to them: they give and obey orders equally. The Principalities arrange their citizens in order and include their subjects' prayers in their own. The Powers, with their arms from heaven, subdue the rulers, or rather the despots, of this aerial region. The Virtues establish connections with the laws of Nature, pay her her due and remodel things of old with new forms. The Archangels reveal mysteries, lay bare secrets, uncover the hidden, or rather bring news to earth of what lies concealed and unfold for earth the mysteries of heaven. The great army of Angels, above the Archangels in obedience but below them in power, fulfills the obligation of obedience to all those mentioned, brings news of lesser import to the world and hurries to and fro performing various services for us. Here the subjects dwell in the city of the high king. To these citizens is entrusted the preservation of the heavenly state. Amongst them this law stands ratified — that one shall be in command, that this one be an active representative and carry out the wishes of the others.[45] Every fool learns from the book of the divine mind what must be done, reads there

[44] For a detailed account of the nine Choirs of angels, see *Hierarchia*, ed. M. T. d'Alverny, *Textes Inédits*, 229-235; cf. *Quoniam Homines*, ed. P. Glorieux, 283 ff.

[45] It is pointed out in *Hierarchia*, 225, that "one angel is greater than another". Logically there would be one who would be greatest.

what is to come, consults God, seeing each and everything in the mirror of the deity. No angel on his own claims title to a domain so great.

Here dwells the one whose life has made him god-like, whose virtue has made him holy, who on earth merited the favour of Olympus, one earthly in body, heavenly in mind, mortal in flesh, a god in life, living a life based in heaven, externally savouring of the earthly, internally meditating on the heavenly. Such a one was not raised aloft by arrogance, glory from accomplishments, abandoned love of the world. He was not broken by deceiful luxury or excess of wealth; he was not inflamed by a desire for possessions or gnawing envy; he was not defiled by the harassing plague of avarice or the blind desire for honour. Rather, his gifts were prudence, contempt of the world, poverty in worldly goods, a strict rule of life, disdain for the flesh, willingness to lay down his life. His spirit triumphant, he trod worldly goods under foot, rid himself of miserliness and forced his flesh into subjection. An upright life, the reward of virtue and recompense for toil enroll in the angelic companies such as are clothed with the white of virginity, the purple of martyrdom or are enriched with the laurels of the doctor — in a word, those who are not disqualified for the reward of the *aureola:*[46] victory crowns all who looked forward to a common reward. Although they differ in merit and dissimilar lustre and unequal light shine from their merits, equal joy and like happiness are in store for all, even where the rewards differ. Nor is it a matter for wonder if an equally happy requital awaits all to whom there is given one life for service, for whom God is all things to all, the gift and the giver, giving a great variety of things to one and one thing to many.

[46] *Aureola* is the celestial crown worn by martyrs, virgins and doctors for their victory over the world, the flesh and the devil.

Here the Virgin Mary[47] by special honour excels the citizens of the heavenly kingdom. She did not, in accord with the law of birth, lose her virginity: she merited the name of virgin and mother. In her two names, their quarrel buried, unite in harmony, names that are wont to war and contend with each other. Motherhood and maidenhood are no longer at variance but eschewing contention, offer each other the kiss of peace. Here nature is silent, logic's power goes a-begging, all the authority of rhetoric comes to naught, reason totters. This is she who, by wondrous benefit of the divine gift, as daughter conceived her father and as mother conceived her son,[48] keeping the honour of virginity without losing the rights of a mother. In the bed of her womb the supreme Godhead prepared himself a guest-chamber. The very son of the supreme creator wove himself a robe; of his own volition he donned the garment of our salvation and clothed himself in our flesh.

She is the star of the sea, the way of life, the gate of salvation, the model of justice, the path of piety, the fount of virtue, the mother of forgiveness, the cradle of purity, an enclosed garden, a sealed fountain, a fruithful olive tree, a fragrant cedar, a paradise of delights, an ornamented wand, a wine cellar stocked with celestial liquid and offering draughts of nectar from heaven, a flowering rose free from thorns, grace that never knew lapse, a fount clear of mud, a light that dispels dark clouds, hope for the miserable, remedy for the guilty, preserver of happiness, way-home for the banished, path for the one astray, light for the blind, rest for the hopeless, respite for the weary. She is the one who wiped out the results of the first fall and the stains of the

[47] In lines 471-499 Alan borrows from the *Canticle of Canticles*, the *Book of Wisdom*, the Laurentine Litany of the Blessed Virgin and the hymn *Ave Maris Stella (Hail Star of the Sea)* of Venantius (Fortunatus).

[48] Mary is the Mother of Christ, Christ is God, thus Mary is the Mother of God. *Divini muneris usu* refers to the Holy Spirit: Hilary, *De Trin.*, 2, 1, *PL* 10.51A.

first mother,[49] overcoming guilt with virtue, replacing what was overthrown, returning what had been taken away, compensating for what had been ruined, restoring what had been lost, making up for what had been put to flight, giving new joys to follow the sighs of yestereve, shining with the light of a new life for us after the darkness of death. At her coming the golden age returns to earth: crime is succeeded by piety, guilt by grace, vice by virtue, hatred by peace, gloom by joy. As the flower of the rose makes up for the hard thorn, as the engrafted branch by its sweet product makes up for the bitter fruit of the original tree, so she atones for the crimes of the first mother; her own daughter brings about her mother's rebirth so that the guilty woman may be absolved by the pure one, the corrupted by the virgin, the shameless by the modest, the miserable by the happy, the proud by the humble and that her own daughter[50] should give birth to the mother of life. The heavenly court hangs on the expression of her will, ready to carry out with devout mind the command of her with whom the controlling reins of the heavenly Kingdom are shared by Him[51] who is that same woman's father and son. Son and Father, He rules all things with an eternal rule. Under his kingship, the soldier has his triumph in heaven, on earth he campaigns an exile. This is the One Who, entering the penitentiary of our flesh, fettered Himself with the chains of expiation to loose the fettered, became sick to heal the sick, poor to bring aid to the poor, died to bring with His own hands the gift of life to the dead, suffered every pain of exile that Himself an exile, He might bring back the miserable from exile. Thus stripes are undone by stripes, wounds by wounds; thus illness gives judgment against illness; thus death is put to flight by death;

[49] The theme of Mary as the Second Eve is very common in Christian writers.
[50] St. Anne, mother of the Blessed Virgin.
[51] Jesus Christ.

thus the living dies that the dead may live; the heir goes into exile to turn slaves into heirs; the rich becomes needy and the mighty becomes a pauper to enrich the indigent. Thus a freeman becomes a slave to free slaves; the highest seeks the lowest place that the lowest may ascend to the highest. Light grows dark that the night may be lit up; the true sun grows faint in eclipse to make the stars rise again. The physician is ill that the ill may heal the diseased. Heaven adapts itself to earth, the cedar to the hyssop, the giant to the dwarf, light to darkness, rich to poor, well to ill, the king to the slave, the purple to sackloth. He is the one Who, in pity for our lot, left the court of His eternal father, endured His aversion for out lot, fastening to Himself, though innocent, the penalties of our lot and the damaging effects of our guilt.

BOOK VI

When the maiden, entering God's realm and the abodes of the magnificent, wished to enjoy a view and foretaste of the strange new things, the brightness dazzled her eyes and the impact of the strange objects benumbed her mind. Faced with them her vision failed and her mind within was darkened. Thus drowsiness overcame the alert mind of Phronesis and false sleep weighed it down: the trance bathing the mind in drowsiness forced it along the path to sleep.[1] Now she would have fallen headlong and met disaster, had not her companion come to her aid, grasped her with her hands, steadied her as she was tottering, with kindly arms around her strengthened the maiden's limbs, forestalled a fall so disastrous, addressed her in kindly tones and soothed away her numbness of mind. Yet full power of mind was not restored to her. When the queen could not by any means eradicate the harmful stupor and restore full powers of mind, she besought with prayers her own sister to come to Phronesis' aid, drive out the numbness completely, bring back her power of mind and force it to return. This sister,[2] dwelling in the realms of the powers above, examines the depths of heaven and, to the exclusion of all else, clings to the innermost recesses of God. Reason establishes nothing for her; with Reason's role postponed, her own belief and faith suffice.[3] For Reason does not come before Faith; rather Faith anticipates it and Reason finally obeys the dogmas of Faith and follows her as she teaches the Articles of Faith. Reason transfers these divine symbols to paper,[4] imprinting on the mind what she etches with

[1] For *extasis*, see *Quoniam Homines*, ed. P. Glorieux, 121.

[2] The sister is Faith. Cf. *De Pl. Nat.* 446A: W. 456.

[3] Cf. Gilbert of Poitiers, ed. N. M. Häring, 133, 164.

[4] Reading *cartis*.

her pen. Her garment, with distinctive stripes of purple and with an intermixture of snow-white, has a reddish sheen with subdued glitter. With this garment our lady is resplendent and her ensemble bespeaks her mastery over Reason since Reason itself is reflected in her clothing. The garment gives place to a painting which expresses itself completely in figures and in its images takes the place of a written book. Here the vocal painting gives a new life to the teachers of old, through whom our faith spread through the whole world and shone with glorious titles of honour. Here Abraham,[5] the father of our faith, lays aside the role of father; hastening to obey his Father in heaven, he refused to be a father to his son. In him Nature and Faith at variance carry on a battle and draw one mind to irreconcilables. For Nature tells the father to spare the son. On the other hand Faith takes a firm stand and orders him to spurn his son in order that Nature may show deference to the Father in heaven. The father, then, wills what he does not wish. Now trying to spare him, now willing to sacrifice him, he finally abandons the alternative he longs for. Nature, then, submits to Faith and sadly yields to the victor what it would not consent to yield under physical compulsion. To strengthen Faith Peter[6] flashes with the light of virtue and his virtue shines in his close companion. Armed with merit of life and the gift of wisdom, Paul[7] exerts pressure by blandishments, reasoning, threats, virtues and offers the pagans admittance to the faith. Not only by miracles but indeed by reason, does he overcome the recalcitrant and he is not satisfied to ply the narrow path assigned him. He desires more and delights to build a road of reason. There protected with the

[5] The account of Abraham is in *Genesis* 11.27-25.7. The account of the command of God that he should sacrifice his son, Isaac is in 22.1-14.

[6] Prince of the Apostles. Cf. Prud., *Peri.* 12.3-6.

[7] The Apostle to the Gentiles. Prud., *Ib.*

breastplate of Faith and the arms of justice, Laurence[8] conquers enticements, threats, penitentiaries, blows, death and overcomes his torture by fire. Equal in his deserts as a fighter and a soldier in the same army, Vincent,[9] subduing the world, in his victory treads everything under foot and fighting against those who survived him, has his victory in death. Although a tracery of beauty embroiders Faith's garment, yet no wantonness discredits her dress; rather it was such as a matron's years call for, a matron who is reaching the turning post[10] towards old age, full of days, her head sprinkled with grey hair and the hoar frost of age. Yet the early stages of old age do not furrow her face: that face which betokens the age of youth belies her years but the grey hair tell a different tale; thus her beauty of countenance takes issue with her grey hairs.

This woman, on her own initiative and touched by her sister's prayers, directs her steps to the place where Phronesis, afflicted with the drowsiness of lethargy, lies listless and, presenting the image of death, experiences a living death and a dead life. But when Faith came and recognized Phronesis from the clear indication of the signs, she saw her in a maze and was amazed at the patient. Pitying her misfortunes she is grieved, rids herself of her sternness of mind and bursts into tears: her aloof grandeur of soul is somewhat tempered and made grow soft, her austerity vanishes and pity takes full possession of her soul. Thus she advanced further and approached the patient more closely. She makes enquiries into the source of the lethargy, explores every

[8] St. Laurence, martyred at Rome c. 258 A.D. The legend that he roasted on a gridiron goes back to the middle of the fourth century. Cf. Prud., *Ib.* 2.15-17.

[9] St. Vincent, martyred at Valencia in Spain in 304 A.D. There was a tradition that he was martyred in the same way as Laurence. Cf. Prud., *Ib.* 4.77.

[10] The *metae* were the turning points for the chariots at either end of the Roman Circus. A race was normally seven laps. *Matrona* and *senium* are so indefinite that it is impossible to guess just how old Fides is in Alan's view. See Intro., p. 31.

avenue, carefully investigating the place, time, cause, symptoms of the disease. Finally she tracks it down and discovers that Phronesis is suffering the derangement of lethargy, as the outwards signs of listlessness indicate. Having discovered the etiology of the affection and found the source of the disease, she asks further what health-giving element can isolate the cause of the listlessness, wipe out the plague, overthrow the pestilence and rout the disease. She prepares, then, to dislodge the drowsiness by threats, prayers, noise of clapping, shouts[11] but this kind of sleep resists. It is no cause of wonder if the disease contemptuously refuses to leave when confronted with these remedies. This was not the drowsiness of ordinary sleep, but an image of death which darkens life's light and deadens the vital element to a greater extent than ordinary sleep but less than death: it is more than lethargy but less than death although an unmistakable prelude to it. Since such treatment fails to dislodge the disease and cannot overcome its great virulence, the listless patient is given a rare draught, prepared by heavenly hands, seasoned with relish, sweetened to taste of flowing honey, pleasant in aroma, savouring of drugs[12] from far-off places, rejecting earth's seasonings, pledging health in a draught with fresh incense from heaven. This spreads through her body, encircles the vital parts, enters the veins, searches out the sinews,

[11] In primitive times disease was regarded as an entity within the patient and methods were used to scare and dislodge it. Skulls of Terramare folk have been found with neat holes drilled in them, no doubt to let a headache out. Such beliefs hardly existed in Alan's milieu. See Lorne C. McKinney, *Early Medieval Medicine, with special reference to France and Chartres*, (Baltimore 1937). M. T. d'Alverny thinks that Alan had an interest in medicine and possibly some training in it: *Textes inédits*, 105; *Entretiens sur la Renaissance du 12e siècle* (Paris 1968) 120. For an interesting and detailed case-history, see Peter of Blois, *PL* 209.126A-128B. For various meanings of *lethargus*, see Peter Dronke, "Boethius, Alanus and Dante", in: *Romanische Forschungen* 78 (1966) 119-125.

[12] For *species* with the meaning of *drugs*, see Macr. *Sat.* 7.8.8.

makes its way into the marrow. On its entry Phronesis revives; as she regains consciousness and the shuddering fear is completely removed from her mind,[13] the stupor itself is astonished that medicine can do this; dislodged it is amazed that such a disease yields to medicine. But however clear the mind's eye within becomes, the bodily eye nevertheless is still weak and cannot bear the fiery brightness or the great flash of Olympus. The resourceful maiden, then, has recourse to a device of her own. She presents Phronesis with a mirror[14] that is outstanding, symmetrical, of a reddish hue, reflective, polished, very broad of surface, equipped with images. In this mirror is reflected everything which the fiery region encompasses: in it shines clear everything which the heavenly universe holds, but the appearance of these things differs from the real objects. Here one sees reality, here a shadow; here being, here appearance; here light, there an image of light. This mirror holds Phronesis' attention and steadies her eyes lest a light too strong for them strike them, injure them and tire both mind and eyes. The mirror acts as an intermediary to prevent a flood of fiery light from beaming on her eyes and robbing them of sight. By use of this mirror her eyes recover, find a kindly brightness and enjoy the clear, gleaming light. As her eyes explore the mirror, Sophia sees there all that the divine world embraces. While she sees some things new to her, looks in wonder at everything, finds joy in the complete whole, the strangeness of the objects produces new joys. Her mind as well as her eyes is delighted and rids itself of the mists of delusion as joy suffuses it. Every symptom of her affliction disappears. If her understanding of any aspects is

[13] There should be a comma, not a period, after *horror* in line 110.

[14] The first use of such a mirror is in the account of Perseus' slaying of Medusa. He could not look on her face and used instead her reflection in a mirror. Cf. the Mirror of Providence in Bern. Silv., 2.11.19. ff.

less than complete, the lady standing at her side gives her fuller instruction, makes good the defects in her understanding, lays bare what is hidden and lays open what is closed. Here she saw the soldiery of the angelic multitude and of the council of heaven, the palm of victory as well as the sweet triumphs of the saints, the varying merits and the fruits of their labours. She stands in awe before the merits of the Virgin, adores the child she bore without having the flower of her virginity fade or wither from the burning heat of lust. She stands transfixed with admiration at the manner of conception and birth and the untouched flower of virginity: she cannot discover whence motherhood comes to one who has had no dealings with a man. She has recourse to the laws of logic. Logic denies the rights of motherhood to her whom virginity grants the honour of virgin; in the same way it would trip up in the race for virginity the mother whose offspring argues her parenthood and traces itself back to its mother by right of birth. That line of reasoning falters: she finds herself face to face with a virgin-mother and sees that logic's arguments are refuted. In deeper wonder she is further perplexed and, in greater difficulty, asks by what ordinance of heaven, by what blessed law the father is begotten by the daughter,[15] God by earthly power, the permanent by the transitory, the cedar by the bloom, the sun by a star, the fire by a spark and how the rock exudes liquid honey. She is astonished that God clothes himself in our shape and that the lord of flaming Olympus dwells in our huts, that the flower of the rose lies hidden beneath the sea-weed, that clay covers the gem, that the violet is hidden in the hemlock, that life dies and the sun darkens.[16] She asks what are the adhesives, the bonds,

[15] See Bk. 5. n. 48.

[16] At the death of Christ, the sun failed and there was darkness over the earth. St. Matt., 27.45; St. Mark. 15.33; St. Luke, 23.44. In the context, however, these words should refer to the Incarnation of Christ and may be another metaphor for what the Incarnation involved for the Son of God.

the fastenings here and what is the origin of their power to unite the human to God, to join the divine to the mortal, God to man and what arrangement leagues God with man. While Phronesis is wondering at each of these things in turn and trying to investigate them as a whole by the laws of her reason, the lady standing at her side warns her against vainly imagining that there were here human laws, earthly covenants, processes of nature, successions known to us — here where nature has no power but all decrees are silenced, laws feel fear, ordinances are benumbed, the will of the supreme creator holds solitary sway and exempts its decrees from our canons, ordinances are in dread, rule yields to the creator, canons have no say and the master issues orders. Not Reason but Faith alone is taken into account there; there the heavenly cause transcends other causes, the supreme law prevails over lesser laws and legal compacts. Let Faith, then, suffice; let Reason drop her investigation here; let Faith guide the reins of Reason.

Prudence accepts this advice, submits to the instruction, follows Faith and hands over to the heavenly agent everything that she perceives to be beyond our law and to operate on a plan of exemption from our ordinances. Under these instructions Prudence takes to the road with greater haste. The queen guides her steps and indicates the speed by her own pace. Lest the hidden regions, the forking footpaths, the twisting cross-paths, the jarring road stay the maiden's steps. Faith appoints herself her companion — Faith who brought back to Phronesis her banished mind, who restored her sight, to whom the numbing disease yielded, from whom no road lies hidden, no place is concealed, to whom the crazy path offers no difficulty, whom the byway does not lead astray. Accompanied by these Phronesis presses on her way with more security, goes past the forking roads, the confusing places, the unknown footpaths. She would not be able to deal with the tortuous places but both sisters supply her with strength when she falters, steady her step, lighten the burden of travel, alleviate the pain, dispel the distaste. The mirror given Phronesis protects her eyes from every impact of light lest the heavenly splendour intoxicate her or the glare rebound on her eyes. Finally weary, trembling, wondering, the maiden completes the prescribed course, enters the lofty palaces of the eternal king and rejoices at having overcome the difficulty of the work now finished. But her eyes are astounded by everything which the message in the mirror offers. Nothing that flashes there is mortal, transitory, waning, earthly: there is reflected only the eternal, the heavenly, the permanent, the immovable, the fixed. Here she sees ungenerated species,[17] views celestial ideas, the form of man, the first beginnings of things, the causes of causes, the seeds of reason, the laws of the Fates, the procession of destiny,[18] the mind of the Thunderer. She sees why God rejects some, predestines[19] others; equips this one for life, withdraws his favours from that one; why poverty humilitates and straitens some, oppresses the needy and their need has only tears for relief; why a channel from rich resources pours every wealth on others and the rich man swims in an ever-increasing river of gold; why wisdom enriches some, poor sense beclouds others, together with an improverished mind and a

[17] *ingenitae species*. Cf. Augustine, *De Diversis Quaestionibus*, 83, 46, *PL* 40.29-30.

[18] In *Dist.* 786C, *Fatum* is defined as "the succession of temporal things, proceeding according to Divine Providence". This brings up the problem of reconciling God's Providence or God's foreknowledge with man's freedom of will. This problem worried Boethius and finally baffled him. *De Cons. Pr.* 2 - *Met.* 3 (Stewart-Rand 371-381). *Fati series* is mentioned at p. 342. Cf. Thierry of Chartres, ed. N. M. Häring, 273.15.

[19] In *Dist.* 909B, Alan gives an explanation of *praedestinatio*. In one sense it means that God eternally preordained that justifying grace and eternal glory should be the lot of his elect. The use of the gerundive, *conferendam*, indicates that there is little possibility of their refusing this grace. *Praedestinatio* also means the ordinary justifying grace that is available to everyone on earth. Its other meanings are prophecy of a future good and its correlative, knowledge of a future good. What Prudence understands, then, is why God gives special graces to some and not to others. Alan then goes on to deal with inequalities on the temporal level.

beggarly will; why a clear beauty of appearance lights up Adonis[20] while Davus has a misbegotten face; why Hector[21] flashes in arms, Ulysses[22] sparkles with the ray of cunning, why Cicero is an orator, Tiphys,[23] a sailor, Myro[24] a sculptor, Pollux[25] a boxer, Cato[26] intransigent, Naso[27] a poet. Yet these are not the only things that delight Phronesis' eyes. Her vision ranging farther afield caresses her eyes with further novelties and on its return brings back wondrous tales. Here she sees the gleaming water sparkle forth from an overflowing spring which, rich in water and more striking than any stream, surpasses the stars in brightness, excels the honey in taste: Paradise yields to it in delights, balsam proves inferior in odour, nard gives it preference of place. A stream, originating there and losing sight of no element that this spring contains, achieves completely the rank of the spring and matches it rank for rank: however a charm just as great graces the overflowing spring. The spring produces the stream, stream and spring send forth the flowing river which retains the flavour of both spring and stream. Although spring, stream and river are distinct, they unite in one and the substance of the three is the same, a simple essence, with like taste, one colour, one and the same sparkle, like appearance.[28] There is, too, a sun, like the spring, that excels our

[20] A very beautiful youth, loved by Aphrodite and killed by a boar. There are other versions.

[21] See Bk. 4. n. 30.

[22] See Bk. 1. n. 25.

[23] The helmsman for the Argonauts in their search for the Golden Fleece.

[24] See Bk. 2. n. 50.

[25] One of the Gemini, brother of Castor. According to Ovid, *Fasti* 5.700, Pollux was a boxer. Cf. Bern. Silv., 1.3.45.

[26] See Bk. 2. n. 73.

[27] Ovid.

[28] *fons, rivus, flumen* make up a ternary, a combination used to help understand the Trinity. See Anselm, *Epist. de Incarnatione* 14, ed. F. Schmitt, 2.13; Abelard *Theologia Christiana* 4, *PL* 178, 1287B; Augustine, *De Fide e Symbolo*, 9.17, *PL* 40.189. This is followed in lines 254-261 by another ternary — *radius splendor, calor.* See *Contra Haereticos*, 406D-407A; Gilbert of Poitiers, 46, ed. N. M. Häring, 111.

sun in light. This sun sheds a ray which the earthly sun adores, which the heavens and the stars revere, to which earth prays. That sun never has to set, is never subject to eclipse, is never affected by darkening clouds. A solar ray coming from this sun is equal in light to its generator and by its brightness proclaims its father: it is the same sun, the same species, one light, coeternal brightness, never in the least falling below its original source, a different sun but not another thing, one sun and one thing, abiding with its progenitor, light in harmony with light, brightness in harmony with brightness, brilliance that forgets not its source-fire. The ray together with the sun gives forth heat that burns as it soothes, soothes as it burns, assuages as it glows, caresses as it inflames, tempers as it burns. The heat dries up the rivers of evil, cleanses from filth and from vice, distills the gold of virtue. The heat removes the chill of sin, the flame of anger, the winter of torpor, the heat of Venus. Thus heat drives out fire, flame is countered by flame, heat by heat, the coal by the glow. The mind touched by this heat bursts forth in flowers and with the blessed bloom of the virtues of soul, this heat purples the land as it accompanies the return of the heavenly Spring.

Phronesis long wonders at these things, repeatedly examines each thing of which her eyes give her a foretaste and, relying on the sisters' guidance, she makes her way up to the citadel of the high King. Here dwells the King of the pole himself, who encompasses all things with the laws of his kingdom, who by his divinity holds in check the celestial powers, at whose nod the heavens tremble. Near to God, then, she can scarce endure His immortal radiance, can scarce abide the light that floods the court of His majesty. However, the surface of the mirror which she places before her eyes protects her from its flash, dulling the light by means of reflection. Then on bended knees, with suppliant mien, in a restrained and lowered voice and with timid bearing, the maiden prays the eternal King, gives a foretaste of the words of salvation and her voice permeated with fear trembles. The Father of the gods, conceding his own rights to the agent of salvation, bids her stand and cease from her fear and trembling lest the terror impede her mind and speech. The maiden raises herself, controls her mind and partly stays her fear: her spirit takes its place with her body; it is raised up and draws level with the body's stance. Thus the spirit, once depressed, now regains its strength and speech follows her uplift of soul. The soul breaks out in the following terms and words pour forth:

"Should we consider our groans, the boredom of our lot, earthly misfortunes and earthly fate, birth into a fleeting world, ever-imminent death, life beset by failures and the outlook from our day of birth, which of us would embark on a course so arrogant that she should presume to hold converse before the eyes and face of God, that the blight of night should talk to the light of day, that the slave should accost the king, the beggar should accost the mighty, that the created should bring complaints against its creator? But we know that you are the fount of love whose innate goodness banishes the sting of envy, whose love united with justice tempers its rigours and does not allow it to range far and wide. In exile we take refuge with you when earth drives us out, the world persecutes us, man rejects us, every thing living condemns us. Thus the world, if one may with reverence say it, exempts itself from your laws when it violates our rights by heinous deeds and it even threatens you with war, for your interests are at stake when the neighbouring house is ablaze.[29] Nature observes these misfortunes and faults of a decaying world. She sees that virtue is subject to vice, covenants to fraud, friendship to

[29] Hor., *Ep.* 1.18.24.

quarrels and peace to fanaticism. She bemoans these excesses, mourns these errors, bewails these abuses and is grieved that earth lies under a cloud. In many instances, too, she censures her own deeds,[30] is anxious to offset her guilt by a superior deed and by new creations of her arts, and to wipe out the disease by new medicine. She still scarce knows how she may overcome the evil, uproot the disease, excise the rotted members to prevent the healthy part from being involved, bar the way to vice to prevent it from destroying the whole world. Finally, however, trusting in what was said in a conference with her sisters, she is following the better course by coming to the conclusion that she should use her powers to fashion one complete work in which she may come to the aid of her reputation. To compensate for the long-standing wreckage of mankind, she wishes to form a new man who, by pre-eminence in beauty and excellence in character, will transcend the rest of men, cut back all excesses, walk the royal path, observe the mean, avoid extremes, so that at least one bright star may shine upon a world which lies buried in the dark night of error, that virtue may thus revive, that Nature in this man may find forgiveness for her mistakes, that she may be able to grant to one what she is unable to grant to a number and may earn in at least one a just claim to approbation and a title to fame: now she lies condemned in many things and loses her rightful dignity when but her ghost remains. But designs do not hold fast to any course unless your favour approves them, strengthens the undertaking and realises the desire by your gift.[31] The work of Nature would languish and come to a halt long before completion,

[30] Reading *facta*.

[31] Reading *tuo*.

retaining the repulsive elements of the ancient mass, unless your right hand hasten to support the work, guide the hand that is weak, direct the writer's pen, make good the traveller's deficiencies. Nature assigns herself the fashioning of the body; she asks of you the boon that remains and the gift which you alone possess: she seeks a soul; this alone calls for the understanding of the heavenly artificer and needs his file. The earthly construction calls for our handiwork but the soul with a heavenly origin does not recognise it and assigns its origin to you alone.[32] By your command then, let a divinity from heaven visit the world of mortality and let a spirit from heaven enter a body. Placed on earth let it live in heaven in its blessed mind and sojourn on earth only by reason of the body. Rich in the resources of virtue, abounding in heavenly love, let it subject the tyrant of the flesh to reason. Let your work proclaim you; let it declare who its creator is; let the product bespeak the producer. Let the divine being so come down to us that, by the very tokens of his virtues, he may exert his influence on the morals of others. Let Nature's bereavements move you at least — the exile of modesty, the loss of good, lowering of morals, the wavering of probity, the banishment of faith, contempt for law and our prayers. If we are factors of weight and importance in affairs, do not further confuse those already confused: we too were once happy. If the crisis in affairs does not at all move you, at least let your love that is freely given influence you. Accept the prayers we offer and give weight to devout entreaties. If you abandon entirely the prayers of those who are exiled from their father's home, we are deserted and conquered, we lose our entire official role and we abandon our arts."

[32] Reading *tibi.*

The ruler of the court of heaven assents to these prayers and expresses his mind in the following words:

"Maiden, mother of the world, sister of the gods above and my daughter, heavenly in origin, yet an inhabitant of earth: on earth you alone have a feeling for things divine and possess the image of my godhead; you alone relieve the boredom of the world and wipe away its tears with your consolation. Your will does not in degeneration fall away from the supreme mind: for the daughter sighs in unison with the father's desire and the offspring, in harmony with her father, follows his wish. Reason has for long recommended this to me, that I should show regard for earth by one gift and bless the world by the godlike presence of a heavenly man, who in himself would have a treasury of virtue to match every worthy office he would hold, that at least the upright man[33] who tends to stray may flourish and, though withered by the vices of others or rather by now deflowered, he may in this one flower have a second Spring. If I reckoned according to their deserts the vices of earth, the wickedness of the world, the crimes of the universe and wished to mete our full punishment, I would again cover the land with floods, again envelop the mountains in surging waters and the whole human race would perish in the deluge. No one's merits of life would exempt him from the flood; no second Deucalion[34] would survive and no second Noah[35] would close up an ark. Rather the

[33] *saltem mundus.* Normally one would think that *mundus* here would mean the *world*, but it cannot have that meaning if we retain *saltem.* Here *mundus* must mean the basically good man and the *aliorum* of line 395 indicates this.

[34] When Zeus flooded the earth in wrath at the sins of men, Deucalion and his wife, Pyrrha, were instructed by Prometheus to build an ark and they alone escaped the flood.

[35] *Genesis* 6.5 ff.

world, which lives a life of continuous crime, would, as its manner of life deserves, perish by a single punishment. Failing this, a strange fire would consume the sins of earth and involve mankind in a single disaster; the universal plan for this great disaster would not grant exemption to one single soul nor could the pest of sin pass away by any other pestilence. But because mercy overrules the process of justice and the rigor of judgement, abated by love, gives way, I will not make the punishment equal to the crimes, the requital to the faults. I will not purge the pestilence with a sword nor the disease by excision, but swayed by the sweetness of your prayers and pitying your exile, I shall give the world more desirable remedies. By divine favour a spirit from heaven, enriched with heavenly gifts, will be sent down from heaven to earth, will be a stranger in the earthly sphere. Received as a guest of the flesh, this new visitor will have a covering of clay. It remains that your hands should accommodate this soul with a worthy resting place, that the court should fit the king, lest the new guest suffer contamination from his lodging, lest the decayed shell spoil the nut, the contents be impregnated with the flavour of the crumbling vase."

Further cheered by these words, the maiden forgets her own toil and complains no more about the difficulty of her travels, returns full thanks and adores the deity of heaven. God himself pursues the task and proceeds to realise his determination. Accordingly, He calls Noys to prepare for him an exemplar for this divine being, an archetype of the human soul, so that the spirit, rich in every virtue, may be made to conform to its form and may, overshadowed in the passing cloud of flesh, lie concealed in the shade of the body. Then on the King's instructions, Noys scrutinises exemplars of each and every thing and searches for a new archetype. Among so many species she has difficulty in finding the one she seeks; finally the object of her search presents itself to the seeker. In its mirror everything of grace finds a home — the beauty of Joseph,[36] the wisdom of Judith,[37] the patience of just Job,[38] the zeal of Phineas,[39] the modesty of Moses,[40] the simplicity of Jacob,[41] the faith of Abraham,[42] the piety of Tobias.[43] Noys presents this form to God to use as exemplar in forming the soul. He then took a seal and gives the soul a form along the lines of its form; He impresses on the pattern the appearance called for by the archetype. The image takes on all the powers of the exemplar and the figure identifies the seal. The Fates attend the creator and perfect the product's beauty: they are not repelled by malicious envy of the soul's endowments but greet its birth with many a gift, closing the appointed sequence with happy omen.

Enriching the product with these gifts, the creator gives it to Phronesis, warns and instructs her, adding threats to these warnings and instructions, that she is not to be remiss in preserving the great trust but must escort it with unusual care, directing her course along a better route, lest the soul, touched by Saturn's icy chill,[44] experience excessive cold or be parched in Mars' heat, or affected with Dione's sweet itch, begin to dally or go to and fro before the moon's currents. Then Noys drenches the soul with

[36] *Ib.* 39. 6 ff.

[37] The greater part of the Book of Judith (8.9-14.11) is an account of her ingenuity and power of persuasion.

[38] Reading *patientia.* Bossuat's *potencia* will not fit into the metrical scheme.

[39] Phineas, a Jewish priest, son of Eleazar and grandson of Aaron. For his zeal see *Numbers* 25.11 ff.

[40] *Exodus* 3.13; 4.1.

[41] This probably refers to Jacob's dealings with his uncle, Laban. See *Genesis* 29.15 ff.

[42] *Genesis* 12.1 ff. is a record of Abraham's faith.

[43] It is doubtful if any recorded character has a better claim than Tobias to *pietas*, the virtue that regulates man's attitude to God, parents, children and rulers.

[44] Cf. Ovid, *Met.* 9.2.58.

celestial dew and anoints it with a type of ointment which stops all encroachments of Air and the storm-winds of disease, stays the chill of avarice, the heat of disgraceful lust, the pang of envy, and moderates anger.[45]

Having gained her wish, then, the maiden descends from heaven on high, hastens her steps and returns to the place from which she came. She reaches the heavens glowing with stars. Reason comes to meet her, praises her for having gained her wish and looks with wonder on the gifts of the creator above. Then Prudence thanks, bids farewell to and leaves the companions by whose guidance she made her way on high. She returns again to the chariot and the well-known charioteer, joyfully sets out again on the old trail. She bypasses the places nearest to Saturn, warily eludes the old man,[46] follows a path apart, keeps far away in her flight from him and takes a distant road so as to be able to resist successfully his fury. The spirit, however, would have experienced Saturn's rage, had not the smeared ointment countered it and the celestial dew overcome and subdued his vehemence. In like manner she eludes the pests of Venus the heats of Mars and the Moon's sphere. Finally, overcoming every obstacle, Prudence, long and hopefully awaited in her sister's prayers, completes the unmeasurable journey and returns. She presents Nature with the gift from heaven. Nature looks with wonder at the artisan's skill revealed in it, and praises the blessed gift. The favour of the giver is praised in the praise of the gift.

[45] Ptolemy speaks of the influence of the planets on the soul: Saturn in *Tetr.* 3.13 (Robbins 353); Venus, 3.13 (Robbins 357); Moon, 3.14 (Robbins 353). Noys washes and anoints the soul to protect it against the demons and fallen angels of Air.

[46] Pauly-Wissowa, *RE* 2.3,218-228.

BOOK VII

The band of virtues comes to meet Phronesis, clings to her in embrace, entwines their arms about her neck, kisses her, celebrates her return, that is crowned with success since her labour bears fair fruit that brings a happy end to her toil: fear that checks hope has not yet begun to dispose of joy and laughter but the triumph over difficulty absorbs fear and joy follows the fulfillment long sought in prayer. With skill and zeal, then, Nature seeks ideal matter from which to shape an outstanding lodging, a dwelling in the flesh that the spirit from heaven may enter, a shining dwelling worthy of its guest, She collects from earth[1] all the more purified parts it contains, all the pure parts that water rightly lays claim to, all the purer parts that pure air chooses for itself, all the refined parts that purer fire keeps for itself. She separates these from the whole and again collects the separated parts into one and, when she thus has a foretaste of the product to come, she makes ready the material for the human body, raising the standards of the work that is to follow. The element of fire supplies material to be treated and fire here lies still and will cause no upheavals, though it customarily disturbs the whole repose of a body and stirs up a greater than civil war. Pure blood draws its components from air and no longer runs riot with pride of special race, but this humour, blood, maintains peace with the others[2] and vents no rage against its fellows. The water-like liquid,[3] inferior to these, runs its course downwards and now

[1] The body will be composed of the four elements — earth, water, air and fire in their purest form. See Thierry of Chartres, ed. N. M. Häring, 442.

[2] The four humours in the human body are blood, black bile, yellow bile and phlegm. See William of Conch, *Glosae super Platonem*, 58, ed. E. Jeauneau (Paris 1965) 128.

[3] Lines 28-33 give a description of the renal and digestive functions. Cf. Bern. Silv., 2.14.137-148.

refuses to turn aside and cause disease although it ordinarily is very close to actual rottenness and is the cause of various deadly maladies. Here excrement gets rid of the sediment from the humours and functioning with greater regularity, cuts down its natural tendencies. The material drawn from these Nature mints into something precious and fits the features of the human body to her material. Earth[4] marvels at its beauty and the very beauty of the gods[5] is astonished to behold its equal on earth. Nature's bounteous hand showers it with all the riches of beauty; having granted these endowments Mother Nature was almost a pauper since she has granted to one set of features her gifts of grace and treasures of beauty. In this beauty another Narcissus[6] lives; in this face a second Adonis[7] comes to life. If another Venus saw this face again, she would fly into her customary passion. This ranks as a greater sign of beauty and endowment of form — that the body does not swell in obesity but rather tends to leanness. Thus he has everything in due order and his beauty is not maimed in any aspect; indeed there is nothing further or greater that Nature could grant him. Nothing is imperfect since the author is all-perfect and could have willed no more than what would fulfill every need. It would not have been fitting for the one who could have done more to have done less.[8] This beauty, then, displays such excellence that it could expose itself for commendation to envy and win praise from an enemy. After Nature's right hand enriched the material with human features, Concord joins[9] soul to flesh and unites discordants by a stable

[4] Reading *terra.*

[5] Reading *deorum.*

[6] See Bk. 2. n. 2.

[7] See Bk. 6. n. 20.

[8] Lines 50-52 are missing in many manuscripts.

[9] *federat.* It is difficult to get an English translation for this post-classical verb. It carries the idea of separate entities united for a common purpose. For the idea see Mart. Cap., 1.1.9-12.

bond. By a subtle bond and rare cohesive she fits the simple to the composite, the subtle to the dull, binds them in an acceptable compact and weds the divine to flesh. It is thus that she joins night and day, Ether and Earth. Thus contraries live in peace, discordants lay aside the contention natural to them and flesh no longer threatens war, as it yields to the spirit, though not without many a murmur. The spirit no longer loathes and abhors the corporeal garment but rejoices in such lodging and shelter. To help Concord complete her work more effectively, the maiden who pledges us the doctrine of numbers and the one who shows us the connection between voices and the bond between sounds[10] assist in the undertaking, strengthen the marriage bond between spirit and flesh, bind them together by numbers, unite them in a reliable pact so that the substance from heaven weds flesh.[11] A new man, then, is formed. Mighty Nature is surprised at the power she has shown in dealing with this man and in her amazement can scarcely believe that the work she has done with her own hands is really hers. Plenty conveys the above endowments to the youth, pouring the gifts of Nature from a full horn and putting no limit to the amount in a service so great. The horn which no presents, small or great, have previously exhausted is completely drained: in this work it puts itself to the test and takes the measure of its power. Favour approaches with her endowment lest the great gifts of the previous givers miss the commendation of perfect praise. Favour bestows her favours on these gifts, grants them the power to please and swift-footed Fame breathes upon the many presents. Although Fame customarily corrupts truth by falsehood, here she can only tell the truth; she discards her ancient ways and of her attributes retains only her name. It is not here a question of

[10] Arithmetic and Music.

[11] Boeth. *De Cons.* 1.M.5.43; 3.M.9.10 (Stewart-Rand 158, 164).

praise without fit subject or fit subject without praise: a subject worthy of applause saves the praise from being hypocritical. Youth bestows the welcome gifts of joy. Though wantonness is her customary attendant, she discards it, adopts grave ways and patterns herself on the characteristics of an aged man. With grave character Youth makes the transition to Old Age. Thus the youth is in the robust years of bloom; but because he is mature in mind, sense prevails over years: the fruit comes before the first flowers, the river before the brook. Intelligence vies with age as they fight in different styles; the latter betokens a youth, the former shows maturity. Laughter is here but it is not the one that spiteful mockery often begets out of time, that envy of soul fathers, that the expression of false love manifests to the world or fickle wantonness so often displays. This was the laughter that shows deep seriousness, displays itself on the face with restraint, distorts the mouth by no cachinnation, is marred by no misuse but is such as subject, place, time and person call for. Chastity joined the ranks, extensively abates the passion of Luxury and turns aside the sweet poison of Venus. The pleasing satisfaction from Chastity quenches incest's recurrent thirst, diverts the flow of lust and overcomes Dione's daughter not by argument but by flight.[12] Hippolytus[13] returns to life, a second Elias[14] comes on earth and another new Joseph[15] rivals the one of old.

Modesty, the mould and guardian of purity, adds her special endowment and the gift that surpasses the other gifts. But in giving it she does not forget due measure; indeed a limit encloses

[12] Dione's daughter is Venus. Flight was always the advice given to a man trying to escape the seductive charms of a woman.

[13] See Bk. I. n. 28.

[14] Elias, the Hebrew prophet, who worked so hard to restrain the excesses of contemporary rulers.

[15] The Joseph here is the spouse of the Blessed Virgin and the foster-father of Christ.

each and every thing by its definite control. She integrates the whole man, moderates his actions, measures his speech, determines his silences, weighs his attitudes, considers his habits and curbs his senses. She earnestly urges him to do nothing that would give rise to disgrace, that would cause shame to mark his brow[16] and feelings of guilt to rack his mind or infamy to impair his claim to fame. She shows what is to be kept a secret and from whom and when, and what should be told lest by silence he stifle what should be expressed[17] or, flush with too much talk, blurt out secrets and drawing the bolt, leave his mouth ajar. She outlines the correct posture for his head and tastefully raises his face to an equally correct level, lest with face aloft, turning towards the beings above, he seem to spurn our mortal race and disdain to look upon our type of life, or with face turned overmuch to earth, show the signs of an inactive and vacant mind. It is raised, then, to a somewhat moderately controlled position and neither rises nor falls beyond due measure. Constancy, making her wishes known, forbids buffoonish gestures, rejects an excessively grave gait lest wantonness betray the buffoon or excessive rigidness exhibit habitual pride. She warns the man not to stoop to thrusting forth base arms like a buffoon nor to work his forearms in unseemly gestures nor, in a display of pride, so to position his elbows that something bow-like is produced.[18] She secures his gait with regular tread to prevent him from mincing his steps and touching the earth with his toes but barely making contact with earth-bound things. Lest hair, over-ornamented with excessive treatment, reach the level of feminine excess and rob his sex of its honoured position, or lest it hang dishevelled, deformed by deep dirt and deprived of due

[16] Cf. Augustine, *Sermo* 160.5, *PL* 38.876.
[17] Cf. Gilbert of Poitiers, ed. N. M. Häring, 54.38.
[18] This seems to refer to the hands-on-hips stance.

attention, and show the youth too much of a philosopher, she insists on a style between both extremes and arranges the hair in a style of her own selection. She does not make the style of his dress shine with excessive splendour or degrade it with drabness; she observes the mean in all things. Lest the eye should hunt abroad what should be shunned or the ear, enchanted by the sweet singing of a honied voice, should lead the mind astray or the nose beguiled by a scent be lowered to debauchery, she disciplines the eyes and ears and curbs the nose. Lest the taste, revelling in sweet savour, beguile the mind with excessive flavour, she moderates the sense of taste. She arranges the sense of touch to prevent it from straying from the right path and inciting the mind within when, carrying the standards of our Dione's daughter, it goes abroad in search of preliminary bouts with Venus.[19]

Reason comes next with no less a supply of gifts and sheds every one of them on him. Now for the first time is she lavish with her presents; she who formerly was sparing with her gifts ceases to spare them; these gifts, however, return with interest. She admonishes him with warnings from a mature mind and bestows on the youth the character of a man full of years.[20] She instructs him not to adopt any sudden course of action, to undertake no venture without preparation, to think over every action first, to take thought before he acts and first examine his projects, to separate the true from the false, to distinguish between the honourable and the base, fleeing vice and pursuing virtue; to make promises rarely, to give more frequently — indeed to have the gift anticipate a request for it and not to leave the gift to be purchased at the price of a plea; if he promises anything, to make the gift equal to, or greater than, the promise,

[19] Cf. Bern. Silv., 2.14. 105-108.
[20] See Introduction p. 30.

lest a hope greater than the reality suppress the donee's joy. She tells him to have fulfilment follow close upon promise lest the gift come late and the donor's procrastinations take from the gift's value and the giver's favour and lessen the gift; not to dissipate his energies on various projects but to concentrate and fix his mind on one good, lest trying everything he attain nothing; not to let his mind rush everywhere in such a way that it is nowhere; not to let the new shoot wither from frequent transplantings; not to let the disease grow more resistant from experimenting with several remedies; not to let his opinions support everything to such an extent that they support nothing, so approve of all things that they lose every thing; not to seek stimulation from popular acclaim nor to reject it if it is tendered, unless it wears the colours of hypocrisy and tries by speech to cheat for profit: for the one who despises all acclaim smacks of excessive sternness; the one who, in his devotion to popular favour, seeks its each and every delight shows himself too impressionable. She warns him not to listen with credulous mind and an ear that drinks up approval to the praises of hypocrites, the lies of common talk, the sound of the flatterer's trappings when he lays on his sophistic phrases and, with a sweet song of praise, harps in the ear of the rich and offers praise for sale at the scales for gifts.

After the endowments and great gifts of Reason, Honesty unlocks her treasury and pronounces the youth the special keeper of her resources; she deposits with him all that she owns and transfers to him the right to all her goods. She advises him to shun those of ill-repute lest his reputation be subjected to strain or the proximity of contagion damage his good character, to flee vice, love Nature, condemning what villainy has spawned or an evil will has brought forth and embracing whatever Nature has created, guarding not against men but against monsters and shunning reproach; so to check vice as to refrain from impairing the noble things of creation; not to let his light be hidden and shine grudgingly for the common good nor his virtue be confined and produce less fruits; to have an interior life of his own which few have and an exterior life which many have, living his interior life for himself and his exterior life for the many; to regard himself as sprung from the world, show himself all things to all men[21] and know that in this he is wise; not to let the places frequented blacken his reputation, nor times nor manner of life nor abundance of goods render him suspect. Honour joins the above-mentioned, tinting the foregoing with her light and preventing them from suffering any unseemly blemish and she hallows everything with the grace of her gift. Decorum clothes all with her special dress, illumining the works of her sisters to the same extent as the rose brings honour to its kindred flowers, Lucifer to the fires of heaven, the carbuncle to the splendour of precious stones.

Phronesis, lending her aid, rains down all the gifts of Sophia. She does not bestow those riches which often blind the minds of the mighty, degrade the dignity of authority, impair laws and delay justice. Rather she gives a treasury of intellect and all riches of soul. The one who receives these will have no further need; indeed once enriched he ever has an abundance. The love of these riches is proper, the possession of them is noble, use of them is advantageous, distribution of them is even more advantageous and their fruits are abundant. This is the store-house of heaven, the treasury of the sky, the overflowing favour which enriches the learned, in lavish spirit seeks generous possessors and disdains the miserly. Hoarded it vanishes; scattered abroad it returns. Unless it is converted to the general good, it slips away and gathers great force as it goes. Rust does not eat away these riches nor fire devour them nor pilfering thieves lessen them nor shipwreck sink them nor robbers seize them nor

[21] 1 Corinthians 9.22.

enemies deplete them. Not only does Phronesis bestow her own gifts: she goes further and bids her hand-maidens bring forward whatever they can and indulge in a kind of contest in pouring out their gifts. The introductory discipline of Grammar fulfils Sophia's injunctions and comes down in her entirety to the youth. She is not thus reduced in standing but rather grows greater and gains stature in him. To the youth's endowment she contributes everything that her rules determine, her canons prescribe and the judgments of her preceptive art enjoins, so that he may not coin words without regard for grammar or make mistakes in speech like a barbarian. Thus he follows the path of correct speech and correct writing,[22] a path marked by no barbarisms, acquires that art, condemns errors and preserves inflections. The band of poets, pouring nectar from the Pegasean spring[23] over the man, teach him how to join words in metrical feet and compose a poem in pleasing rhythm.

Logic with cunning power comes next and is not chilled by her puny[24] gift: indeed she is all-agog to strew her riches on him and removes all checks on her gift-giving. She teaches him how to enter the subtle battle of reason, check the opposing party, smash the forces of the adversary, use reason to protect his own side, track down truth, rout falsehood, rebut schismatic and heretical brethren and pseudo-logicians by logic and expose sophists.

At hand are the refinements of Rhetoric and its ornaments of style by which words shine like stars, a discourse clothes itself in beauty and the conclusion shines in a flood of light.[25] These resources for a discourse, these refinements and beauty of

[22] Cf. John of Salisbury, *Met.* 1.12, ed. Webb. 31.

[23] Hippocrene, the fountain of the Muses. The winged steed, Pegasus, by a blow of his hoof caused the spring to open on Mt. Helicon.

[24] Logic by herself was of little consequence. See Bk. 1. n. 18.

[25] Cf. Boeth., *De Cons.* 2. pr. 1.21 (Stewart-Rand 174).

speech, the power of Rhetoric spreads abroad. It adorns the youth's speech and makes his words distinguished by many a change of style. She tells him to make his utterances concise, to compress deep thoughts within a brief discourse, to encompass much in few words, not to ramble on in a prolix harangue but work towards the end that his speech be brief, the ideas rich in meaning, the discourse eloquent and fruitful in a large offspring of ideas.[26] Or if, perhaps, the discourse runs on in a torrent of words, let the ideas flash farther still,[27] let the abundant harvest serve as an excuse for the forest of foliage, the yield of rich grain compensate for the floating chaff and the sense for the loquacity.

That art[28] bestows its resources, the art which enquires, according to definite laws, into the seeds of things, their compacts, their interpenetration, their causes and their bonds, investigates numbers and every result of theirs by which all things are held fast and are drawn together by their alternations and all things are bound together at once by numbers and keep the peace as agitation disappears. Thus laying bare the secrets she had from Minerva, she makes the man her heir, reveals to him all she possesses that can be known, all that her power pours forth, to let him know what is the rationale of numbers, what efficacy and power are in numbers, what force so great holds sway in numbers that a stable bond binds everything by a knot of number.

Music uncovers her riches, grants the man her gifts with right goodwill, adopts him and assigns all her goods to him as to an heir. She shows him which voice clashes with which, which harmonises with which. She teaches him the affinities of voices, the contentions of sounds, which voice attracts the ear, which intoxicates it.

[26] Longinus, *On the Sublime* 7.3., says that there is no sublimity in a piece of writing, "if the thoughts which it suggests do not extend beyond what is actually expressed."

[27] The imagery is from a thunder-storm. The flash of lightning can be seen far beyond the rains and the sound of the thunder.

[28] Arithmetic.

That art[29] unfolds her hands and stretches them out with gifts, the art which measures the space of earth, the expanse of sea, the movements of the air on high, measures the boundaries of the heavens and marks every heavenly body by definite limits. The high does not hinder her, the unmeasurable does not slow her, the deep does not hold her back. She teaches the youth how to enclose the earth in space, measure the air, fix the limits of the sea, encompass the sky within boundaries and describe the round shape of the earth.

The science of the stars arranges to take lodging with him and finds no chamber more pleasing. She teaches him what movements govern the heavenly bodies, sets the stars in motion and what spirit stirs the orb of heaven. By the glory of this pure gift, Wisdom enriches the man and sets a distinguishing mark on him. With a more god-like breath, however, the divine science of heaven,[30] the way of truth that knows not falsehood, the science which, rejoicing in its dependence on Faith alone, relies on no art and refuses to take refuge in human reason, smiled charmingly on him when the heavenly fire still kept his soul among the beings above and her serene brightness suffused him and he was not yet subject to the pressures of our lower air and the repulsiveness of our world. She teaches him to follow what is of heaven, avoid what is transitory, live by the law of heaven,[31] direct his mind on high, shrink from the earth, ascend in mind to heaven, check the violent outbursts of the body, combat the excesses of the flesh and bring unlawful tendencies into subjection to reason.

Piety coming next gives her entire self and offers herself as a

[29] Geometry.

[30] Theology.

[31] For the *ius poli* as opposed to the *ius fori*, see *Dialogus Ratii et Everardi, ed. N. M. Häring, Mediaeval Studies* 15 (1953) 250.

gift; she hands over so much to the man that he, now the foster-child of so much pious affection, is thought to be Piety herself. She teaches him to plane away blemishes from the mind, get rid of all the clouds of hatred, let his mind become tractable; if it is once anointed with the oil of piety let it be in such a way that his firm and constant mind never stray from the right, lest, if the youth slackens in piety, he grow soft, the softness feminise great deeds and the weakened mind lose its manly firmness. She teaches him to regard as his own the tears, troubles and misfortunes of the unhappy, not to consider himself happy while he sees the grounds for grief persist in so many cases. She instructs him to defend widows, console the unhappy, support the needy, feed the destitute and befriend orphans.[32]

Adding her gifts, Faithfulness by many an endowment proves that she is the Faithful One; she reserves to herself no part of herself, rather, she produces everything and her gifts argue that she is faithful. She teaches him to avoid deceit, to despise fraud, to keep with inviolate loyalty pacts of friendship, the law of trust, the plight of love, not to hide under a deceptive name the role of false friend or hypocrite. She further warns the man not to seek friends who will be footmen of fortune, move off, stand by or flee with her, follow the changes of events and fate, leave with the fleeting Spring of fortune and shun the Winter and the storm-clouds of misfortune. She instructs the youth never to buy a friend by a bribe or hunt for love with a gift as bait, for love procured at a price disappears when favours cease and friendship lasts as long as the largess. Such love continues as long as it can contribute to the size of the gift. There is no true Faithfulness there where a bribe bestows love; it is not love

[32] The services listed here formed part of the knight's code. See H. O. Taylor, *The Mediaeval Mind*, (Cambridge, Mass. 1949), Vol. 1.517-573. The defence of widows is enjoined in *Isaias* 1.17.

that bestows the gift when the market-value of the thing given and the usefulness of the gift are put in the scales to weigh the love. She warns him to ignore the venal procedure of request and bequest and seek a friend he can so embrace in true love and inviolate loyalty that his love wins the love of the other and the other's love brings in new loves. Let appreciation, she advises, respond to appreciation: let there be a mutual bond of friendship which neither Fortune, acting the step-mother, can dissolve nor misfortune shake nor fame break; let him seek one to whom he can entrust himself completely, make known his wishes and reveal his whole mind, to whom he can entrust the secrets of his innermost soul, so that, storing his treasure of mind in him, he has no secret that he would not reveal to him, in order that his friend from a token of this kind may weigh his friendship and repay it in the same measure.

Next comes the virtue[33] which takes delight in scattering gifts and pouring out wealth and spreading abroad a mass of riches. She refuses to suckle property or feed cash; neither does she allow treasure to lie idle and inactive in her possession nor glut her purse with coins but compels it to disgorge whatever money it has at any time swallowed. Once she was very frugal, now she is lavish to one person, surpasses herself and outdoes her own powers in regard to him. She urges him to keep his mind aloof from all gifts; drop them from his hands[34] and not succumb to the love of riches; spurning wealth in his soul and triumphing over it in his mind, to trample on riches in such a way as to prevent their trampling on him; not to let his hand reach quickly out for bribes, not to let the snare of avarice close with tight grip on the gift in hand, not to send gifts in quest of a corresponding recompense; not to thirst for gain nor let a gift

[33] Largitas — Generosity.

[34] Reading *manu*.

given successfully beg rewards but to pour out gifts far and wide without hope of return and let nobility alone and simple kindness of soul condition the present and season the use of the gift.

After the others Fortune's daughter, Nobility, kinswoman of Chance that is ever at hand, would have willingly and gladly given her gifts, if anything entirely her own, that she could by Nature's law control, had fallen to her lot. But since she has power over nothing except what Fortune supplies, she does nothing without consulting Fortune: in fact the daughter decides to make her way to her mother's abode, sets out on her journey and successfully makes her way over the long road.

There is a rock in mid-ocean on which the sea forever beats, which the conflicting waves charge, which is harassed in various ways and pounded with a never-ending assault. Now it is totally hidden, buried in the waves; now shaking off the sea, it breathes in the air above. It maintains no one aspect; minute after minute transforms it with successive changes. When Zephyrus[35] blows his gentle breath over everything, the rock sprouts choice flowers and rejoices in an abundance of greenery. But soon fierce Boreas[36] ravishes the flowers and ruins the greenery: *finis*[37] is written to the flower's history just as it opens and the flower is mocked by a moment of life. In the same way raging Aquilo[38] plunders everything, mows down the flowers with the sword of cold and wipes out a former joy. Here grows a varying grove and trees that differ. This remains barren, that one bears fruit; one rejoices in renewed foliage, another leafless laments;

[35] West-wind.

[36] Borth-wind.

[37] *Explicit* is not strictly a Latin word. It is found at the end of Mss. and is probably ab abbreviation for *explicitum est* or *explicitus est* (sc. *liber*), *the work is finished.* The use of the word goes back at least as far as the time of St. Jerome. See *Ep.* 28.4, *CSEL*, 54.229.6. The corresponding word at the beginning of a Ms. is *incipit.*

[38] Aquilo is really the Greek *βορέας*, the North or slightly N.N.E. wind.

one flourishes, quite a few wither; one blooms, others are bloomless; some rise on high, the rest hug the ground; one sprouts, the others decay. Thus various accidents alter them and they all alternate in successive changes. The fall of the dice brings here many things that run counter to the normal.[39] The cedar, brought low, and sinking to a pygmy's height, ceases to be a giant and the dwarf myrrh assumes giant stature: thus one takes the form of the other. The laurel pines, the myrtle bears fruit; the olive withers, the willow becomes fruitful, the pear tree is barren, the apple-tree is bereft of fruit, while in produce the elm contends with the vine. Here the thorn-hedge, armed with its darts, threatens careless hands with wounds and the prickly yew hurts them. Here Philomena rarely sings, the lark seldom thrills: more often the horned-owl, the harbinger of misfortune and herald of grief, foretells sad chance. Here two streams[40] flow down, differentiated by unlike rising-places, different appearance, diverse shades of colour, dissimilar taste and separate source-springs. One has very sweet water, gives honey-sweet draughts, leads many astray by its sweetness. A draught of its waters causes a greater thirst for them; it intoxicates those who drink from it, nay while the water is slaking thirst, it is producing it; a drink from the stream gives a thirst for the stream and it causes dropsy in countless drinkers. It bickers along with faint murmur, murmurs in a sweet whisper and flows

[39] *per antifrasim.* See Mart. Cap., 4.360. Alan uses the phrase loosely. It refers to a contradiction between the literal and actual meaning of a word, e.g. *Parcae, the ones who spare,* means the Fates who spare no one. Cf. Jerome, *Ep.* 7. 8, *CSEL* 55.115; Augustine, *De Doctrina Christiana* 3.29.41, *PL* 34.81. The connection of *Parcae* with *parcere* has no etymological basis.

[40] The account of the streams comes from Mart. Cap., 1.1-15. The account there is more straightforward and easier to understand. There are three streams of Fortune, connected by rivulets; an amount of water keeps flowing from one stream to another. Alan's account is extreme and gloomy. There is unadulterated joy or unadulterated woe and the joy lasts but a short time.

over the rock in a quiet stream. At the head of this river many keep their place and there is no opening for them to go further. They scarcely touch and barely taste the sweet waters of the river. They long to feast further on this great delicacy, they long to be more fully immersed in the stream, to have all their limbs drenched in its waters.[41] Others go further: these an ampler stream holds immersed in a deep eddy and deeper water carries them along. However, when they have been touched with the great sweetness of the stream, a gentle wave carries them back and sets them on the bank again.

The other river tumbles down in fast-flowing fall, black with sulphurous waters. The water by its bitterness causes wormwood to grow and its raging heat resembles a furnace. Its colour clashes with the eyes, its flavour with the taste, its crash with the ears. Zephyrus does not ripple these waters but Boreas, making the waters heave from their depths, raises them to mountain height, proclaiming a war between the waves and involving kinsfolk in battle. On the river's bank floods of tears are overwhelming many who are afraid of being sunk in the deep torrent of the raging river and of having to bear the violence of its flood. Many people go down into this stream, are buried in the deep waters and are carried along by the swollen river. The flowing water now sucks men in, now spews them out. Those it plunges into the waters, these it allows a short respite, but the abyss so sucks in most that they cannot retrace their steps and escape to the world above and no tracks are left to mark the way back. This river, running with various windings, enters the flood of very sweet water,[42] forces that stream to degenerate and makes it share its corruption. The cloudy darkens the clear, the bitter sours the sweet, the warm spoils the cool, the fetid ruins the fragrant.

[41] Reading *perfundi.*

[42] Reading *predulcis aquae.*

BOOK VIII

The house[1] of Fortune, clinging on high to a sheer rock and threatening to tumble down, sinks into a steep slope. It is subject to every raging wind and bears the brunt of every tempest of heaven. Rarely does the gentle breeze of Zephyrus make that house calm and clear and rather seldom does its soft, kind breath wipe out the storms of Notus[2] and the cold of Boreas. One part of the house sits atop the mountain rock, the other crouches on the rock's base and as though on the verge of sliding off, shows signs of falling. One part of the house glitters with silver, shines with gems, is alight with gold; the other part lies debased with worthless material. The former part prides itself on its lofty roof; the latter stands uncovered in a gaping cleft. Here is Fortune's abode, if indeed the unstable ever abides, the wandering takes up residence, the moving becomes fixed. For Fortune complete rest is flight, permanence is change, to stand still is to revolve, to be in a fixed position is to run to and fro, a fall is an ascent. For her reasoned procedure is to be without reason, reliability is to be reliably unreliable, devotion is to be devotedly undevoted. She is fickle, unreliable, changeable, uncertain, random, unstable, unsettled. When one thinks that she has taken a stand, she falls and with a counterfeit smile she feigns joy. She is rough in her gentleness, overcast in her light, rich and poor, tame and savage, sweet and bitter. She weeps as she smiles, roams around as she stands, is blind as she sees. She is constant in fickleness,

[1] It is very difficult to get a clear idea of a house from a writer's description of it. There are more than thirty reconstructions of Pliny's Laurentine Villa, all based on the detailed account given by him in *Ep.* 2.17.

[2] The South-wind was warmish but was not liked because of the heavy rains and wind-storms that accompanied it. Ovid, *Am.* 1.14.12, *Met.* 1. 264; Vir., *Aen.* 6.355. Boreas, the north-wind is traditionally associated with cold.

steadfast in faltering, true to falsehood, false to truth, unchangeable in changeability. She keeps this constant rule — that she is not constant; she faithfully maintains this one principle — that she knows not how to be faithful; she remains true to this one tenet — that she always proves false; she is settled on this one thing — that she ever goes her unsettled way. Her appearance with its twofold aspect misleads the viewer. The front of her head is covered with a rich growth of hair, the back bemoans its baldness. One eye dances mischievously, the other overflows with tears; the latter is dull and heavy, the former sparkles. Part of her face is alive, aflame with natural colour; part is dying in the grip of pallor; as the charm of the countenance fades, the face grows dull and its beauty melts away. One hand gives a gift, the other takes it away; one increases the gift, the other[3] diminishes it; one offers it, the other withdraws it; one hand grips tightly, the other loosens its grip. Her steps are unequal, retrograde, reeling, wandering: as she advances she goes backwards; at once fast and slow on her feet, she falls far back as she goes forward. Now she shines forth in finer toga, now slumming, she wallows in the clothes of the poor; now left without a dress to her name, she offers herself to the public and is seen bemoaning her honours of old. She keeps her wheel in fast motion and no rest brings an end to the toil of movement, no leisure-time stops the motion.[4] For when that labour, as it often does, tires her right hand, her left hand takes its place, comes to the aid of its weary sister and plies the wheel in faster motion. Its whirl is ravenous, its swoop is fast, its attack on two fronts. It envelops mankind, exempts no one from its downward spin but forces all to put up with the antics of fate and drives

[3] Reading *haec*.

[4] See the representations of "Fortune et sa roue", Plates 65-86 in P. Courcelle, *La Consolation de Philosophie dans la Tradition Littéraire* (Paris 1967).

men down into all kinds of misfortune. It increases the pressure on some, lightens the burden for others; hurls some down, raises others up. While Croesus[5] is at the top of the wheel, Codrus[6] is at the bottom. Julius[7] is on his way up, Magnus[8] on his way down, and Sulla[9] is at the bottom. Marius[10] is coming up but, with a turn of the wheel, Sulla is on his way back and Marius is being forced down. Thus the wheel sweeps everything up in turn and spiralling Fortune changes our fates.

Gay Nobility makes her way to Fortune's territory that is marked by the above-mentioned ensemble, greets her mother on arrival, touches briefly on the reason for her journey and in humble prayer beseeches her mother, if she holds anything outstanding and worthy of approbation that might grace a work of virtue and suit the product of Nature, not to deny her this thing. She points out that what Nature makes, grace makes anew,[11] character moulds, virtue shapes, prudence enriches, sense of duty endows, dignity favours, goodness adorns, reason crowns, beauty sets apart and the virtues en masse rush to its service.

[5] Last king of Lydia. So many anecdotes were current about his wealth in Roman times that his name was used to designate a wealthy man. Ovid, *Tr.* 3.7.42. Cf. Bern. Silv., 1.3.41.

[6] A king of Athens of dubious historicity. There is a reference to his poverty in Bern. Silv., 1.3.41. Cf. Juvenal 3.208. For the *summa* and *infima*, see Boeth., *De Cons.* 2. pr. 2.30 (Stewart-Rand 180).

[7] Julius Caesar.

[8] See Bk. 2. n. 31.

[9] A brilliant, but ruthless and dissolute politician and commander who went so far as to lead an army on Rome and capture it. Power for a time see-sawed between him and Marius but Marius was finally defeated and murdered.

[10] Marius, like Sulla, had a long and involved career as an army man and political figure. Alan's reference is probably to the question of the command in the war in the East. Sulla had the command. Marius intrigued with Sulpicius Rufus who passed a law transferring the command to Marius. Sulla resorted to arms to annul the transfer. Marius fled to Africa.

[11] For the important concept of *creare* and *recreare*, see *Expositio Prosae de Angelis* and *Sermo de Trinitate*, M. T. D'Alverny, *Textes Inédits, 200, 216, 224, 258.*

After this statement Fortune, lightening the gravity of her countenance with a restrained smile, replied to her daughter as follows:—

"The act of Nature, the product of virtue, does not need our work. So distinguished a work of God, enriched by each and every endowment of Nature and blessed by divine gifts, needs no act on our part and lacks no power that would bring it honour. What will the god of chance be able to do where nothing is subject to chance? What can I ever changing do where permanence protects the object? What can I, ever on the move, do where the object is fixed and firm? What can the inconstant do where everything remains constant? Gold does not need iron nor light darkness. In the same way the act of Nature, the work of virtue, the product of the heavenly Artisan does not need my help and does not call for the services of my skill. Yet, lest envy seem to goad me to rage against this good work or pride to stay me, I will bring gifts. Such as they are, I do not hold back any of them, lest the giver rather than the gifts be put to shame and the defects in the gifts be charged to a counterfeit giver. I will add what is mine, if indeed anything may be called mine or I may properly be said to give anything to anyone. God forbid that I should give anything: rather I lend my services for a time and never have I given anything that I could not regain at will. However, in this instance I will try to overcome my defects and gain myself strength. I will change my native trickery and put aside the irksome changes connected with me. I will make myself stable, cutting out change as far as I can. I will set about becoming sagacious, wise, discreet, truthful and steadfast — I, who so far have been foolish, improvident, lying, precipitate; I will change my former habit of aberration and for a short while will be proud of my work".

After this Fortune eagerly set out on her perilous course and hastens on the journey she has begun. Nobility accompanies her on her journey and follows her mother's steps. Passing over the road of ill-defined edges, doubting her direction, led by chance, instructed by error, Fortune went in search of Nature's home. Wandering, rushing, changing, straying, she finally and with difficulty chanced upon it. The whole court was surprised and astonished at her arrival. Although the change of dress, déclassé look, random motions might well terrify the viewer and turn the dumbfounded mind from the right path, still Nature does not tremble in fear. At sight of Fortune she is struck with a momentary astonishment but her firm presence of mind does not forsake her. With Fortune, then, prescribing limits, Nobility brings forth the gifts and endowments and graces with her favour a youth blessed by Nature's gift, virtue's service, heaven's[12] bequest, prostrated by no taint of sin. Yet her gifts shine with less splendour when placed side by side with the previous ones; indeed they scarce show any splendour when they are crowded by objects of brighter light. Thus the lesser flame seems dim beside the furnace; thus a star, when it shares the sky with Phoebus, lies unseen. However, as an honour and token of favour, he has conferred on him impressive nobility, illustrious lineage, free-born parents, unrestricted liberty, noble birth. As Fortune proceeds to lay out other endowments, Reason stands beside the giver, lest perhaps the gifts of this one spoil those of the previous givers and the glory of many objects should be lost by the defects of one. She does not allow Fortune to besprinkle prosperity with adversity, joy with sorrow. She compels her to be false to herself, takes her natural self away from her, makes the false true, the untrustworthy trustworthy, the slack firm.

[12] Reading *coelesti.*

makes the blind to see and the wanderer to settle down for a while. Fortune, then, bestows her resources but Reason does not allow her gifts to go beyond, or fall below, due measure:[13] she measures the wealth and weighs all the riches, lest, if too great a flow of these pour forth, it drag the mind down headlong, the torrent of wealth engulf it, turn it aside to unlawful practices and emasculate its actions.

That heavenly and divine being had now been made perfect in all things. Slippery Rumour was already crying the work of Nature throughout the world and the report had already reached many ears. Gloomy Allecto shuddered at these reports. She did not, however, give them easy credence but she is finally compelled to believe them against her will, when events and rumour force acceptance. She wails that wiles are listless, she moans that groans are stilled, she is pained that pains are dulled. When man rejoices, she weeps; when the world laughs, she mourns; when the world blooms, she droops; when virtue blossoms, she withers; when human affairs flourish, she pines; when man is in charge, she is in exile.

The above-mentioned pest without warning sends out a call for her attendant pests. At her command there gather together in united assembly[14] the lords of Tartarus,[15] the rulers of night, the

[13] For *ultra ... citrave*, see Thierry of Chartres, ed. N. M. Häring, 573.

[14] The members of Allecto's council here are based on her council in Claud., *In Ruf.* 1.28-38. From here to 9.379, there is considerable confusion and signs of hasty and unrevised writing. When Alan proceeds to deal with the Vices in detail, he keeps much of Claudian's terminology but follows the method (but not the divisions) of Prudentius in the *Psychomachia.* A number of prominent Vices are named; each has a retinue of minor Vices. There is an account of the marshalling of the hosts of Vices and of the actual battle. Fiery Licentiousness is featured prominently in the marshalling but does not appear in the battle. Foolishness (*Stultitia*) appears as a prominent Vice with a retinue in the marshalling; in the battle she appears in the retinue of Imprudence (*Imprudentia*), who is not listed in the marshalling. The Sting of the Flesh (*Carnis Stimulus*) takes part in the battle but is not mentioned in the marshalling. The same holds true for Need (*Carentia*),

fosterers of iniquity, the artificers of crime, the teachers of mischief, loss,[16] trickery, fraud, want, theft, robbery, violence, anger, rage, hatred, discord, quarrels, disease, gloom, wantonness, excess, poverty, extravagance, pride, envy, fear, old age. This storm of crime, mob of vice, assembly of evil, multiple plague and public pestilence rushes down to the halls of Tartarus, where Erinys holds sway, Allecto gives orders and Megaera dictates the laws. When the raging mob, discordant tribe, dissonant assembly, motley multitude, unsightly race had taken their seats Allecto, with voice swollen with pride and words bespeaking haughtiness, while a murmur was still making the rounds of the audience, breaks into the following speech:

> "What mean this justice, this order, this restraint? Whence this quiet? What is this great rage for peace that Nature should decide to outlaw our enactments, have the world serve her, condemn the guilty, protect the just, although our power is greater than her strength and Nature identifies herself with the lower elements less than our conclave does? Subdued so often by the laws of our regime, will she

Weeping (*Fletus)*, Moan (*Gemitus*), Wailing (*Planctus*), Tears (*Lacrimae*). Misfortune (*Casus*) is with Lowliness (*Ignobilitas*) in the marshalling but with Grief (*Luctus*) in the battle. Defects (*Defectus*) changes from Discord (*Discordia*) to Old Age (*Senectus*): however, its meaning with Discord is probably Defections. In 9.329 we find "What remains? Fraud alone". At 9.353, having dealt with Fraud, he proceeds to give an account of Avarice. Discord is "the one who has been the chief cause of the mad folly, the one who first lit the fires of trouble" at 9.30. At 9.270 Excess (or Venus, if we read *quae* for *qui*) "was the outstanding figure in the battle and the beginning and origin of the entire war".

In his other works Alan gives the traditional Christian theories on Virtues and Vices. See *De Arte Praed.*, 114D-174B; *Reg.* 667C; *Sermo de Trinitate*, M. T. d'Alverny, *Textes Inédits*, 257-259; *Sermo de Sph. Int.*, *Ib.* 306. Any attempt to fit the Virtues and Vices of the Anticlaudianus into a Christian framework would involve more of a strain than the words could stand.

[15] The penal department of Hades.

[16] *Teachers* applies only to mischief, not to the rest of the list.

still be able to effect a change again and bind our neck in chains? For shame! Will incest be gone and modesty in power? Will crime languish and a sense of duty rule the world? Will avarice concede victory if the enemy of avarice should pour out her gifts everywhere? Will the official voice of fraud be silenced, while honesty holds sway in the land? Will resentment submit to a silence imposed by peace? Will peace quietly dislodge our regime to which protective prescription of such long standing establishes our claim, which actual possession bestows on us and guards what is bestowed by a just title? But shame on us if we join the train of justice, we whom it ill befits to live a life of justice or turn to supplication. Instead of law, then, we must choose force; let violence instead of virtue be our standard. It is fitting that we should adopt might instead of right, dictate armed revolution and write laws in blood. Mother Nature has armed one youth, without experience in war and inferior in strength to take the field against us who are mature in years and lords of war. In the same way a young stag vents its rage on a bear, a twig takes up arms against the oaks, a vale against the mountains, a hare against young hounds, does against the tiger. If we should wish to check the strong by the strong and to hammer out a nail with a nail,[17] could not one sent by us thwart anyone, one whom Tisiphone has cherished from her earliest youth and Erinys suckled at her own breasts? Could not a new Sulla,[18] a second Nero[19] prevail over the laws, another Rufinus[20] again stir up the ancient frenzies, a

[17] There is a Latin proverb, coming from Greek, *clavo clavum eicere, to drive out one nail by another.* Cicero quotes it in connection with dislodging one love by another: *Tusc.* 4.35.75.

[18] See n. 9 supra.

[19] See Bk. I. n. 35.

[20] See Introduction, p. 33.

new Catiline[21] upset the world? But if our tribe is united together, it will the better wipe out Nature's new onslaughts, will humble her fresh pride, returning what has been aloft to its old ruins. With uniform din, then, unified warfare, similar fury, let us carry strife and wars to him who, though alone and a boy with too little realisation of the nature of war, is being armed against us and the tamarisk seeks to destroy the cedars."

When she had said this the entire crowd with a shout proclaim their assent and vow to follow their mistress wherever it may lead. Fulfilment follows hard upon vow. Discord thirsts for the arms of war, is first to long for the commotion and prepares to take part in the preliminary skirmishes of the first battle. Her servants stand by, carry out her orders as she gives them and make ready the insignia of war for their mistress. Envy supplies the horses, Rage the chariot, Fury the arms, Violence as charioteer, Contention as armbearer, Anger as attendant, advance in front their mistress. Terror, however, keeps at her right side as she advances and Damage clings to her left; Defection follows after her; Death, with his tread that brings life's sunset, marches in the rear and Death's faithful Achates,[22] Pallor, and Slaughter accompanied by unremitting

[21] Brother-in-law of Marius whom he murdered as Sulla's lieutenant. He was an ambitious demagogue. There was always enough suspicion attaching to him to prevent his being elected consul but not enough evidence to secure a conviction against him, particularly when he had the aid of prosecutors like Clodius. Finally he took up the cause of the luckless and dissatisfied, espousing equally the cause of the bankrupt veterans of Sulla and the owners whose land had been grabbed for them. This did not get him the consulate. He then organised a conspiracy, involving elements throughout Italy. He fled from Rome and joined a band of outlaws in Etruria. Sufficient proof of his conspiracy was obtained and the leaders were put to death. An army marched out against Catiline. He was defeated and killed near Pistoria in 62 B.C.

[22] Faithful companion of Aeneas.

Grief. These are the companions that Discord drags to the fray; she alerts all of them and instils in her allies the love of war.

After these, Poverty,[23] originating with the lower classes, takes up arms and goes along with hanging head, poor attire, sad tread but reckless of her life. Shaken by no fear of death, broken by no dread, she rushes in and anxious to sell her life for the death of many, shows unusual daring since the poor and needy know no fear. She goes as a foot-soldier, surrounded by a countless crowd of infantry: to her standards rushes the crowd from the proletarian cohort — Pain, Toil, Thirst, Hunger, Fasting,[24] Cares. Infamy follows next, surrounded by her own monsters. Her standards are borne by Contagion of life, censurable Acts, Life of notorious tendencies; Contempt accompanies her, Shame clings to her steps, Murmur creeps along the ground, Reproach hurries along, Fame,[25] reversing her role, overflows in praise and loud Laughter breaks into smiles. Mor-

[23] Some have expressed surprise at finding Poverty listed as a vice. Huizinga(75) thinks that this would be the attitude towards Poverty before Europe felt the influence of St. Francis of Assisi. De Lage(56) explains its presence among the Vices by the fact that it is plebeian. The Virtues in Book 1 are personifications of qualities or factors that would help in the formation of a perfect body. The Vices here include anything that could injure the New Man. However, he now a soul and is open to attack on a second level and can be aided by Virtues of a different kind. Apart from this, Poverty in itself is an evil and a breeder of Vice. The Poverty of Spirit mentioned in the Gospel (St. Matt. 5.3) is detachment from worldly goods. Alan gives the traditional Christian teaching on Poverty in *Sent.* 248A-C.

[24] This is more difficult to explain. Fasting appears as a Virtue in Prud., *Psycho.* 244. It certainly has the approbation of Scripture in both the Old and New Testament. Its apponent in 9.105 is *Saties, Abundance.* As it appears in the retinue of Poverty, it could mean the Fasting necessary to make a small amount of food last a long time. It is also possible that Alan was covertly inveighing against the extremely large number of days on which Christians were bound to fast. See list in Du Cange, 4.285-288. Alan realised that there were many indifferent and evil types of Fasting and only a few good types. See *De Arte Praed.* 176D-178C.

[25] Fame should celebrate the good; here she praises the evil. The word-play between *Fama* and *Infamia* is typical of Alan.

bid, sad, trembling, weak Old Age,[26] full of years, leaning on a staff, without the support of strength of mind, stirs up wars and in the heat of a new war grows young again. Weakness, Disease, Weariness, Boredom, Failure accompany Old Age on his[27] way: they are afire with love of war and wish to live the life of the camp. Grief is inflamed as he rushes into arms; clad in a rent mantle, bedewed with tears, he furrows his face with his nails. Gloom, Lament, Sorrow, Depression, Disaster are enthusiastic in his service, profess their military allegiance to their master: ministers and king together are hot for war. Fiery Licentiousness, attended by a large clientele fans her native fires to a hot love for war. Perjury takes an oath to help her, false Love vows its aid as do Fickleness of mind, lying Wantonness, insipid Sweetness, savoury Sorrow, sick Pleasure, adverse Prosperity, sad Joke, bitter Joy, rich Poverty, poor Wealth. After the others Excess presents himself, mounted on a superb steed, proud of gesture, outstanding in attire, with a superfluity of talk, corruptive in action. He comes before the furore of war and supplies all with resentments to justify the war. Under his leadership, Drunkenness, Pride, Boasting, Indigestion, Pomp carry their standard and voice threats of war.

The ever-present tinder-box of evil deeds,[28] the tyrant of the flesh, the goad to sin, the flame of transgression, the source of guilt, the enemy and plunderer of our reason flies into a great rage for battle and a fury for war: Guilt, Malevolence, unlawful Passion, ruinous Pleasure take up arms to help him. No smaller host, no less packed assembly of chiefs equip Foolishness with arms: her companions are Laziness, Frivolity, Indolence, trifling

[26] The appearance of Old Age as a Vice makes the sense in which *Vice* is used quite clear.

[27] Although *Senectus* feminine, Alan was thinking of its embodiment as an old man as the *domini* of line 258 shows.

[28] Lust.

Talk, Chatter, Leisure, Sleep. Impiety shows no less rage; priding herself on her large army, she thirsts for war with deeper longing and rejoices to find no passage except by shedding blood. Iniquity, Massacre, Crime, Violence, Slaughter dwell in her camp and acknowledge her leadership in war. With darts in her quiver and deceitful bow, Fraud is armed and shows her rage. Her companions are twofaced Deceit, Craft, unlawful Artifice, deceptive Cunning. A more evil band of clients accompanies Avarice - constant Worry, greedy Usury, foul Robbery. She, with sleepless care and avid mind, reckons which money is out hunting for wealth, which lies idle in the strongbox and is not serving the interests of its mistress. Lowliness,[29] follows her, Disgrace follows Lowliness' footsteps, Rejection clings to her, Scourge is ever present, Scarcity applauds, Failure dogs her steps. Burdensome, dejected and spiteful though she is, she gains more favour with her mother, Fortune, and pleases her more than Nobility: the love for Nobility grows proportionately colder and more languid and Mother Fortune wishes she could change her former deeds; she gives complete preference to her second child and tries to undo what was formerly done.

Rumour, carrying her news, takes wing and wedding falsehood to truth, announces that the Furies have joined in conspiracy against the gods above, the realms of the dead against heaven, that the Manes[30] and the lord of Erebus[31] have unloosed Tartarean Chaos, reject the rule of Erebus' brother[32] and no longer grant peace to the world. She invents horrendous things as she tells of things more horrible than monsters, piles

[29] *Ignobilitas*. She has neither the advantages of noble birth nor a plentiful supply of the goods of her mother, Fortune.

[30] Spirits of the dead.

[31] Pluto.

[32] Night.

crime on crime, adds fury to the Furies and proclaims that the Eumenides have more than their usual power. She fills out the rage of Tisiphone and increases the fury of Megaera. A more cruel Pluto arises from below; Erinys[33] looms larger; the janitor[34] of the underworld no longer has three heads, he now assumes a hundred. Allecto doubles her quota of snakes.

Nature stands firm in her intention and is not shaken by any harassment of fear. She rids her mind of dread, her spirits rise, her readiness for war is intensified, and the same attitude takes possession of the Virtues. The celestial hero arms himself, the blessed offspring of the heavenly beings who is to face this great contest alone in a new kind of war. The Virtues give the hero arms, supply him with strength and equip one man with all their insignia. Peace gives greaves, Probity grants spurs, Piety a breastplate, Prudence a helmet, true Faith a missile, Reason a sword, Constancy a shield. Hope bestows horses, guiltless Fear adds the reins, Concord fulfills the duty of arm-bearer, Rumour, like a crier, sounds the trumpet and crowns the hero's glory with praise. Reason fights on his right; Constancy takes her place on his left. Modesty arranges the entire throng and Prudence checks the din of the infantry. In like fashion each and every Virtue bears arms, swears to aid the hero, gives every honour of Mars to the youth whom Nature is sending to war, grants him their excellence in war and their role in the struggle.

Already the plagues of Erebus, the contaminators of crime, the monsters of the underworld, Pluto's subjects, the fosterlings of night, Tartarean Chaos, come forth, pour over the earth; already they are wrapping our day in the thick darkness of night and struggle to extinguish the bright light of the world.[35] Light

33 Tisiphone, Megaera, Erinys refer to the Furies.

34 Cerberus. Apparently Alan did not know that, according to one tradition, Cerberus had a hundred heads. See Hor., *Car.* 2.13.34.

35 Erebus was the brother and husband of Night.

itself is astonished at the strange onslaughts and at the fact that night itself has now more than its usual power and a longer duration and does not observe its proper cycle nor make way for Phoebus. Light, however, balances its losses by this one consideration - that on the other side unending light abides, cut off by no darkness and there is uninterrupted day where that heavenly assembly, the band of Virtues and the ranks of Nature, are under arms. Now the lines of battle are in view of each other; now enemy beholds enemy and the sight inflames their souls with rage. Their spirits begin to take fire; a growing feeling of boldness excites their minds; resentment flares up; already in imagination the squadrons are triumphing over one another; already are imagining wounds inflicted and suffered. The ardour in the soul joins battle before the steel in the hand. The hordes of Vices, chafing at delay, hasten to make the first hostile move, stir up the first furore; the whole cohort roars its anger in mighty shouts, attacks the enemy with insults before swords, has a foretaste of war in the insults, taunts him with gestures, shouts and threats. The gestures, shouts and threats do not break him down. Firm in his lofty design, the youth stands boldly confronting them and his constancy of mind overcomes fear. When their words, threats and gestures proved powerless, words give way, there is no longer any place for them; rather deeds succeed threats and the war of words gives place to a war of weapons. Already the symbolic war is taking on the flavour of actual warfare and actual events bear witness to the battle of souls.[36]

[36] Reading *pugnas animi res ipsa fatetur.*

BOOK IX

Now the infantry rush into battle,[1] now they dare to shed first blood, now they seek to pour the first libations of gore and inflict the first wounds of war. Clouds of dust arise; a strange shower falls heavy on earth as missiles rain down, while the shower of dust spreads out; clouds of missiles shut out the sky and strange lightning flashes from the gleam of new steel. Discord, inflamed in mind, raging in spirit, afire with fury, makes the first attack on the hero, undertakes the first encounter, destined to fall in the first tumult. Violence urges on her steeds, Contention supplies her with arms, Resentment furnishes her with an arrow; Fury prepares her bow, Envy, her sword, and she shows more eagerness for war than the others. The arrow, harbinger of war, which Discord shoots with all her strength at the New Man, wings its way and seeks the enemy with headlong rush. The shot, however, deceives the hopes of the hand that fires it; the shield knocks the arrow aside and the boss wards off the entire attack. Then that New Man concentrates all his powers of soul and all his strength and devotes his entire attention to the war. He looses the reins, he plies his horn-hoofed steed with the spurs. The prancing courser is not

[1] Tastes change in literature. The catalogue of ships and men in *Iliad* 2 has little appeal for a modern reader. Only a professional student of the Bible would have any interest in the lists in *Chronicles* 1. Yet when these works were written, there was an interest in these things. Knights and knight-errantry were flourishing in the twelfth century. People were delighted by the accounts of the feats of knights. Few to-day have any interest in them. Parodies on them, from Cervantes' *Don Quixote* to Mark Twain's *Connecticut Yankee*, have made them appear silly. As far as I know, the last one to write a serious and sympathetic account of them was Charles Mills, Esq. in *History of Chivalry or Knighthood and its times.* (London 1826). Book 9 depicts the New Man in the paraphernalia of a knight and, like a knight, engaging in battle with evil and fearful forces and, of course, winning every engagement.

slack of pace through laziness, sluggishness nor tiredness from overweight. He takes part in the battle with the same enthusiasm for action as his master and joins in trampling on the troops of the enemy. The New Man, then, moves against the opposing ranks and, as he hastens to face the enemy, frees his sword from its sheathe. He does not thunder forth threats but flashes lightning from his sword alone. He puts everything to the test of steel, does not carry on the fight in words but in blows and the enemy is thwarted on several fronts. He singles out from the rest the one who has been the chief cause of the mad folly, the one who first lit the fires of trouble. Attacking her, then, with his sword, he tears the life from her body and forces the death of her whose life was the death of the world: her death alone stays the death of the world. It is not enough to see her dead: her opponent demands more. Beheading her with the sword, he unhooks her head from the trunk. It is but right that the head should not be united with the trunk in one through whom the first contention, hatred, madness, dissension, strife, the first conflict and rage, the first fears and the first desire for war arose. That one, then, lies dead on the ground who once caused the death of others. With her death the power of her dependents perishes; the punishment of one rebounds on many; the affliction of the head makes its way down to the members. Now Fear itself is afraid, Contention is silenced, Anger is chilled, Rage is tamed, Violence settles down, Envy itself perishes, Animosity fades away, Fury surrenders its arms. The Virtues are at hand to help the New Man: fired to battle-heat by the same goad, they take up arms against what is left of the enemy. Some they annihilate, others they put to flight, they make war on all. Animosity is annihilated by real Trust, Contention by Concord, Anger by Peace, Rage by Self-Possession, Fear by Hope. Poverty, with power in the fray not less but greater than the others, is roused to anger. She does not thunder with her sword nor threaten war with the lightning flash of arms nor gleam with coat of corslet nor have her side protected by a shield nor her face by a helmet. Rather she is hardened by many a callus and refined by no touch of art. A club, still showing its old features and original shape, takes the place of arms but her intensity supplies the deficiency in arms and her boldness makes up for her lack of weapons. Poverty rushes upon the New Man and threatens death with her club. She poises the club and when it is poised, she strikes. He is dazed by the stroke as his helmet gives way before a blow so heavy. Constancy, however, with her sword diverts the blow to some extent as it nears its mark. Poverty, then, is inflamed with greater fury and rages with a mighty din when she sees that her club vents its ire in vain and does not measure up to her expectations. Then she doubles, nay, multiplies her strokes, but her club is frustrated in the very act of striking. For as often as Poverty interposes the strokes of her club, Strength with her sword repels her charges. When she sees that her attacks are ineffectual, she urges her dependents to war with greater vehemence. Hardship rushes in, Hunger presses onwards. Thirst springs forward, Fasting enters the lists, sleepless Care rises to the combat, clods of earth, stones, sticks and missiles from an oak tree's trunk supply Hardship with arms. Armed Hunger grabs reeds, supplies Thirst[2] with missiles and the others rage with like arms. But the New Man makes the first charge, first goes to meet the enemy. He first attacks Poverty, relying on the swift flight of his horn-hoofed steed and his own efforts. He concentrates his power in his spear and fells her with it: fallen she remains lying on the ground. He attacks her as she lies there. He does not, however, probe her heart with the steel nor cause her head to roll with the sword nor saturate his arms with gore, disdaining to end the enemy's life with a death worthy of note and to counterbalance her fall with a distinguished

[2] Reading *siti.*

demise. He tramples her under foot, mashing her face as she lay there and pounding her felled form with his horse's hooves. Poverty, long insensitive to the feelings of the world,[3] has to die but death gains no spoils of soul in her: just a mind is left and death, checked and worsted by mind, grows depressed. Mind long and strenously resists death but finally departs with him. When Poverty thus yields to death and to the rights of fate, she impoverishes her retinue by her death. Her company is in need. The wealth of the one who was rich while Poverty lived vanishes and with her death all his resources disappear. Her fellow-citizens whom she formerly enriched in her poverty are reduced to need. Toil is drained and inactive. Thirst flees, Hunger throws down her arms, Fasting flees, Care vanishes. Thus the lower troop loses ground with the fall of the higher and the people perish at their master's death. Pain is put to flight by Rest, Fasting by Abundance, Care by Peace; Plenty overcomes Hunger, Thirst is put out of action by Fruitfulness, Need is overcome and leaves the field.

Infamy, anxious to make up for the fall of her companions, stands forth with increased courage, tries to blazon the death of her companions and satisfy her grief by the slaughter of her enemies. She rushes to attack the New Man but prefaces the attack by a speech and barbing her abuse with words, she says:

> "For shame! Will a race with the power of age, intelligence, caution, strength and arms give way before the weak soldiery of one youth and will yon boy triumph over our race?"

Without further speech, she dispatches a missile in his direction, giving a practical demonstration of the threats she is voicing. The missile, speeding with its message, beats the air but does

[3] This shows that by Poverty Alan had in mind the Cause of Poverty.

not, as a substitute for an official dispatch, bring news of peace, nay, it is an act of war. Infamy, speeding on her way, follows the missile, races it and attacks the enemy with her sword, desiring to help the arrow with the steel, so that if the hero's arms should chance to parry the arrow or the arrow's violence rage with restricted fury, the rampaging sword might make good the arrow's cooling fury. The arrow, then, remembering the right hand that shot it, sped to the New Man's forehead, but his helmet blocked its passage, held it off, prevented its entry and barred its way. Infamy, wishing to make up for the failure of the arrow, comes to its aid with naked sword. But Favour standing between diverts the blow from the helmet; the sword falls short in its stroke and is a poor compensation for the deficiencies of its partner, the arrow. When her band of followers sees that their leader's attack is of no avail, they are fired with deeper rage and thus snatch arms with greater vigour. Contagion enters the battle, Murmur rushes in, Reproach rises to the fray, Disgrace presses forward. The New Man, however, does not become despondent in soul, does not break down in the face of the enemy, does not panic, does not stumble around from wounds received. Rather he takes away for a time from Fame the horn on which she is sending forth a thundering proclamation of his glory and using this as a weapon, he strikes the enemy, shows his power by the many wounds inflicted and clears a way out for himself by repeated blows. Shame dies in the fall of the enemy, Murmur lays aside his arms, Reproach grows silent, Disgrace can feel no anger, Contempt dies, Contagion leaves the field. Thus Favour wipes out Disgrace, Fame wipes out Shame, Renown takes the place of Murmur, Praise of Reproach, Honour takes contempt as her spoils of war, Strength takes Contagion.

However sluggish, full of years, doting and crumbling from inactivity, Old Age is, she tends to find a new warmth in war, a new youth in arms. Now carried by her enthusiasm, she no longer seeks the aid of a staff and supported by battle-rage asks for no guidance. She is strong in weakness, robust in illness, rich in distress, powerful in sluggishness, quick in indolence. Close to her end, near to approaching death, with a crop of grey hair and a face furrowed with wrinkles, Old Age rushes upon the New Man that fronts her. At first she does not attack with the sword nor do battle with the dart nor thrust with the lance but tries by what one might call a type of wrestling to throw him to the ground, take away his horse and have her sword range free against a foe despoiled of arms. His horse, however, maddened by the warning touch of spur, rushes upon her and dashes the unfortunate dame to earth. She, however, rising up regains both her strength and resolve. She turns her hand to arms and places her hope in them. However, her helmet is decayed from want of use; it grows old from an overlay of dirt and now mouldy, shivers from the bite of scabrous rust. The shield reckons its years by its layers of rust and stripped of its ribbing, does not prevent the spear from entering. Rust, eating into the brittle chains of the breastplate, erodes them and separates the once joined scales. Her sword, stuck in the scabbard, is dulled and does not come out easily after its long rest. Old Age tries to unsheathe it but the decayed sword contemptuously rejects such means of coming forth and refuses to obey the hand that presses it, preferring to enjoy quiet inactivity rather than experience the many disturbances of war. However, the sword is finally drawn from its compartment: dull, blunt, embedded in filth, no longer remembering the rage of battle, this blade seeks peace not war - if indeed it may rightly be called a blade and not the shadow of a blade. Old Age, armed with the sword, attacks the hero, calls on the sword to wound him but the sword, no longer remembering wounds, strikes in vain, does not know the openings that permit wounds but, in many a crazed blow, is stopped dead against the helmet. Old Age, then, seeing that her fury is of no avail, is astonished and grieves that she is being conquered without inflicting a wound. Near though she is to death, she is willing to hasten what is fast approaching and draws the enemy's sword upon herself. The New Man, pitying her and deciding not to repay the enemy her just deserts, grants life to her who does not wish to live and denies the destined end to one who desires her destiny. He stays his steed, tightens the reins and uses the weapons of words against Old Age to restrain her wild emotions and oaths. He proceeds to speak in these words:

> "Why are you trying to bring about what has been determined, you for whom death, close at hand, is determining your last hour, for whom life is death and death is life? Why do you beg for what has been granted you? Why do you foolishly ask for what Nature is preparing for you, for what death near-by is threatening? Enjoy what remains of life and do not seek to anticipate the day that is near. Let a gain of further life be your consolation for death and let life compensate you for what you will lose at death."

Old Age is defeated, flees, renounces war, lays down the sword, throws off the shield, removes the helmet and satisfied with its staff alone, withdraws. Weakness loses its strength, Disease grows faint and leaves the battle, Languor falls ill, Decline is stopped in its tracks, Failure sinks, Boredom becomes tired.

Weeping is present and sees that her companions are wandering about aimlessly and yielding in the fight: she bewails the failure of her own party in the war. Grief mourns with rent garments; as she is impatient, she hastens her steps, approaches the enemy agressively and tries to undo the knots of his helmet to make a passage for the sword to enter and inflict a wound. But Laughter comes to his aid, with her sword she severs the arm from the trunk; the hand sticks fast to the helmet, dies as it clings there and deprived of its natural power,[4] grows stiff. Now

[4] Reading *vigore*.

Moan bemoans its losses; now Grief overflowing turns back on itself; Weeping weeps with its entire attendant band; Wailing wails; Tears are moistened. Now Pain itself is in pain, having lost the alleviations for pain. Depression is depressed; Moan dies down; Ruin is ruined and all the violence of Grief disappears. Sorrow is overcome by Joy, Depression by Glory, Wailing by Happiness, Moaning by Humour, Failure by Success and Laughter routs the prudishness of the evil-minded.

Venus herself rages. Her rage is more violent, her wickedness greater, her attack more destructive, her power more oppressive. While she bewails the fact that the ranks of her fellow-fighters are weary and their lines growing thin and that the enemy squadrons are increasing in number and ardour and while she is grieved that her madness has come to an end, nevertheless, she hastily snatches up and hurls at the enemy a lighted torch which counterfeits the very likeness of the thunderbolt which is wont to dissolve stones, pulverise rocks, melt iron, set cliffs on fire. Trembling with fear of this fight, this war, the New Man wishing to avoid this battle, fears to stand his ground. Flight looks after his interests and by flight's advice he escapes the coming blows. The lighted torch comes down, dies in the air and loses its strength when there is nothing left to feed its hot flame. The New Man, however, in Parthian[5] fashion, shoots an arrow at Venus while he is retreating and it does not miss its mark. It first strikes and causes a wound and thus finally brings about her death; nor can Desire urge any opposing argument when Venus is thus thwarted. Thus in a new kind of war new laurels fall to the New Man. While he flees, he puts to flight; while he gives away, he has his way; while he is falling, he is rising; he

[5] The Parthians were superb cavalry-men. One of their accomplishments was the ability to let loose a shower of arrows on the enemy while riding away. Vir., *Geor.* 3.31. Hor., *Car.* 1.19.11; 2.13.17.

conquers while he is being conquered; he has courage while he fears; he wins the battle while he is leaving the field; though absent, he exerts pressure; though anticipated in the attack, he gets ahead of the enemy. The Cytherean is astounded at her fate as she dies and she does not believe that her end is at hand although death itself is calling to her. Since it is usual for others to go to death through her influence, she can hardly believe that she can die. However, seeing that her fate is at hand, faced with death, she breaks into these complaints:

> "Alas, my band, so often victorious, goes awry in a single action; so often triumphant, that band is now defeated which has had no experience of failure but which Fortune has now failed. Now my well-known heat grows cold, the heat from that furnace of mine which burns the fires of the sun, inflames Neptune beneath the waves, drives Bacchus to his orgies, with its fire blasts Jupiter like lightning, ravishes the gods above of their divinity and drives many masters to slavery. Now my arms lie idle, my arms through which Achilles, counterfeiting a girl in his degenerate clothes, was once overcome and yielded.[6] The descendant of Alceus,[7] degenerate in arms, exchanges his staff for a distaff, his arrows for a day's supply of wool, his quivers for a spindle and basely unsexed himself completely in womanish action.[8]"

[6] Alan is mistaken in this reference. When the troops were mustering for Troy, Achilles' father or mother persuaded him to hide in Scyros dressed as a girl. Venus has nothing to do with this. While there he performed the usual tasks of a maiden of the household.

[7] If Alan wrote *Alcides*, he was mistaken. It should be *Aeacides*: Aeacus was Achilles' grandfather. Alan took the legend from Ovid, *Ars Am.* 1.689-696. Ovid gives the correct reason for Achilles' change of dress and also uses the correct patronymic for him.

[8] Both Ovid and previous writers tell of Achilles' affair with Deidameia on Scyros and an old tradition relates that she bore him a son. Neoptolemus. Alan's statement that he "unsexed himself completely" is ludicrous. His entire treatment of the story about Achilles shows the signs of haste and lack of revision referred to in Bk. 8. n. 14.

Thus she spoke and gave up life and voice together. Excess, who was the outstanding figure in the battle and the beginning and origin of the entire war, is now afraid, now he wishes to quit the field, now his high-flowing ideas are lowered, now the enthusiasm of his spirit cools as he sees the death of his companion. Nevertheless, his poised spear wings its way but it goes awry in his attack on the enemy. The hand that hurls it directs it poorly, and with poor guidance, it goes off course, turns aside from the enemy and does not even touch any part of his shield in its flight. Then Moderation brings help to the New Man; she bares her steel, throws the enemy ranks into confusion and breaches their lines. Moderation wars against Excess, Pride is attacked by Sober Reason, Vengeance by Tolerance, Debauchery by Temperance. The battle goes in favour of the Virtues; Victory fights on their side. Thus Pride is conquered; Debauchery quits the field, Gluttony gives up, Indigestion surrenders. The Sting of the Flesh, carrying on his struggle in unseen warfare, attacks the New Man from the rear and essays a secret onslaught on him. However, Reason, ever on the alert, adverts to these attacks: she does not remain idle and inactive but blocks the Sting of the Flesh, restrains his ferocity and stays his fury. Nevertheless, he long withstands Reason's powers, fights a drawn battle with her and in his struggle puts up a strong resistance. Finally he is conquered and yields to his enemy. Imprudence swoops down on the New Man with a more bitter attack; she observes no laws of warfare but, swirling in the whirlwind of war, keeps nothing in mind but the love of battle. She wishes to wrench from the top of a rock a large stone fixed in place by its own mass, a stone under which Achilles would totter, the descendant of Alceus[9] would groan, and Atlas would grow faint. But her strength gives way beneath the burden; her violence, overcome by the weight,

[9] Hercules.

is dulled and beneath the mass she suffers a grievous fall. Prudence opposes her, conquers her when she is already overcome by the weight and compels her against her will to take a holiday from war. Indolence is defeated by Industry, Frivolity by Seriousness, Damage by Advantage; Zeal puts Leisure to flight, Sense dooms Foolishness, Silence overcomes trifling Talk.

Impiety no longer restrains her anger and agitation of mind.[10] She advertises herself by war and announces herself by brawls: she indulges in a brawl of words and carries the brawl to its completion in blows; she puts to the test of the sword what she maintains by speech; she roams around in the random battle and her fury is greater than the fury of the battle.[11] She turns aside from the accepted ways of war, maintaining that the law of warfare is that it has no law and that its covenant is to ignore covenants. When her raging sword fails to wound, she snatches up an axe, intending to make up for the sword's failure by use of the axe. She strikes the hero and exhausts her strength on him, but the New Man unconcerned stands his ground under the axe's heavy impact. Piety stands by but does not use her sword in the combat. Rather she wishes to temper the war by winning words and pleas. However, the battle's ardour is further enkindled under the shower of pleas and prayers add fuel to the fire of fury. But when blandishments, words of goodwill and pleas have proved of no avail, Piety abandons honeyed words, seizes her sword and proceeds to meet war with war and steel with steel. She frustrates the axe's work by interposing her shield and causes the several blows to rebound. Finally, Impiety, overcome by the many toils, grows faint, yielding in the battle and overcome without being attacked. Who remains ? Fraud alone. She seeks her consolation in war and resorts to her old subterfuges

[10] Reading *retinet* and putting a semi-colon after *Impietas*.

[11] Reading *furit*.

and deceits. She tries to bring the furies of war against her enemy in a debased contest, a cringing war, a deceitful attack. Although she is not kind, Fraud entices him with kind words. Thus she offers these pleas, propitiates him with sweet words and cloaks her artifices with the ornaments of Rhetoric:

> "Youth, whom earth favours, on whose side heaven fights, on whom God smiles, on whom the heavens wait, whom the whole universe applauds, to whom the entire world prays, spare what is left of the combatants, those who have survived by chance and with difficulty and let not the lion's anger rage against calves. Why try to vanquish the vanquished? Why seek to carry on war against those powerless in war? It is enough to have shown that one can do it and a noble mind desires nothing beyond the power to conquer."

While with fawning pleas she fakes the words of a suppliant, she secretly draws her sword, quite quickly bares the blade and with repeated strokes calls on the steel to wound. The helmet measures its strength against the steel, shows its contempt for the blade and does not deign to yield to such steel. On the other side Faithfulness bears arms, counteracts the plots of Fraud, lays bare her deceptions and reveals her secret stratagems. When Fraud sees that neither her deceptions nor her cloaked deceits have any power, she quits the field, betakes herself to flight, lays her arms aside and gains a further span of life by flight.

There remains Avarice with her din: on her the whole rage of the battle fury devolves; alone she faces the dangers of this great war; alone she rages; by herself she confronts a large number; in her alone hopelessness begets hope. She hurls against the New Man darts afire with many a flash of silver; the javelins pelt him like hail, spears rain down and the arrows in flight resemble a cloud. Pestilential Avarice, then plants a forest of javelins and a crop of arrows in her enemy's shield and covers him with those arrows. But the javelins rather lightly penetrate the shield and do not stick fast in the buckler. The Virtue[12] which rains down gifts, spreads her largess abroad, does not bury her money nor imprison her resources in a strongbox but generously pours out her riches without hope of return, cuts a path with her sword through the grove of javelins and hews down the forest. She presses hard on Avarice, keeps up the fight unremittingly, snatches the sword which Avarice holds, overcomes the enemy with her own arms and compels the arrows to vent their rage on their owner. Avarice, then, is vanquished and flees. Fortune's daughter[13] remains the sole survivor of the fight but Fortune forces her away from the war and urges her daughter not to decide to stir up family disputes: she warns her that a daughter should not indulge in a quarrel with her mother or sister stir up a conflict with sister. She agrees with her mother's advice and deserts the enemy since she does not know on which side she could with more justice bear arms. Thus making her submission to neither, she serves both.

Now crime's cohorts are defeated, silently take their arms back to their domains, are astonished at their defeat and can scarcely credit what has happened to them. They do not believe what is before their eyes and flee in indignation to the Stygian shades below. The battle ceases, Victory falls to the New Man. Virtue rises, Vice sinks, Nature triumphs, Love rules, nowhere is there Disagreement but Agreement everywhere. For that blessed man guides the earthly kingdom with the reins of law, that man

[12] *Largitas*, Generosity. See Bk. 1. n. 10.

[13] Fortune has two daughters, Nobilitas and Ignobilitas. They refer to a man's lot by birth or acquisition and have no reference to nobility or ignobility of soul. *Ignobilitas* (which I have translated as *Lowliness*) is mentioned as a Vice in Bk. 8.296. There is no mention of Nobility among the Virtues preparing for, or taking part in, the battle. Here Alan is presumably referring to *Ignobilitas* and indicating that in a war nobleman and commoner may be found on the side of justice or in the opponent's camp.

whom licentiousness does not impair, pride does not overcome, crime does not sully, the goad of wantonness does not urge on, guilt from fraud does not taint. The Virtues now set up camp on earth, rightly acquire domain there and guide the world; the stars and the abodes at the poles are now no more pleasing to them than the earthly sphere. Now earth vies with heaven, now the world clothes itself in heavenly splendour, now the Olympians bedeck the earth. No longer is the field reclaimed with the hoe or scored by the ploughshare, no longer does it bemoan the scars inflicted by the curved plough to make it, however unwilling, obey the greedy husbandman and return the seed with high interest. The tree does not need the knife nor the vineyard the pruning-hook. They bear new fruit of their own accord and surpass in their fertility the husbandman's prayers. Hope is outdone by richness of fruit; the tree produces fruit and the vine-branch bears grape-clusters gratis: vine-shoots are amazed at grapes that have come into existence without their help. The rose, emerging from its tegument, covers the gardens with crimson. It bears no suggestion of a mother-thorn but is brought into existence and comes forth spontaneously and proceeds to new growths without seed. Thus, too, the other flowers smile and blooms in fresh youth colour the earth with various hues.

Long life to you, o book, over which I have toiled and sweated long and continuously, you whose fame slander already impairs. Do not try to rival the poets of old but rather follow with reverence the steps of the ancients and let the lowly tamarisks take second place to the laurels. Now the ship, avoiding Scylla and the monster, Charybdis, sails on a calm sea to the harbour. Now the mariner rejoices at the sight of land; now the runner is at the winning post; the anchor is fast in the harbour. However, the mariner, after negotiating the heaving sea, trembles and fears attacks on land: he fears that, though he has been safe asea, he may be shipwrecked and lost ashore, that spite may rage against him or slander sink her teeth in him who, as he brings his work to a fitting conclusion, has drained his energy in writing and borne the burden of the toil. If spite pours out her whisperings for the present and wishes to ruin the reputation of the poet and waylay his newly-won honours, at least she will be silent after his death.

APPENDIX

Peter of Compostella and Alan of Lille

Peter of Compostella *Beiträge* 8. 4 (Münster 1912) 61-68.	Alan of Lille
GRAMMATICA	
Prima quidem, que ver florum venatur honorem.	
Et nec virgineum veneris flactura pudorem	Nec proprium frangat Veneris fractura pudorem.
Auferat, ac lactis torrente carere putetur,	Sunt tamen in multo lactis torrente natantes .... (2, 391-2)
Infantes cibat iste cibus nec pigra moretur.	Infantem cibat iste cibus (2, 395)
Tres adit illa gradus, quibus amplior eius honestas	
Crescit, et immenssa eius prima potestas;	
Ordo, genus, species, pars, instrumenta, facultas,	Officium, species, genus, instrumenta, facultas (2, 418)
Qualiter ars normas referat sub canone multas.	
Queritur hic quid sit numerus, quid litera pura	
Vel duplex, cur se ratione figura	Deffendens sese propria racione, figura ... (2, 422)
Defendit vel cur elementi iram nomen	Cur sibi mendicet elementi littera nomen (2, 428)
Vendicat, autve sonum vocalis possidet omnem,	Cur tenui deiecta sono poscencia vocem
Cetera mutescunt; cur metro iura duarum	Cetera mutescant (2, 434)
	Qualiter in metro vires et iura duarum
Vendicat una sibi; cur com muta liquidarum	Vendicat una sibi (2, 444)
Una facit longam; cur vox induit una	Quomodo diversas species vox induit una (2, 446)
Diversas species vel sensus duplicat una;	
Cur gravis acentus premit, erigit alter acutus,	Quam gravis accentus infra demittit, acutus
Et circumflexus giratur ad infima ductus.	Erigit, in gyrum fert circumflexus ... (2, 447-8)
Verba ligat metris, et carmen pigere rimo	Turba poetarum docet illum verba ligare
	Metris et dulci carmen depingere rithmo (7, 259-260)

Noscitur et pueros informat canone primo	
Cur pertita vigens scribendi destinat artem,	
Sive loquendi recte cuius regula partem	.... sic ergo loquendi
Evocat, aponit, componit, dividit, unit,	Recte scribendique viam sectatur et artem (7, 255)
Coniugat illa gradus, quos declinatio munit.	

LOGICA

Virga secunda quidem sequitur penetrabilia mentis	Virgo secunda studet, intrat penetralia mentis (3, 2)
Suscitat ad pugnam, pugnans armatur elenchis.	Monstrat elenchorum pugnam .. armet elenchum (3. 34, 35)
Queritur hi, quid vis, quid maxima, quid locus artis,	Quid locus in logica dicatur ... quid maxima ... vis argumenti (3, 42-44)
Quid genus aut species, cuius moderamine partis	
Demonstrative vel temtativa potestas	
Inferet aut fallit, topicum cur duplice gestas	
Res ratione probat, partitur, colligit, unit.	
Singula cur tunicis veri fallacia munit	
Falsa vel abscondit fur artis falsa sophista;	.... artis fur .../Falsa
Vel genus in species partes are dividat ista.	Quid genus in species divisum separat (3, 67)
In totum cur rem descripcio pingit eandem,	Quo modo res pingens descriptio claudit easdem (3, 65)
Aut sua descripta cur difinitio tandem	
Extra se non vult; quid sit substancia rerum,	
De difinito vult id concludere verum.	
Arte sua logica rationis inire duellum	
Certat et incaptis argutum mittere tellum;	
Fallax adverse temptat concludere parti	Hec docet ..../ Adversae parti concludere (7, 265)
Et pseudo = logicos reserare nec inferat arti	Scismaticos .... retundere fratres
	Et pseudologicos (7, 268-269)

Falsa sophista loquax, partem ratione tueri	...... partem suam racione tueri (7, 266)
Nititur ipse suam, nec possit ymmagine veri	Cur pseudologicus, artis fur, artis adulter
Falsum concludi, vult denudare sophistas,	Falsus et ypocrita furtivus predo, sophista (3, 38-39)
	.... et denudare sophistas (7, 269)
Verum septari, falsumque recindere mistas	.... recidit/Falsa ... (3, 36-37)
Explanans metados ubi nulla sit ars specialis,	
Quin non indigeat artis moderamine talis.	

RHETORICA

Tertia virgo nitens vultum splendore colorat,	
Quasi sertum roseum pilus arte pollitus honorat;	... miraque politus/ Arte iacet crinis (3, 151)
Nullus et in facie candor peregrinus inheret,	Sed partim vultus candor peregrinus inheret (3, 155)
Exemplans auri speciem coma fluxilis heret.	Exemplans auri speciem (3, 151)
Nec velut arridens delegat lumina sursum,	Nunc oculus sursum lumen delegat in imum (3, 161)
In latus oblicans nec mergit ad infima rursum.	In latus obliquans, anfractus querit et umbram (3, 163)
Vestis eam vestit vario variata colore;	
Serta nitent sertique valor precurrit honore.	
Queritur hic que causa, quis ordo, queque potestas,	Hic velud in libro legitur, quis finis et actor
Forma vel officium, vel quem demostrat honestas	Forma vel officium, que causa, quis ordo (3, 170-171)
Finem vel cause genus ad quem pervenit apte,	.... et ad quem
Quo tendat vel quid delibet utile capte	Deveniens finem deliberet utile iustum (3, 175-6)
Afirmet rectum, justum dijudicet artis.	
Que partes, vel qualiter ars vel sancio partis	
Rectorice concludat opus, vel dissipet, urgat,	
Qualiter innumerisque modis oratio surgat,	
Qualiter optato conclusio singula fine	Quomodo concludens conclusio singula fine (3, 196)
Dirigat ac robur sumat sententia digne.	

Quis locus, aut tempus, quid sit complexio facti,	
Que vel quot species que viris causa peracti:	
Quid fugat aut sistat dubii sermonis habenam.	Legitimo claudit, sistens sermonis habenas (3, 197)
Quomodo censuram faciet narratio plenam	
Nec nimis obscuram; que vis vel questio juris,	
Quis casus, vel consilium, que sancio duris	
Afficit in penis occasio, causa, facultas,	
Liberet aut dampnet, nec culpas linquit inultas.	
Cultus rethorici precepta modosque colorum	
Explicat orator; nan sub sermone leporum	
Verba nitent sermone brevi concludere multa,	Succinte docet illa loqui sensusque profundos
Plurima sub paucis cun sententia scientia fulta	Sub sermone brevi concludere, claudere multa
Mostrat et in vario presignit verba colore,	Sub paucis (7, 276-278)
Sermonum variata modis stipata decore:	
Ut redimat paleas granum sensusque loquelam	Excuset foliis silvam, paleasque vagantes
Et breve prolixum verbum censura procelam,	Ubertas grani redimat sensusque loquelam (7, 283-284)
Temperies turpe pulcrum discrimen honestum,	
Et vicium virtus et rerum copia questum.	

ARISMETICA

Virgo prima nitet, cuius iam copia mentis	
Scribitur in vultu sensus aurora lattentis	
Exit in exterius gracilis, sutilis, acuta.	Ergo decora, decens, gracilis, subtilis, acuta (3, 276)
Ambit eam vestis, cuius concordia ducta	
In numerum crescens, numerandi predicat artem.	.... numerandi predicat artem (3, 300)
Ostendens, que lex numeri, que regula partem	Que numeri virtus, que lex

Congregat in totum, vel quis numeratus habetur, Vel numerus numerans, vel qua ratione vocetur	Quis numerus numerans... quis numeratus (3, 316) Quo iuris merito vel qua racione vocetur
Mars impar numerus, par scientia; cur sapientum	Femina par numerus, impar mas, virgo Minerva; Cur animam, celum, racionem, gaudia, vitam Impare sub numero prudentum dogma figuret;
Dogma parem numerum mortem, sed in inpare tentum	Cur corpus, terram, sensum, lacrimabile, mortem Par numerus signet ... (3, 319-324)
Fert numerum vitam, que linea, que figura Quis quadrus, quis piramis, aut que linea pura; Que virtus numeri, cum quo deitatis idea Rebus signa dedit, non a vero pharisea Astra movens, elementa ligans, ad cuius asillum Limes fedus amor exemprar forma, sigillum. Ponitur in mundo partus inmitata parentis, Inviolata manet, se gignit, origo latentis In se fit numeri, se de se multiplicando Virgo parit, partusque suus virgo superando,	Hic erat ad cuius formam deitatis ydea Impressit rebus formas... (3, 309-310) Astra movens, elementa ligans (3, 305) Principium, finis, exemplar, forma, sigillum (3, 308) Incorrupta manet, partus imitata parentis (3, 313) Sese multiplicat, de sese gignit et in se Incorrupta manet (3, 314-315) Quomodo virgo parit... (3, 313)
Vel superatur ab his, vel cur extrema ligentur	Quis numerus propriis completur partibus aut quis Vel partes superat vel ab hiis superatus habundat; unde/Provenit ut vicibus mediius extrema ligentur
Sub vicibus mediis, vel cur necpti perhibentur	Cur duo quadrati medio nectantur in uno Vel solidos nectat iunctura duobus (3, 329-332)
Uno sub modio duo quadrati, vel ab ortu Radices primo simul extrait, omnia portu Concordi religans mundum regit, ordinat illum, Singula componens, coadunat, adauget asillum. Indegat et numeri causas et semina rerum,	.... et ad primum radices extrahit ortum (3, 318) .... semina rerum Legibus inquirit (7. 285, 287)

Querit et efectus certis concludere, verum	.... numerisque ligantur/Cuncta (7, 289-290)
Legibus actemptat numeris cur cunta ligentur,	
Que ratio numeri, que vis, qua lege tenentur	Que racio numeris (7, 294)
Omnia sub numeris stabili sub parte ligata,	Ut numeri nodo stabilis liget omnia nexus (7, 296)
Et numeris contempta suis, sunt cuncta creata.	
	MUSICA
Virgo secunda decens vario sub cenmate fatur.	Scemate sub vario monstrans quid musica possit (3, 413)
Que species artis, que vox, qua lege ligatur	
Musica, quo iure loquat, anni tempora motat	que musica colligit horas
Sidera distinguit, menses, annalia dotat,	Distinguit menses, locat anni tempora, cogit
Ordinat excessus tempus discriminat, horas	Excursus, elementa ligat, iungitque planetas (3, 415-417)
Colligit, excursus cogit citansque sonoras	
Inducens furias proprium nescire furoram	coegit.../Furiasque suum nescire furorem (3, 405)
Predicat atque sui dulcem parit ille saporem.	dulcemque soni parit illa saporem (3, 399)
	Quae vox ad vocem fit duppla vel in diapason
Quis sonus aut est in dyapason cantus ad illum,	Quis resonat cantus, vel quis sexqualter ad illum
	Sit sonus aut illi concors sonet in diapente;
Aut quis sex qualiter sonus est, vel prebet asillum.	Que vocum iunctura parit diatessaron, in qua
	Cum tribus una sonans vox litigat, imo iocatur (3, 434-438)
Ut concors illi cantus sonet in dyapente.	
Que vocum iunctura tiplex unaque sequente	
Dat diatesaron in tribus una sonans tamen una	
Non cantus generat, sed vocum consona pugna.	Cantus non gignit vox una sed unio vocum (3, 427)
Vocum divicias ambit rixasque sonorum,	Musica divicias aperit (7, 297)
	Monstrat amicicias vocum rixasque sonorum (7, 301)
Ostendens que vox turbet, vel quis modus horum	
Aurem dumulcet, vel vocum federa partem	
Quam resonando tenent, que vel vox vendicat artem.	

GEOMETRIA

Tercia virgo decens precedit ymaginem florum. Iam prati faciem vires inmitata sororum, Prosilit in campum, metitur magna profundum; Indegat alta, subit, scrutatur singula, mundum Circuit, astra meat, mare circinat, infima terre Ambit, et ostendit, que simplex linea vere Curva sit aut recta, que circumflexa vocetur, Quid sit treteganus cur angulus omnis habetur	que linea curva Recta vel equalis que circumflexa vocetur (3, 489-490) Quid sit tetragonus, quid forma triangula (3, 493) cur angulus omnis
Rectus et obtusus et acutus, cur perhibetur Equorum laterum triganus que forma triangula detur Aut circumducta centrum dat; qua ratione Equalem formam sibi forma triangula prone Invenit, aut quid sit centrum, que consita plano Vel contempta superficies; cur eleufuga sano	Aut obtusus hebet, aut sursum tendit acutus, (3, 496-7) Equorum laterum trigonus describitur (3, 501) aut quid/Circumducta sua describat linea centro (3, 495) Queve superficies plano contenta (3, 491) Cur huius tyrones artis eleufuga terret (3, 506)
Vis intellectu capitur; quis prebuit artem Commensurandi claudens immensa, refrenans Ampla, sequens parva, sub pondere singula frenans; Vel quid sit puctum quis linea, quidve figura. Quidve superficies, cur urget eleufuga datura Arte sub hac dociles, quid mensura retinetur Clausum sub triplici, quid strion esse probetur	Que mensurandi doctrinam fundit et usum Edocet, immensum claudit, spatiosa refrenat Parvaque consequitur (3, 485-487) quid sit mensura triplici clausum, quid sterion (3, 493-494)

Virgo quarta vigil vultusque reponit in altum,
Alta petit, terrena fugit, dat ad ardua saltum.
Queritur hic quid sint astrorum nomina, motus,
Signa, potestates, discursus ab ordine totus,
Que loca, que cause, que vis, que spera, quis ortus,
Ad quos astra meant vel sunt ducentia portus.
Quid sit celum, quid auxis, quid spera vocetur
Quis polus axem terminat, aut resecare probetur
In partes speram, cur mundi forma ligetur
Quinque paralelis, cur zonis machina mundi
Ambitur variis extremis, fligora fundi
Partibus in mediis, estus lateralibus eius
Temperiem certat, ut sit concludere peius
Aut melius clima — probat hoc habitatio rerum —,
Linea cur oblica meat sortita severum
Motuum signiferi duodeno pingere celum

Sidere testetur, vel qua ratione gemelum
Motum consequitur, vel qua sub lege planeta
Devius, aut vagus est dircursus non sine meta
Circulus aut quare curvatus utrumque colurum
Possidet, aut que spera iovis que semita durum
Martem saturnunque vehit; quos improbat actus;
Quis limes venerenque iovem non peste subactus
Ducit, ut opositos effectus quilibet horum
Inferat in mundo; cur cun moderamine morum
Virtus nascendis infunditur a superiori;
Cur venus hos lacerans urit, dum cedit amori.

Que docet astrorum leges, loca, tempora, motus,
Signa, potestates, discursus, nomina, causas (4, 19-20)

Qua racione meant stelle (4, 36)

quis polus axem/Terminet (4, 22-23)
mundusque ligetur
Quinque parallelis cinctus zonisque quibusdam (4, 24-25)

Cur obliqua means declini limite ducta
Linea signiferi duodena sydere celum
Pinguat (4, 32-34)

Cur decurtatus concludat utrumque colurum
Circulus (4, 29-30)

quo limite currit
Stella Iovis (4, 45-46)

SELECT BIBLIOGRAPHY

Ancient and Medieval Works

Abelard	*Theologia Christiana.*
Aelian	*Varia Historia.*
Aeschylus	*Prometheus Vinctus.*
Alan of Lille	*Anticlaudianus; De Arte Praedicatoria; De Fide Catholica Contra Haereticos; De Planctu Naturae; De Sex Alis Cherubim; De Virtutibus et Vitiis* (redactio brevior); *De Virtutibus et Vitiis et De Donis Spiritus Sancti* (redactio longior); *Elucidatio in Cantica Canticorum; Epistola Magistri Alani quod non est celebrandum bis in die; Expositio Prosae de Angelis; Expositio super Symbolum Apostolicum et Nicenum; Expositio super Symbolum Quicumque; Hierarchia; Liber in Distinctionibus Dictionum Theologicalium; Liber Parabolarum; Liber Poenitentialis; Rhythmus de Incarnatione Christi; Rhythmus de Natura Hominis Fluxa et Caduca; Sermo de Sphera Intelligibili; Sermones; Summa Quoniam Homines; Theologicae Regulae.*
Alberic of Trois Fontaines	*Chronica.*
Ammianus Marcellinus	*Rerum Gestarum Libri.*
Anonymous	*De Ultimis Syllabis.*
Anselm	*Epistula de Incarnatione.*
Apollonius of Rhodes	*Argonautica.*
Appollodorus (Mythographus)	*Bibliotheca; Epitome.*
Apuleius	*Florida; De Deo Socratis; De Dogmate Platonis.*
Aristophanes	*Aves; Nubes.*
Aristotle	*Analytica Posteriora; Analytica Priora; De Caelo; Meteorologica; Poetica; Rhetorica; Sophistici Elenchi; Topica.*

Athenaeus — *Δειπνοσοφισταί* [Coena Doctorum].

Augustine — *De Civitate Dei; De Diversis Quaestionibus; De Doctrina Christiana; De Fide et Symbolo; De Trinitate; Enarrationes in Psalmos; Sermones.*

Avitus — *De Mundi Initio; De Originali Peccato.*

Bacon, R. — *Opus Tertium.*

Bernardus Silvestris — *De Mundi Universitate, sive Megacosmus et Microcosmus.*

Boethius — *De Arithmetica; De Consolatione Philosophiae; De Musica; De Trinitate; Contra Eutychen; Interpretatio Euclidis Geometriae; In Topica Ciceronis Commentaria.*
Liber de Divisione; Posteriorum Analyticorum Aristotelis Interpretatio; Priorum Analyticorum Aristotelis Interpretatio; Topicorum Aristotelis Interpretatio.

Bonaventure — *De Sex Alis Seraphim.*

Calcidius — *In Timaeum Platonis.*

Callimachus — *Hymnus in Dianam (Artemidem).*

Catullus — *Carmina.*

Celsus — *De Medicina.*

Charlemont, C. — *Series Sanctorum et Beatorum Virorum Sacri Ordinis Cisterciensium.*

Cicero — *Brutus; De Inventione; De Finibus Bonorum et Malorum; De Natura Deorum; De Optimo Genere Oratorum; De Oratore; Epistulae; In Verrem; Topica; Tusculanae Quaestiones.*

Clarembald of Arras — *Tractatus super Librum Boetii; Tractulus super Librum Genesis.*

Claudian — *In Rufinum; Panegyricus dictus Probino et Olybrio Consulibus.*

Diodorus Siculus — *Bibliotheca.*

Dionysius of Halicarnassus — *De Compositione Verborum.*

Donatus — *Ars Grammatica.*

Ennodius — *Epistulae; Opuscula.*

Euripides — *Antiope* (fragmentum); *Electra; Hippolytus; Orestes.*

Garnerius — *Sermones.*

Gerard of Cremona — *Liber de Causis.*

Gilbert of Poitiers — *Expositio in Boecii Librum Primum de Trinitate; Expositio in Boecii Librum Secundum de Trinitate; Expositio in Boecii Librum de Bonorum Ebdomade.*

Giraldus Cambrensis — *Topographia Hibernica.*
Godfrey of Saint Victor — *Fons Philosophiae.*
Gregory the Great — *Sanctus Pater Benedictus; Homiliae in Evangelia.*
Gundisalvus — *De Scientiis; De Divisione Philosophiae.*
Hermannus Contractus — *Chronicon.*
Herodotus — *Historiae.*
Hesiod — *Theogonia.*
Hilary of Poitiers — *De Trinitate.*
Hildebert — *Epistolae.*
Homer — *Ilias; Odysseus.*
Horace — *Ars Poetica; Carmina; Epistulae; Sermones (Satirae).*
Hugh of Honau — *De Diversitate Naturae et Personae; Liber de Homoysion et Homoeysion.*
Hyginus — *Fabulae.*
[Iamblichus] — *Theologumena Arithmeticae.*
Isidore of Seville — *De Ecclesiasticis Officiis.*
Jerome (Hieronymus) — *Epistulae.*
John of Altavilla (Jean de Hanville) — *Architrenius.*
John of Garland — *De Triumphis Ecclesiae.*
John of Salisbury — *Entheticus; Metalogicon.*
Joseph of Exeter (Joseph Iscanus) — *De Bello Troiano (Frigii Daretis Ylias).*
Juvenal — *Satirae.*
Longinus — *De Sublimitate.*
Lucan — *Pharsalia.*
Lucretius — *De Rerum Natura.*
Macrobius — *Commentarii in Somnium Scipionis.*
Map, W. — *De Nugis Curialium.*
Martianus Capella — *De Nuptiis Philologiae et Mercurii.*
Michael Psellos — *De Daemonum Operatione.*
Nicomachus of Gerasa — *Introductio Arithmetica.*
Ovid — *Amores; Ars Amatoria; Fasti; Epistulae ex Ponto; Metamorphoses; Tristia.*
Otho of Sankt-Blasien — *Continuatio Sanblasiana.*
Pacuvius — *Antiopa.*
Persius — *Satirae.*
Peter of Blois — *Sermones.*
Peter Cantor — *Summa de Sacramentis et Animae Consiliis.*
Peter of Compostella — *De Consolatione Rationis.*

Philip of Bury	*Philobiblion.*
Pindar	*Epinicia (Olympia).*
Plato	*Parmenides; Protagoras; Res Publica; Timaeus.*
Plautus	*Comoediae.*
Pliny the Younger	*Epistulae.*
Plutarch	*De Gloria Atheniensium.*
Priscian	*Institutiones Grammaticae.*
Probus	*Instituta Artium.*
Propertius	*Elegiae.*
Prudentius	*Peristephanon; Psychomachia.*
Ptolemy	*Almagest (Mathematica Syntaxis); Tetrabiblos.*
Quintilian	*Institutio Oratoria.*
Richerus	*Historiarum Libri IIII.*
Rufinus of Aquileia	*Commentarius in Symbolum Apostolicum.*
Seneca	*Epistulae; Quaestiones Naturales; Thyestes.*
Servius	*Commentarius in Artem Donati.*
Sidonius Apollinaris	*Carmina; Epistulae.*
Solinus (Gaius Julius)	*Collectanea Rerum Memorabilium.*
Sophocles	*Aiax.*
Statius	*Achilleis; Silvae; Thebais.*
Stephen of Bourbon	*Tractatus de diversis materiis predicabilibus.*
Stephen of Tournai	*Rhythmus.*
Suetonius	*De Vita Caesarum.*
Tacitus	*Agricola; Annales; Historiae.*
Terence	*Comoediae.*
Thierry of Chartres	*Glosa super Boethii Librum de Trinitate; Lectiones in Boethii Librum de Trinitate; Tractatus de sex dierum operibus; Tractatus de Trinitate.*
Varro	*De Lingua Latina.*
Victorinus (Marius)	*Liber de Definitione.*
Virgil	*Aeneis; Bucolica; Georgica.*
Walter of Châtillon	*Alexandreis.*
William of Conches	*Glosae super Platonem; De Philosophia Mundi.*
William of Malmesbury	*De Gestis Regum Anglorum.*
Xenophanes	*Fragmenta* (Diels).

Modern Works

Alan of Lille, See Alverny, M-T. d'; Bossuat, R.; Dreves, C. M.; Glorieux, P.; Hödl, L.; Huizinga, J.; Longère, J.; Lottin, O,; Moffat, D. M,; Wright, T, Häring, N. M.

Alonso, M. A., *Domingo Gundisalvus, De Scientiis* (Madrid-Granada 1954).

Alszeghy, Z., "Ein Verteidiger der Welt predigt Weltverachtung," in: *Geist und Leben* 35 (1962) 197-207.

Altamura, A., *Philip de Bury, Philobiblion* (Naples 1954).

Alverny, M-T. d', "Alain de Lille et la Theologia," in: *L'Homme devant Dieu, Mélanges offerts au Père Henri du Lubac* 2 (Aubier 1964) 111-128.

——, *Alain de Lille, Textes Inédits* (Paris 1965).

——, "Le Cosmos Symbolique du XIIe Siècle," in: *Archives* 20 (1953) 31-81.

——, "Maître Alain — 'Nova et Vetera'," in: *Entretiens sur la Renaissance du XIIe Siècle* (Paris 1968) 117-135.

——, "Les Pérégrinations de l'Ame dans l'autre Monde d'après un anonyme de la fin du XIIe Siècle," in: *Archives* 13 (1940/2) 229-299.

——, "Un Sermon d'Alain sur la Misère de l'Homme," in: *The Classical Tradition, Literary and Historical Studies in Honour of Harry Caplan* (Ithaca 1966) 515-535.

——, "Variations sur un thème de Virgile dans un sermon d'Alain de Lille," in: *Mélanges offerts à André Piganiol* (Paris 1966) 1517-1528.

Arcoleo; S., "La Filosofia della Natura nella Problematica di Alano di Lilla," in: *La Filosofia della Natura nel Medioevo, Atti del Terzo Congresso Internazionale di Filosofia Medioevale* (Milan 1965) 255-259.

Anselm See Schmitt, F.

Atkins, J. W. H. *Literary Criticism in Antiquity* (London 1934).

Auvray, L., "Un Poème Rythmique et une Lettre d'Etienne de Tournai," in: *Mélanges Paul Fabre* (Paris 1902) 279-291.

Avery, B. R., See Zimmermann, O. J.

Bacon, Roger See Brewer, J. S.

Baldwin, C. S., *Medieval Rhetoric and Poetic* (New York 1928).

Barach, C. and Wrobel, J., *Bernardi Silvestris De Mundi Universitate Libri Duo, sive Megacosmus et Microcosmus* (Innsbruck 1876; Minerva Reprint, Frankfurt a. M. 1964).

Baron, R., "A propos des Ramifications des Vertus au XIIe Siècle," in: *Recherches de Théologie Ancienne et Médiévale* 23 (1956) 19-39.

Barré, H., "La Maternité Spirituelle de Marie dans la Pensée Médiévale," in *Bulletin de la Société française d'Etudes mariales* 16 (1959) 87-118.

Baumgartner, M. *Die Philosophie des Alanus de Insulis*, in: *Beiträge* 2 (Münster 1896).

Benno of Osnabrück, See Francke, K.

Bernardus Silvestris, See Barach, C.

Boethius, See Friedlein, G.; Stewart-Rand.

Bossuat, R. *Alain de Lille Anticlaudianus, Texte critique avec une Introduction et des Tables* (Paris 1955).

——, "*Quelques Personnages cités par Alain de Lille,*" in: *Mélanges du Moyen Age dédiés a la Mémoire de Louis Halphen* (Paris 1951) 33-42.

Brewer, J. S., *Fr. Rogeri Bacon Quaedam Hactenus Inedita* (London 1859).

Bubnov, N., *Gerberti postea Sylvestri Papae II Opera Mathematica* (Berlin 1899).

——, *Accedunt aliorum Opera ad Gerberti Libellos aestimandos intelligendosque necessaria* (Berlin 18 99).

Callimachus, See Pfeiffer, R.

Cappelli, A., *Cronologia, Cronografia e Calendario Perpetuo* (Milan 1930).

Charlemont, C., *Series Sanctorum et Beatorum Virorum Sacri Ordinis Cisterciensium* (Paris 1666).

Chenu, M-D., "*A la Mémoire renouvelée du 'Doctor Universalis', Alain de Lille,*" in: *Citeaux 13 (1962) 67-70.*

——, "Conscience de l'Histoire et Théologie au XIIe Siècle," in: *Archives* 21 (1954) 107-133.

——, "Grammaire et Théologie aux XIIe et XIIIe Siècles," in: *Archives* 10 (1935/6) 5-28.

——, *La Théologie au Douzième Siècle, Etudes de Philosophie Médiévale* 45 (Paris 1957).

——, "L'Homme et la Nature. Perspectives sur la Renaissance du XIIe Siècle," *Archives* 19 (1952) 39-66.

——, "Nature ou Histoire? Une Controverse exégétique sur la Création au XIIe Siècle," in: *Archives* 20 (1953) 31-81.

——, "Platon à Citeaux," in: *Archives* 21 (1954) 99-106.

——, "Un Essai de Méthode Théologique au XIIe Siècle," in: *Revue des Sciences Philosophiques et Théologiques* 24 (1935) 258-267.

——, "Une Théologie axiomatique au XIIe Siècle. Alain de Lille," in: *Citeaux* 9 (1958) 137-142.

Cilento, V., *Alano di Lilla, Poeta e Teologo del Sec. XII* (Naples 1958).

——, *Medio Evo monastico e scolastico* (Milan 1961).

Clarembald of Arras See Häring, N. M.

Claudian, See Platnauer, M.

Cornog, W. H., *The 'Anticlaudian' of Alain de Lille, Prologue, Argument and nine Books, with an Introduction and Notes* (Philadelphia 1935).

Courcelle, P. *La Consolation de Philosophie dans la Tradition Littéraire* (Paris 1967).

Curtius, E. R., "Dante und Alanus," in: *Romanische Forschungen* 62 (1960) 28-31.

——, *Europäische Literatur und lateinisches Mittelalter* (Bern 1948; tr. Trask, W. R., *European Literature and the Latin Middle Ages* (London 1953).

Delhaye, Ph., "La Vertu et les Vertus dans les Œuvres d'Alain de Lille," in: *Cahiers de Civilisation Médiévale* 6 (1963) 13-25.

——, "L'Enseignement de la Philosophie Morale au XIIe Siècle," in: *Mediaeval Studies* 11 (1949) 77-99.

——, "Le Péché dans la Théologie d'Alain de Lille," in: *Sciences Ecclésiastiques* 17 (1965) 7-27.

——, "Pour la 'Fiche' Alain de Lille," in: *Mélanges de Science Religieuse* 20 (1963) 39-51.

Delage, R., *Alain de Lille, Poète du XIIe Siècle* (Montreal and Paris 1951).

Dick, A., *Martianus Capella* (Stuttgart 1925: reprint with additions by Jean Préaux, Stuttgart 1969).

Dimier, M. A., "Mourir à Clairvaux," in: *Collectanea Ordinis Cisterciensium* Ref. 17 (1955) 272-285.

Dimock, J. F., *Topographia Hibernica, Giraldi Cambrensis Opera* 5, Rolls Series 21.5 (London 1867) 3-138.

Dionysius of Halicarnassus See Roberts, W. Rhys

Dölger, F. J., "Das Sonnengleichnis in einer Weihnachtspredigt des Bischofs Zeno von Verona," in: *Antike und Christentum* 6 (1950) 1-56.

——, *Die Sonne der Gerechtigkeit und der Schwarze* (Münster 1918).

Dreves, G. M. and Blume, C., *Ein Jahrtausend lateinischer Hymnendichtung* (Leipzig 1909).

Dronke, P. "Boethius, Alanus and Dante," in: *Romanische Forschungen* 78 (1966) 119-125.

——, "Dante's Earthly Paradise: towards an Interpretation of *Purgatorio* XXVIII," in: *Romanische Forschungen* 82 (1970) 467-487.

Dugauquier, J. A., *Pierre le Chantre, Summa de Sacramentis et Animae Consiliis,* in: Analecta Mediaevalia Namurcensia 7 (Louvain 1957).

Duhem, P., *Le Système du Monde,* 3 (Paris 1954).

Dupuis, A., *Alain de Lille, Etude de Philosophie scolastique* (Lille 1859).

Elorduy, E., "La Motivacion de la Virtud en la Edad Media," in: *Revista espanola de Teologia* 3 (1943) 63-113.

Engelhardt, G. J., "An Emendation in Anticlaudianus," in: *Speculum* 23 (1948) 110-111.

Escoffier, J.-P., *Calendrier Perpétuel* (Paris 1880).

Francke, K., *Benonis aliorumque Cardinalium Schismaticorum contra Gregorium VII et Urbanum II scripta,* in: MGH *Libelli de Lite* 2.366-422.

Friedlein, G., *Anicii Manlii Torquati Severini Boetii de Institutione Arithmetica Libri Duo; De Institutione Musica Libri Quinque* (Leipzig 1867: Minerva reprint, Frankfurt a. M. 1966).

Gams, P., *Series Episcoporum* (Leipzig 1931).

Garin, E., *Studi sul Platonismo medievale* (Florence 1958).

Gerbertus, See Bubnov, N.

Gilbert of Poitiers, See Häring, N. M.

Gilson, E., *La Philosophie au Moyen Age*, 2nd. ed. (Paris 1947).

——, "Le Moyen Age et le Naturalisme Antique," in: *Archives* 7 (1933) 5-37.

Giraldus Cambrensis See Dimock, J. F.

Glorieux, P., "Alain de Lille, docteur de l'Assomption," in: *Mélanges de Science Religieuse* 8 (1951) 5-18.

——, Article on Alan in *New Catholic Encyclopedia*.

——, "L'Auteur de la Somme 'Quoniam Homines'" in: *Recherches de Théologie ancienne et médiévale* 17 (1950) 29-45.

——, "La Somme 'Quoniam Homines' d'Alain de Lille," in: *Archives* 20 (1953) 113-359.

Godfrey of Saint Victor, See Michaud-Quantin, P.; Synan, E. A.

Gompf, L., *Daretis Yliados Libri Sex*, in: *Joseph Iscanus Werke und Briefe, Mittellateinische Studien und Texte* 4 (Leiden 1970) 5-217.

Gregory, T. *Anima Mundi. La Filsosofia di Guglielmo di Conches e la Scuola di Chartres* (Florence 1955).

Green, H. R., "Alan of Lille's Anticlaudianus, Ascensus Mentis in Deum," in: *Annuale Medievale* 8 (1967) 3-16.

——, "Alan of Lille's 'De Planctu Naturae'," in: *Speculum* 31 (1956) 649-674.

Gundissalinus, See Alonso, M. A,; Haring, N. M.

Häring, N. M., "A Commentary on the Pseudo-Athanasian Creed by Gilbert of Poitiers," in: *Mediqeval Studies* 27 (1965) 23-53.

——, "A Latin Dialogue on the Doctrine of Gilbert of Poitiers," in: *Mediaeval Studies* 15 (1953) 243-28 9.

——, *Commentaries on Boethius by Thierry of Chartres and his School* (Toronto 1971).

——, "Der Begriff der Natur bei Gilbert von Poitiers," in: *La Filosofia della Natura nel Medioevo, Atti del Terzo Congresso Internazionale di Filosofia Medioevale* (Milan 1965) 279-285.

——, "Der Literaturkatalog von Affligem," in: *Revue Bénédictine* 80 (1970) 64-96.

——, *Life and Works of Clarembald of Arras* (Toronto 1965).

——, *The Commentaries on Boethius by Gilbert of Poitiers* (Toronto 1966).

——, "The Creation and Creator of the World according to Thierry of Chartres and Clarenbaldus of Arras," in: *Archives* 22 (1955) 137-216.

——, "The Liberal Arts in the Sermons of Garnier of Rochefort," in: *Mediaeval Studies* 30 (1968) 45-77.

——, "The Liber de Homoysion et Homoeysion by Hugh of Honau," in: *Archives* 34 (1967) 129-253.

——, "The Liber de Diversitate Naturae et Personae by Hugh of Honau," in: *Archives* 29 (1962) 103-119.

——, "Thierry of Chartres and Dominicus Gundissalinus," in: *Mediaeval Studies* 26 (1964) 271-286.

——, "A Poem by Alan of Lille on the Pseudo-Athanasian Creed," in: *Revue d'Histoire des Textes* (1974).

Hauréau, B., *Histoire de la Philosophie* (Paris 1872).

——, "Mémoire sur la vie et quelques œuvres d'Alain de Lille," in: *Mémoires de l'Académie des Inscriptions et Belles Lettres* 32 (1886) 1-27.

——, *Notices et Extraits de quelque Manuscrits Latins de la Bibliothèque National* (Paris 1890-93).

Hermes Trismegistus, See Nock, A. D.-Festugière, A. J.

Highet, G., *The Classical Tradition* (Oxford 1949).

Hödl, L., *Die Geschichte der scholastischen Literatur und der Theologie der Schlüsselgewalt* (Münster 1960: Beiträge 38.4).

——, "Eine unbekannte Predigtsammlung des Alanus von Lille in Münchener Handschriften," in: *Zeitschrift für Katholische Theologie* 80 (1958) 516-527.

Hugh of Honau, See Häring, N. M.

Huizinga, J., *Uber die Verknüpfung des Poetischen mit dem Theologische bei Alanus de Insulis* (Amsterdam 1932).

Hutchings, C. M., "L'Anticlaudianus d'Alain de Lille, Etude de Chronologie," in: *Romania* 50 (1924) 1-13.

James, M. R., *Walter Map's 'De Nugis Curialium'* (London 1923).

Javelet, R., *Image et Ressemblance au douzième siècle de Saint Anselm à Alain de Lille* (Strasbourg 1967) 2 voll.

Jean de Hanville, See John of Altavilla.

Jeauneau, E., *Guillaume de Conches, Glosae super Platonem* (Paris 1965).

——, "Macrobe, source du Platonisme chartrain," in: *Studi Medievali*, 3a Serie 1.1 (1960) 3-24.

——, "Nani gigantum humeris insidentes, Essai d'interpretation de Bernard de Chartres," in: *Vivarium* 5.2 (1967) 79-99.

John of Altavilla, See Wright, T.

John of Garland, See Wright, T.

John of Hanville, See John of Altavilla.

John of Salisbury, See Webb, C. I. C.

Joseph of Exeter, See Gompf, L.

Keil, H. Grammatici Latini (Lipsiae 1850-1870)

Knowles, D., *The Evolution of Medieval Thought* (London 1960).

Landgraf, A. "Zum Werden der Theologie des zwölften Jahrhunderts," in: *Zeitschrift für Katholische Theologie* 79 (1957) 417-433.

Lebeau, M., "Découverte du Tombeau du bienheureux Alain de Lille," in: *Collectanea Ordinis Cisterciensium Reformatorum* 23 (1961) 254-260.

Lecoy De La Marche, A., *Anecdotes Historiques, Légendes et Apologues tirés du Recueil Inédit d'Etienne de Bourbon, Dominicain du* XIIIe *Siècle* (Paris 1877).

Lesne, E., *Les Ecoles de la fin du* VIIIe *siècle à la fin du* XIIe, *Histoire de la Propriété Ecclésiastique en France* 5 (Lille 1940).

Longère, J., *Alain de Lille: Liber Poenitentialis* in *Analecta Mediaevalia Namurcensia* 17, 18 (Louvain 1961).

——, "Alain de Lille Liber Poenitentialis, Les Traditions Moyenne et Courte," in: *Archives* 32 (1965) 169-242.

Lottin, O., "Le Traite d'Alain de Lille sur les Vertus, les Vices et les Dons du Saint-Esprit," in: *Mediaeval Studies* 12 (1950) 20-56.

Manselli, R., *L'éresia del male,* in: *Collana di storia* 1 (Naples 1963).

Map, Walter, See James, M. R.

Martène, E., *Veterum Scriptorum et Monumentorum Amplissima Collectio* 6 (Paris 1729).

McKinney, L. C., *Early Medieval Medicine with special reference to France and Chartres* (Baltimore 1937).

Michaud-Quantin, P. *Sommes de Casuistique et Manuels de Confession au Moyen Age (XII-XVI Siècles),* in: *Analecta Mediaevalia Namurcensia* 13 (Louvain 1962).

——, *Godfroy de Saint-Victor, Texte publié et annoté,* in: *Analecta Mediaevalia Namurcensia* 8 (Louvain 1956).

Mills, Charles, *History of Chivalry or Knighthood and its times* (London 1826).

Moffat, D. M., *The Complaint of Nature,* tr. *Yale Studies in English* (New York 1908).

Moore, P., *The Observer's Book of Astronomy,* revised edition (London 1967).

Ninck, M. H., *Die Bedeutung des Wasser im Kult und Leben der Alten,* 2nd. ed. (Darmstadt 1960).

Nock, A. D.-Festugière, A. J., *Corpus Hermeticum* (Paris 1945).

O'Brien, M. J., *The Socratic Paradoxes and the Greek Mind* (Chapel Hill 1967).

O'Donnell, J. R., *Bernardus Silvestris* in: *New Catholic Encyclopedia.*

——, "The Meaning of 'Silva in the Commentary on the *Timaeus* of Plato by Chalcidius," in: *Mediaeval Studies* 7 (1945) 1-20.

Parent, J. M., "Un nouveau Témoin de la Théologie dionysienne, in: *Beiträge,* Suppl. 3.1 (1935) 288-309.

Pelster, F., "Der Heinrich von Gent zugeschriebene 'Catalogus virorum illustrium' und sein wirklicher Verfasser," in: *Historisches Jahrbuch* 39 (1918/1919) 253-265.

Peter Cantor, See Dugauquier, J. A.

Pfeiffer, R. *Callimachus* (Oxford 1949).

Philip of Bury, See Altamura, A.

Piehler, P., *The Visionary Landscape* (London 1971).

Platnauer, M., *Claudian,* Loeb Text (Cambridge, Mass. 1956).

Ptolemy, See Robbins, F. E.

Porphyry, *Isagoge.*

Quain, E. A., "The Medieval 'accessus ad auctores'," in: *Traditio* 3 (1945) 215-264.

Raby, F. J. E., *A History of Christian-Latin Poetry from the Beginnings to the Close of the Middle Ages* (Oxford 1927).

Ralph of Longchamp, Ms. Paris, BN lat. 8083.

Rath, W. *Bernardus Silvestris über die allumfassende Einheit der Welt* (Stuttgart s.d.).

Richerus, See Waitz, G.

Robbins, F. E., *Tetrabiblos of Ptolemy,* Loeb Text (Cambridge, Mass. 1940).

Roberts, W. Rhys, *Dionysius of Halicarnassus, On Literary Composition* (London 1910).

Roscher, W. H., *Hebdomadenlehren der griechischen Philosophen und Ärzte* (Leipzig 1906).

Russell, J. "*Interpretations of the Origins of Medieval Heresy,*" in: *Mediaeval Studies* 25 (1963) 26-63.

Schmitt, F. "Epistola de Incarnatione Verbi," in: *S. Anselmi, Cantuariensis Archiepiscopi, Opera Omnia* 2 (Rome 1940) 1-35.

Simon, M., "Les Dieux antiques dans la Pensée Chrétienne," in: *Zeitschrift für Religions-und Geistesgeschichte* 6 (1954) 97-114.

Soto, P. B. *Petri Compostellani de Consolatione Rationis Libri Duo,* in: *Beiträge* 8(1912) 61-151.

Steinen, W., von den, *Notker der Dichter und seine geistige Welt* (Bern 1948).

Stephen of Bourbon, See Lecoy De La Marche, A.

Stephen of Tournai, See Auvray, M.

Stewart-Rand, *Boethius, The Theological Tractates, The Consolation of Philosophy,* Loeb Texts (London and New-York 1926).

Strecker, K., *Moralisch-Satirische Gedichte Walters von Châtillon* (Heidelberg 1929).

Stubbs, W., *De Gestis Regum Anglorum Libri Quinque,* Rolls Series 90.1 (London 1887).

Sulowski, J., "La Philosophie de la Nature chez Raoul de Longchamp," in: *La Filosofia della Natura nel Medioevo, Atti del Terzo Congresso Internazionale di Filosofia Medioevale* (Milan 1965) 320-326.

Synan, E. A., *The Fountain of Philosophy, A Translation of the Twelfth-Century Fons Philosophiae of Godfrey of Saint-Victor* (Toronto 1972).

Taylor, H. O., *The Mediaeval Mind* (Cambridge, Mass. 1949).

Thierry of Chartres, See Häring, N. M.

Thouzellier, C., "Controverses Vaudoises-Cathares à la Fin du XIIe Siècle" in: *Archives* 27 (1960) 137-227.

——, *Hérésie et Hérétiques* (Rome 1969).

Thurot, C., *Extraits de divers Manuscrits Latins pour servir à l'histoire des doctrines grammaticales au moyen âge* (Paris 1869: Minerva Reprint, Frankfurt a. M. 1964).

Trask, W. R., See Curtius, E. R.

Vasoli, C., "Il 'Contra Haereticos' di Alano di Lilla," in: *Bullettino dell'Istituto Storico Italiano per il Medio Evo e Archivio Muratoriano* 72 (1960) 35-89.

——, *La Filosofia Medioevale* (Milan 1961).

——, "*Studi recenti su Alano di Lilla*," in: Bullettino dell'Istituto Storico Italiano per il Medio Evo e Archivio Muratoriano 72 (1960) 35-89.

Venantius (Fortunatus) *Ave Maris Stella* (hymn).

Visch, C. de, "Dissertatio de unico Alano Ripatorii abbate, Antissiodorensi episcopo, ac tandem monacho ordinis Cisterciensis, apud Cistercium anno 1203 mortuo in: *PL*, 210, 10-26.

Waitz, G., *Richeri Historiarum Libri IIII*, in: MGH, Sr. G 3.99-110.

Wakefield W. L. and Evans, A. P., *Heresies of the High Middle Ages* (New York and London 1969).

Walter of Châtillon, See Strecker, K.

Webb, C. I. C., *Joannis Saresberiensis, Episcopi Carnotensis, Metalogicon* (Oxford 1929).

Wetherbee, W., "The Function of Poetry in the 'De Planctu Naturae' of Alain de Lille," in: *Traditio* 25 (1969) 87-125.

William of Auxerre, Ms. Paris, BN lat. 8299.

William of Conches, See Jeauneau, E.

Wright, T. *Joannis de Garlandia De Triumphis Ecclesiae* (London 1856).

——, *Johannis de Altavilla Architrenius.* in: *The Anglo-Latin Satirical Poets and Epigrammatists of the Twelfth Century,* Rolls Series 59.1 (London 1872) 240-392.

——, *Alani Liber De Planctu Naturae.* in: *The Anglo-Latin Satirical Poets and Epigrammatists of the Twelfth Century,* Rolls Series 59.2 (London 1872) 429-522.

——, *Alani Anticlaudianus* in: *The Anglo-Latin Satirical Poets and Epigrammatists of the Twelfth Century,* Rolls Series 59.2 (London 1872) 268-428.

Wrobel, J., See Barach, C.

Zimmerman, O. J. and Avery, B. R., *Life and Miracles of St. Benedict* (Collegeville, Minnesota 1949).

INDEX

TABLE OF CONTENTS